Unequal Britain
Human rights as a route to social justice

Unequal Britain
Human rights as a route to social justice

**Written and edited by
Stuart Weir**

POLITICO'S

First published in Great Britain 2006 by
Politico's Publishing Ltd, an imprint of
Methuen Publishing Ltd
11–12 Buckingham Gate
London
SW1E 6LB

10 9 8 7 6 5 4 3 2 1

ISBN-10: 1-84275-091-7
ISBN-13: 978-1-84275-091-9

Printed and bound in Great Britain by St Edmundsbury Press Ltd, Bury St
Edmunds, Suffolk

Contents

Appendices

Acknowledgements

This book is very much a collaborative effort. Part 1 is the product of years of discussions I have had with Iain Byrne, Paul Hunt, Judith Mesquita and Ellie Palmer, all of whom are in one guise or another at the Human Rights Centre, University of Essex. I owe particular gratitude to Ellie Palmer for sharing her research on socio-economic rights in the courts, which forms the backbone of Chapter 4. Judith Mesquita collaborated with me on Chapter 2 and Debbie Chay, chair of Charter88, briefed me on the laws of the European Union for Chapter 3. Debbie lectures in public and European law at Brunel University and is one of the founding members of Law Tutors Online. Marc Francis, public affairs manager at Shelter, read through Chapter 9 and gave us good advice.

I should also like to thank the authors of the separate chapters in Part 2 for their good ideas in two joint seminars and for comments on Part 1. Mitchell Woolf, consultant solicitor at Scott-Moncrieff, Harbour & Sinclair, who also lectures at Queen Mary, University of London, kindly attended the second seminar and gave us insights into the ideology of the judiciary.

Professor Paul Hunt, Chairman of the Democratic Audit board and formerly director of the Human Rights Centre, has been unfailingly helpful. Professor David Beetham, my principal collaborator at Democratic Audit, played a significant part in shaping the ideas on the connections between economic and social rights and democracy, as have various colleagues at International IDEA who assisted in developing the democracy audit framework for international use, chief among them Professor Peter de Souza, of the Centre for the Study of Developing Societies, Delhi; and Professors Kevin Boyle and Francesca Klug, who in the early days of the Audit joined me in insisting that economic and social rights were integral to democracy.

Professor Stuart Weir
Director, Democratic Audit
June 2006

Introduction

My vision of Britain is of a nation where no-one is left out or left behind, and where power, wealth and opportunity are in the hands of the many, not the few.

Tony Blair, 2000

We in Britain believe that we live in a mature and historic democracy. We rank social justice, or 'an equal society', second only to freedom as the most important attribute of democracy; and we want both in this country.[1] The popular view, that Britain needs a Bill of Rights to protect both political freedom and social justice, was partially met in 1998 when the government passed the Human Rights Act into law. The Act gives effect to the civil and political rights that are enshrined in the European Convention on Human Rights – the rights to life and liberty, to a fair trial, to protection from torture and persecution, to freedom of conscience, to free speech, assembly, association and information, to privacy and respect for home and family, to education and to property, all of which should be enjoyed without discrimination. The government and public authorities are now duty bound to protect and promote these civil and political rights and citizens have a right to go to court for redress if they believe that any of their rights have been violated.

But the public expect more from a Bill of Rights than the protection of freedoms, as a series of opinion polls for the Joseph Rowntree Reform Trust has shown. The public want to secure important economic and social rights alongside civil and political rights. In polls from 1991 to 2004, large majorities of people agreed that a Bill of Rights should protect rights to hospital treatment on the NHS within a 'reasonable time'; rights to join a trade union and take part in a legal strike without losing a job; a woman's right to have an abortion; and the right of homeless people to be housed. Public support for such rights is broadly as high as it is for the traditional civil and political rights that the Human Rights Act now protects.[2]

Public opinion in this country reflects the formal view of the international community. In 1948 the United Nations Universal Declaration of Human Rights asserted that civil and political rights on the one hand, and economic, social and cultural rights on the other, were equal and indivisible. Further, by regarding social justice as an important aspect of democracy, the British public reflects Democratic Audit's view that economic and social rights are integral to democracy. We recognise that civil and political rights play a significant part in securing social justice and equality in the United Kingdom. But at best they only partially protect people from social injustice in very significant spheres of daily life. Rights such as access to paid work with fair rates of pay; good and safe working conditions; secure and decent housing; education for life; access to high-quality health care; benefits, pensions and services for people who are out of work, injured, disabled or elderly; all these are vital not only to the well-being both of individual citizens and of society, but also to the workings of our democracy. For both reasons, these rights ought to be equally accessible to all citizens and governments in this country proclaim their intention to realise them.

The democratic principle of equal citizenship requires that no-one should be allowed to fall below a minimum acceptable level of economic and social existence. Economic and social well-being create self-confident citizens able and willing to play a part in the democratic life of their society, to exercise their civil and political rights, and to enjoy personal and political freedoms. By the same token, poverty – or economic and social exclusion – not only leads to alienation, social tensions and crime, but also hinders people from being active citizens or even registering or using their right to vote.[3] In the view of Democratic Audit, British democracy requires both political equality and social inclusion if it is to work properly and fairly.

Full political equality is out of reach in a British society that has grown increasingly unequal over the past quarter of a century. Social mobility has silted up and even gone into reverse. Yet effective political equality simply cannot be realised without a certain measure of economic equality (though precisely how much is open to debate). Otherwise those at the top will exert or even buy undue political influence while those at the bottom will usually be excluded from the political process altogether.[4] The richer someone is, the more able and likely they are to engage with civil society and politics. The poorer they are, the less able they are to participate. A recent survey of poverty and social exclusion in the UK found that 43 per cent of those who do not participate at all in civic life are poor. Only 18 per cent of poor people participate to any great extent.[5] A study of social exclusion during the 1990s also found that low incomes are often associated with other forms of exclusion, especially from being engaged in a productive, socially valued or political activity.[6]

We adopt the concept of social exclusion as a guiding star because it places poverty within the wider idea of a modern European society of people bound together by rights and obligations that reflect a shared civil, political and moral order. Social exclusion describes not just poor material means, but also people's inability to participate fully and effectively in everyday life and their individual and communal alienation from mainstream society. It embraces a broad range of inter-connected issues and policies – education, health, housing, work conditions, environment and transport as well as employment and social security. Social exclusion can therefore be defined in terms of the denial of human rights – civil, political, economic, social and cultural – which is the prime concern of this audit.

Britain's two-faced approach to socio-economic rights

The current government proclaims the indivisibility of socio-economic and civil and political rights internationally. For example, the Foreign Office devoted a whole chapter to socio-economic rights in its 2003 annual report, insisting that 'the choice between economic, social and cultural rights and civil and political rights is a false one . . . unless people have adequate access to food, shelter and health care they will never be able to enjoy the full range of civil and political rights'.[7]

Giving people in Britain basic socio-economic rights would empower them to seek justice in most aspects of their everyday lives. But government ministers and officials, jealous of their political prerogatives, are unwilling to recognise these rights in law at home, though they pay lip service to them abroad. They fear that giving people such rights would give judges the power to adjudicate upon their policies and substitute their own priorities for those of government. For them socio-economic rights belong in the realm of political policy: they are the stuff of public policies and programmes determined as they see fit by governments put in place democratically at general elections. Governments and the judiciary agree further that socio-economic rights are too vague to be 'justiciable' – that is, resolved and enforced by judges in court – and that their realisation is essentially down to policy choices, legislative measures and resource allocations that the courts are not competent to decide. For example, they argue that it is up to government and public authorities to determine the national budget for housing or to set the rates for social security benefits.

These arguments are attractive from a democratic point of view: after all, it is surely up to elected governments to determine public policies, not unelected judges. But they are essentially superficial. They are based on a fundamental misapprehension of the part that socio-economic rights can properly play in a democracy and the relative roles that governments and the courts should perform in their protection. We shall argue this case in depth throughout this audit. Suffice it to say here that they express a typically top-down view of democratic society. They fail to consider the case for socio-economic rights from the point of view of the ordinary citizen. Such rights would empower relatively powerless people to hold governments and public authorities to account for policies and actions that affect their lives and, where necessary, provide them with the opportunity to obtain redress if, for example, policies on housing were failing to meet the housing needs of the population or vulnerable homeless families were being refused accommodation by over-stretched local authorities; or, to take another example, workers were sacked for going on strike.

It is a mistake therefore to regard the inclusion of socio-economic rights in British law merely in institutional and legal terms (especially as Britain's unrepresentative electoral system undermines the democratic legitimacy of our governments).[8] Rather than detract from democracy in this country, giving people socio-economic rights could deepen British democracy, as our evidence to Parliament's Joint Committee on Human Rights in 2003 argued:

> Incorporation [of socio-economic rights into British law] could provide a human rights framework of shared values within which government and the public could develop and review policies and the allocation of resources for economic and social well-being in the UK and for improving the quality of public services.[9]

Defenders of the status quo also point out that the substance of most socio-economic rights receives statutory protection in Britain. Under current legislation, for example, public bodies are obliged to respect significant aspects of such rights in housing, employment, health-care, education and social security. If they fail to meet these obligations, dissatisfied citizens can seek remedies through judicial review in the courts, and they do. The UK's anti-discrimination laws and regulations in relation to race, sex, disability, religion and sexual orientation provide substantial, though varying, protection of rights at work and across services. The present government is committed to an Equality Act and an Equality and Human Rights Commission. Yet the existing patchwork of laws and regulations does not provide the legal, or constitutional, protection of socio-economic rights that the Human Rights Act does for civil and political rights. Judicial review provides only partial redress for those who believe that their socio-economic rights have been violated. First, vulnerable or marginal groups or individuals who fall outside the scope of the legislation cannot challenge its limitations in protecting their social, economic or cultural rights; and second, very often the obligations placed on public bodies that these groups are seeking to enforce are discretionary, and even when they are absolute duties, the courts often refuse to enforce them.

Britain is signed up to the core international treaty on socio-economic rights, the International Covenant on Economic, Social and Cultural Rights, but our obligations under the covenant have no effective legal force in the UK, as British governments refuse to incorporate it into British law. In 2002, the UK government reported on its compliance with the covenant to the UN body which monitors compliance among signatory states, the Committee on Economic, Social and Cultural Rights (CESCR). The CESCR has repeatedly admonished UK governments for their refusal to incorporate the covenant, and has asked them to put in place arrangements to make sure that they can at least meet their obligations under it. It regularly finds that Britain is failing to meet international standards for the protection of economic, social and cultural rights. Following its review of the UK's official report, and an interactive dialogue with government representatives, the CESCR issued its concluding observations in June 2002,[10] which contain a long list of 'concerns' about the government's failure to provide or protect key rights; worse still, many of these 'concerns' had been voiced in its previous report, published in 1997 to set a benchmark for the new Blair government (see Chapters 2 and 5). The committee expressed particular concern about the persistence of considerable levels of poverty and homelessness in the UK. Its concerns and recommendations elicited some fairly heated responses: the *Daily Telegraph* noted the 'breathtaking effrontery' with which the committee 'has chosen to lecture the United Kingdom on the way in which we run our affairs'.[11]

Widening recognition of socio-economic rights

It has long been common wisdom that there is a north–south divide among democracies on recognising socio-economic rights – that developed northern countries do not need explicitly to protect such rights in Bills of Rights or in their constitutions and so they don't, whereas southern countries need to recognise and protect such rights legally. As ever, common wisdom is only partly true; and the idea makes policy-makers in the UK complacent about their refusal to consider protecting such rights here.

It is true that there is a form of divide, which derives in part from the fact that developed countries tend to have older constitutions than developing or new democracies and are in that respect out of date. Newer democracies, such as Brazil and South Africa, are more likely to incorporate socio-economic rights in law or the constitution. The 1996 Constitution of South Africa, for example, famously entrenched a wide range of economic, social and cultural rights in its Bill of Rights. Socio-economic rights there have been asserted and upheld in the courts, providing a workable model for the UK to adopt (see Chapter 5).[12] But there is also an international trend towards recognising economic, social and cultural rights in legal or constitutional form. Apart from those countries well known for protecting such rights in their constitutions, such as Brazil, India and Colombia, many other countries recognise socio-economic rights in a more selective way. A survey in 2001 found that an estimated total of 109 countries recognise the right to health in their national constitutions.[13] The academic lawyer David Beatty argues that socio-economic rights have proved to be justiciable in different situations around the world and points out that rights to basic levels of health, education, welfare and a clean environment 'find their place with increasing frequency alongside the traditional first generation of rights [i.e. civil and political rights]',[14] citing the provisions of new constitutions in the Czech Republic, Hungary, Portugal and Slovakia, as well as Namibia and South Africa.[15] There is, moreover, Italy, where the constitutional court is, Beatty records, often regarded 'as the most active court in the field of social and economic rights', and Spain, where social and economic rights are protected in the merger of old and new constitutions. Finland has integrated key economic, social and cultural rights into its national constitution, apparently in response to the recommendations of the CESCR, thus translating international obligations into tangible protections at the domestic level. Beatty also points out that the European Court of Human Rights and courts in Belgium, Germany, Japan, the United States and elsewhere frequently deal with social and economic rights.

There are uncertain moves towards recognising and enforcing socio-economic rights in Europe, through the laws of the European Union, through the European Social Charter and (increasingly) through the European Convention of Human Rights and the attempt to agree the EU Charter of Fundamental Rights. But Europe is not alone in giving more recognition to economic, social and cultural rights. They have become more prominent in thinking in the Americas and Africa as well as domestically in many states. In 1998 the General Assembly of the Organization of American States adopted the San Salvador protocol, extending the primarily civil and political rights protections in the American Convention on Human Rights into socio-economic areas. The African Charter on Human and People's Rights, adopted in 1981, recognises four social and economic rights alongside civil and political rights, creating a new framework for the promotion and protection of all human rights in Africa. Aspirational as most of these initiatives are, they are establishing a new credibility for human rights to which the UK could contribute by recognising and realising them at home and abroad.

Unequal Britain

The purpose of this audit is to consider the case for moving on from the unstable statutory delivery and protection of socio-economic rights in the UK to inscribing them in law (we do not fully consider the case for cultural or environmental rights, important though they are). The origins of the book lie in Democratic Audit's submission to the CESCR in 2001 and subsequent evidence to the parliamentary Joint Committee on Human Rights inquiry into UK compliance with the International Covenant on Economic, Social and Cultural Rights.

The book is divided into two parts. Part 1 contains five chapters, written and edited by Stuart Weir with the co-operation of Judith Mesquita and Ellie Palmer. Chapter 1 reviews the current system for securing such rights in the UK through legislation, reviews the current government's policies for realising them, and reports on the CESCR's latest verdict on its progress and failures. Chapter 2 sets out exactly how Britain is supposed to protect socio-economic rights under the International Covenant and the conventions of the

International Labour Organization. Chapter 3 describes Britain's obligations to secure such rights under EU law, the European Convention on Human Rights and the European Social Charter. EU law gives legal protection to some important economic and social rights in the UK. Both Chapter 2 and 3 describe and analyse the British government's arguments against giving all such rights legal protection in the UK. Chapter 4 examines in detail the ideology of the judiciary on socio-economic rights – and its record in protecting them. Chapter 5 surveys Britain's failures to reach international standards on socio-economic rights and suggests that such rights would empower communities and individuals to secure social justice in partnership with the courts and government. This chapter draws upon experience in making socio-economic rights in South Africa justiciable to demonstrate how it might be done in the UK.

Part 2 consists of six chapters that audit the state of social and economic well-being in relation to equality and discrimination, poverty, health-care, housing, education and work. These chapters – by Tufyal Choudhury (on discrimination), Jan Flaherty (poverty), Judith Mesquita (health), Iain Byrne and Andrew Blick (housing and employment) and John Fowler (education) – seek in different ways to relate the realities on the ground to Britain's obligations to protect socio-economic rights under international and European laws and treaties. The authors have also collaborated in the process of identifying actual and potential violations of economic and social rights in Chapter 5.

Most studies of economic and social rights are strongly legal in approach. This audit represents a unique first attempt to combine the legal, political and social approaches to analysing economic and social well-being from a human rights perspective. As such, we have not sought to impose a common approach on the authors of Chapters 6 to 11, since we think that at this stage debate and understanding can only benefit from a variety of approaches. There is also some overlap among these chapters and between Parts 1 and 2, as economic and social rights do not belong in watertight compartments and overlap and interact.

As we have already acknowledged, we have not had the resources to cover cultural and environmental rights and we have chosen for the same reason to examine only five main areas of economic and social life, and even then to do so briefly. We are painfully aware therefore that there are many economic and social injustices which we do not touch upon in this audit. But we hope that in advancing the case for embedding economic and social rights in law, we might contribute to their realisation finally across all aspects of life in this country. Even within the limitations we have agreed, data, laws, court cases and events change too fast to keep up with. We have tried to update this book to the end of 2005, or at least to cover the first two terms of the Labour government and significant policy changes thereafter. But where we have failed, the book will nonetheless be relevant, because though specific details and data change relatively fast, the overall circumstances within which we all live change much more slowly.

1

The 'Anglo-social' welfare state

People do not in general have enforceable economic and social rights in the UK. This country has ratified the United Nations International Covenant on Economic, Social and Cultural Rights (ICESCR), as well as other UN conventions, International Labour Organization treaties and the European Social Charter. These international instruments seek to guarantee social, economic and cultural rights and to impose obligations on those states that ratify them. However, like most other European countries, the UK has not incorporated the ICESCR or the other conventions and treaties into domestic law; thus they do not have legal force in this country. Nor yet does the UK have its own Bill of Rights, which might, if popular opinion mattered, protect socio-economic rights.

Some socio-economic rights are legally protected in the UK, largely those that derive from EU directives, which oblige the UK to give workers positive rights in employment, such as the right to equal pay for equal work, and some positive protection against discrimination at work. Some measure of protection for socio-economic rights is afforded by the primarily civil and political rights guaranteed by the Human Rights Act (see Chapter 4). For example, the House of Lords, the highest court in the land, ruled in November 2005 that the conditions of asylum seekers who were deprived of benefits because they had claimed asylum status late and who were forbidden to find work amounted to 'inhuman and degrading treatment', which is prohibited under Article 3 of the European Convention on Human Rights.[1] Discrimination is prohibited in certain services and activities. But for the most part neither the government nor the judiciary here regard the courts as fit bodies to review public decisions on economic or social affairs, especially if they involve the allocation of public resources. The judges are anxious not to intervene in political issues of any kind; and it is argued, often vehemently, by government ministers that they would otherwise usurp the roles of elected governments and their policy-makers – and ultimately that of the electorate, who in a democracy determine such issues at general elections. Thus the British courts generally do not recognise most socio-economic rights, which are generally regarded as being 'non-justiciable' (i.e. the courts cannot consider issues of economic and social rights as they are outside their scope).

This argument is valid as far as it goes, but it is hardly conclusive. In a mature democracy, such as Britain, it ought to be recognised that a purely majoritarian approach – that is, the expression of the will of the majority at elections is sufficient in itself and may be regarded as 'the voice of the people' – fails to recognise the basic inter-dependence of democratic arrangements and human rights. Human rights are essential to ensure that a state satisfies the basic principles of democracy – namely, not only that the people should wield ultimate control over the decisions that are taken in their name, but also that they should be equal in the exercise of that control. The argument fails on another ground, too: the unrepresentative nature of first-past-the-post elections to the House of Commons places in power, and too often with commanding majorities, governments which have failed to win a majority even among those who vote, as in the 2005 election.[2] In a modern democracy people should have a double relationship with the state: in the first instance, they have the right to vote and the associated human rights that make a reality of the value of their vote; and equally, as individuals, their human rights should be protected to guarantee them not only full participation in their society and its government, but also a full life for their own sake. The vote is too blunt and diffuse an instrument to secure these goals.

Nor can majorities always be relied upon to ensure that all citizens possess the human rights to which they are entitled. This is why it is important that every citizen should be enabled to insist upon their rights and to seek remedy where they are denied. Thus making economic, social and cultural rights justiciable has two functions: first, the state would be obliged to take seriously its responsibilities to all its citizens and the qualities of democracy; second, it would give aggrieved people the means directly to assert their rights and needs and to share in the political decisions that provide the substance of their rights. Governments in the UK and most similar democracies accept these arguments so far as civil and political rights are concerned. But not for economic, social and cultural rights.

The public does not share the official disdain for economic and social rights. The public regards social equality as an important part of British democracy and has long expressed support in opinion polls for a British Bill of Rights that contains socio-economic rights alongside civil and political rights. In 2000, for example, the two top equal items in a popular Bill of Rights were the rights to 'fair trial before a jury' and 'hospital treatment in reasonable time', both having over 90 per cent 'majority backing' (that is, a majority of those who would include these rights in the Bill over those who would exclude them). Other economic and social rights obtained over 50 per cent 'majority backing'.[3] Similarly the Hutton commission on the NHS found that 94 per cent of the population believed that patients should have a 'lot of power' or a 'little power' over the medical treatment that they receive.[4] So the people want to be empowered. But they are not. Instead of giving people economic and social rights, governments have through legislation obliged a variety of authorities, local councils, benefits offices, health trusts and so on to provide benefits and social, health and welfare services and entitlements. But the legislation usually gives these bodies a wide degree of discretion over provision. Very few entitlements are mandatory, and even when they are, the judiciary will collude with the authorities in evading the duty where resources are an issue (see Chapter 4).

There is, however, one promising major development in official rights thinking. The Northern Ireland (NI) Human Rights Commission published a draft Bill of Rights for the province in 2001 that includes economic, social and environmental rights. The commission is consulting widely on this proposal and further drafts and has found strong public backing for including rights to health care, housing and employment in an NI Bill of Rights.[5] The commission's view is that since poverty and social exclusion represent a fundamental denial of human dignity, the protection of social and economic rights is an integral part of the delivery of effective human rights. Its third opinion survey in 2004 found continuing backing for enforceable social and economic rights: three quarters of people responded that such rights were 'essential' or 'desirable' and substantial proportions of Catholics (79 per cent) and Protestants (66 per cent) wished to impose a duty on government and public bodies to deliver them.

The commissioners are due to publish a revised draft Bill in June 2006 and to give their advice to the NI secretary in September. The draft Bill would be binding on the devolved administration, the Northern Ireland Executive and Assembly, and sets out social, economic and environmental rights alongside civil and political rights, including access to health care; protection against destitution; the right to 'adequate housing' appropriate to need; the right to choose religious, integrated or other schooling; the right to 'engage in work'; and protection against a 'dangerous environment'. The commission offers a choice of three scenarios: a set of minimum socio-economic rights only, enforceable through the courts; a wider range of 'not as fully fledged' rights, but making them progressively realisable in a non-discriminatory way as under the ICESCR; or thirdly, a directly enforceable set of minimum rights alongside a wider range of progressively realisable rights. In a progress report published in April 2004, the commissioners comment:

> For a country as wealthy as the United Kingdom there can be no excuse based on resources for not making these rights available to everyone in society and therefore it is appropriate for anyone who is denied the rights to be able to go to court to seek a remedy.[6]

What will the secretary of state make of such sentiments and the provisions of the draft Bill? Informed (and uninformed) opinion in Northern Ireland is not hopeful.

The first welfare state

It is then governments which determine the substance of economic and social rights – and their limits – through their policies and legislative programmes. The welfare state, founded by the 1945–51 Labour governments following the Second World War and then partially dismantled under Margaret Thatcher's governments, is now being re-cast by a New Labour government in a globalised world as the 'Anglo-social' welfare state (see below).[7] The postwar Labour government was moved by the idea of 'social citizenship' and adopted a universal statutory approach to make a reality of the idea. Their new creation, the 'welfare state', would in effect guarantee economic and social rights. A new structure of flat-rate social benefits was introduced; the NHS was founded, on the principle of free health care at the point of need; a programme of high-quality public housing was set in motion; universal state schooling was already set in place; and Keynesian economic policies were adopted to achieve full employment. Subsequent Conservative and Labour governments maintained the basic structures of the welfare state until the end of the 1970s. The Conservatives encouraged private provision in partnership with the welfare state, promoting private home owner-ship with the aim of creating a 'property-owning democracy', and encouraging private education, private and occupational pension schemes and private medical care. Labour governments sought to improve the welfare state incrementally, introducing allowances for dependent children, earnings-related pensions and other reforms.

The weaknesses of the initial approach have since been well documented, but Labour governments' goals were at least inclusive in intent. For a time the welfare state seemed invulnerable, prized as it was by the trade unions. But it was unpopular (the NHS apart), under-funded, statist and bureaucratic; and it often suffered badly in comparison with what the private market offered. Queues were almost its defining characteristic. The crises of the 1970s and the advent of a neo-liberal government under Thatcher exposed the vul-nerability of its statutory framework and the weaknesses of the trade unions. The statutory framework has since been dismantled over time by Conservative and Labour governments, which are pro-gressively shifting the burdens of economic, educational and social care provision onto the shoulders of individuals.

The new welfare state

Since 1997, the New Labour government has made a priority of restoring public services, with the NHS and state education in the van. *Guardian* journalists Polly Toynbee and David Walker published a pre-election audit of economic and social progress in 2005, concluding that, 'by 2005, Britain was a richer and fairer society than in 1997'. They quoted Clare Short as saying that the Blair government was 'creating a Labour country without telling the story'.[8] In this sense, Tony Blair and Gordon Brown have cautiously been seeking to return to a modified version of the 1945–51 Labour government's ideal of social citizenship. This, very briefly, is their model of social citizenship, three or four generations on from the Attlee model. They give private enterprise and provision a far more prominent role in economic and social policy, but have also responded to the needs of a fast-changing workforce by promoting policies for women and child-care that were not in the original blueprint. They have substantially boosted investment in key public services, notably health-care and education, and returned to policies of full employment (though not to neo-Keynesian economics), through increases in public sector employment, a flexible, or employer-friendly, labour market and strong economic objectives including those for growth and employment. But full employment, though an end objective of economic policy, was not made the first priority. Decisions over interest rates, probably the most powerful tool of economic management, were transferred from the Treasury to the Bank of England Monetary Policy Committee. Its brief was to deliver 'price stability – low inflation – and, subject to that, to support the government's economic objectives, including those for growth and employment'.

The mantras of the programmes to improve and modernise public services are 'choice' and 'voice'. To achieve its public service goals, the government has since 1997 engaged upon numerous programmes and schemes and monitored progress through a 'measurement culture' of targets (dominated by the Treasury's public service agreements with departments), league tables and inspectorates.[9] There is a sense in which the whole panoply of inspectors and regulators is a substitute for a participatory democracy in which citizens share in shaping policies, rather than a necessary complement to active citizenship.

In the NHS, the government is seeking to improve care standards, to reduce waiting times and to retain inclusive treatment, while introducing 'choice' and a small measure of 'voice' and contracting out certain treatments to the private sector. Similarly, it has attempted to raise standards in state schools and to introduce an element of 'choice' at secondary level, through giving parents an element of 'choice' of school and introducing specialist schools and privately sponsored city academies (where donors are said to be rewarded with honours and even peerages).[10] At the time of writing, Blair's choice agenda in secondary education is creating considerable turbulence in his parliamentary party. There are widely shared concerns among Labour MPs, party organisations such as Compass and in education generally that the latest plans will open the door to selection, largely on class grounds. In January 2006, a leaked report from the Audit Commission, the government body charged with ensuring the quality of public services, warned that the government's plans to make secondary schools autonomous could 'work against the interests of the most disadvantaged, least mobile and worst-informed parents and children'. New rules to prevent selection 'by the back door' would be needed; the plans made schools insufficiently accountable and focused on providing parental choice that is 'neither realistic nor an issue of primary importance to parents'.[11] In higher education, the government has abandoned universalist policy, by abolishing maintenance grants for all but low-income university students while introducing a regime of variable tuition fees and loans (repayable after graduation). In housing, the shift in emphasis from public renting to private ownership is irreversible, and the government is engineering another shift away from local authorities to registered social landlords in rented social housing. It has allowed house prices to rise in the private sector while failing to invest in sufficient rented, or 'affordable', housing for the hundreds of thousands of people priced out of the private market. The sheer rise in house prices, which the government did nothing to check, deepened not only the housing divide, but also a growing divide in wealth, between the 70 per cent who own their houses and the rest of the population.

Inequalities under the Labour government

The government has been committed to a strategy of discreet redistribution, eschewing more progressive income and wealth taxes in favour of 'stealth taxes' (such as stamp duty on the purchase of houses, which has struck at the wealthier). Tony Blair and Gordon Brown have conspicuously lauded the rewards of private enterprise and have foresworn any notion of systematically taxing them. Their redistributive policies are concentrated on improved public services and benefit policies at the lower end of the scale. The broad strategy that the government has followed was spelled out in the influential manifesto *The Blair Revolution*, by Peter Mandelson and Roger Liddle, two of Blair's closest allies, in 1996. They described the 'massive redistribution of wealth' which had taken place since 1979: 'The incomes of the top 10 per cent have risen by over 60 per cent in real terms. The bottom 30 per cent of the income distribution have seen at best a marginal improvement in living standards.' They argued that the Thatcherite theory that increased wealth 'trickled down' from the very rich to the poor 'simply hasn't worked for the bottom third'. But they rejected the traditional Labour agenda, of overt redistributive taxes on incomes and wealth as expounded in the party's shadow Budget of 1992, arguing that it had 'very little resonance' in modern society and would not have 'helped solve any of the real social problems'. They advocated an emphasis on public services and the need to persuade the better off to 'opt in'.[12] The influence on Blair is evident in the following exchange with Jeremy Paxman on BBC2's *Newsnight* on 4 June 2001, just before the general election:

> *Jeremy Paxman*: Do you believe that an individual can earn too much money?
>
> *Tony Blair*: I don't really – it is not – no, it's not a view I have. Do you mean that we should cap someone's income? Not really, no. Why? What is the point? You can spend ages trying to stop the

highest-paid earners earning the money but in an international market like today, you probably would drive them abroad. What does that matter? Surely the important thing is to level up those people that don't have opportunity in our society.

Paxman: But where is the justice in taxing someone who earns £34,000 a year, which is about enough to cover a mortgage on a one-bedroom flat in outer London, at the same rate as someone who earns £34 million? Where is the justice?

Blair: The person who earns £34 million, if they're paying the top rate of tax, will pay far more tax on the £34 million than the person on £34,000.

Paxman: I am asking you about the rate of tax.

Blair: I know and what I am saying to you is the rate is less important in this instance than the overall amount of tax that people would pay. You know what would happen, if you go back to the days of high top rates of tax. All that would happen is that those people, who are small in number actually, and you can spend a lot of time getting after the person earning millions of pounds a year, and then what you don't do is apply the real energy where it's necessary on things like the children's tax credit, the working families tax credit, the minimum wage, the New Deal, all the things that have helped people on lower incomes.

Paxman: But where is the justice in it?

Blair: When you say 'where is the justice in that', the justice for me is concentrated on lifting incomes of those that don't have a decent income. It's not a burning ambition for me to make sure that David Beckham earns less money.

In April 1999 the government introduced a national minimum wage for those at the lower end of the earnings scale and has raised it several times since. At the same time, ministers have abandoned the previously universalist Labour approach to social security and are boosting a basic low-income support scheme with 'targeted', or means-tested, benefits for old people and families with children (in or out of work), but this has produced consequent problems of low take-up and stigma. The government has also committed itself to end child poverty within a generation and embarked on a focused drive to regenerate poor and disadvantaged neighbourhoods.

But despite its attempts thus to address poverty, an Institute for Fiscal Studies (IFS) report, entitled *Poverty and Inequality in Britain*, argued in 2005 that 'the net effect of seven years of Labour government is to leave inequality effectively unchanged'. The report noted that in 2000/1, according to one method of measurement (the 'Gini coefficient'), inequality 'was at its highest level since at least 1961'. The IFS concluded that the impact of Labour's tax and benefit reforms was merely to 'just about halt the growth in inequality, and certainly not to reduce it'. Inequalities in income in the UK are greater than the EU average and considerably greater than in Germany and France. Wealth inequality has increased under New Labour. Between 1990 and 2000, the share of wealth held by the richest 10 per cent of the population rose from 47 per cent to 54 per cent. The wealthiest 1 per cent saw their share leap from 18 per cent to 23 per cent.

Such figures cast doubt on the central thrust of the government's policies – that poverty and its ills are best addressed by way of improved public services and targeted benefits at the lower end of the income scale. Certainly, the links between inequality, ill health and low life expectancy have been demonstrated by Richard Wilkinson, the social epidemiologist, in his latest study, *The Impact of Inequality*.[13] This systematic and wide-ranging study shows that once a developed society has reached a basic level of GNP, further increases in income (including increases for the poorest) do not improve health and life expectancy may even begin to diminish. This is because inequality and ill health are linked: the more unequal a society is, the more unhealthy its people are, and not merely the poor. What matters within countries is not absolute income, but income relative to others – a measure of status and position in society. Relative inequalities, he argues, affect the quality of life for all and contribute to social ills of all kinds, violence, racism and much else. We may add to that poverty and discrimination. Moreover, Wilkinson shows that it is not necessary to strive for unattainable levels of equality. Even small reductions in inequality can improve a nation's health, as the Scandinavians have demonstrated.

The legislative approach to social citizenship

Overall the government has retained the legislative approach to social citizenship that has long been common throughout western Europe and Scandinavia. While European states have created a tradition of civil and political rights, they adopt a programmatic approach to the substance of economic and social rights. There are signs of a shift towards a more rights-based stance in a few countries. For example, in the 1990s, Finland gave constitutional status to economic, social and cultural rights, while Norway has recently incorporated the ICESCR into domestic law. Ireland's National Anti-Poverty Programme, with its 'poverty-proofing' of legislative and policy proposals, is partly driven by a concern for economic and social rights. But for the most part, western European and Scandinavian countries rely on laws and policies that are designed to promote and protect the substance of economic and social rights, even though they do not put them into effect as enforceable rights. However, the welfare states of 'social Europe' are more firmly embedded in political and public consciousness and their institutions than the British model has been. Polly Toynbee, the *Guardian*'s social affairs expert, has recently commented that 'the public realms in France and Germany still put ours to shame'.[14] Both countries have invested more consistently in superior social security, pension and health services over the years than the UK, though the Labour government has since its first years attempted to close the gap on health and education. The Scandinavians are even more highly taxed welfare states with strong traditions of social justice. Thus the higher levels of investment that Labour introduced after 1999 were necessary simply to catch up with our European neighbours. In services such as the NHS and state education the government has had a decades-long backlog of neglect to make up.

The 'Anglo-social' model

Contributors to an Institute for Public Policy Research (IPPR) review of social justice in 2005 described New Labour's welfare state as 'the Anglo-social' model, combining high employment in flexible labour markets with strong public services.[15] Continental countries such as Germany and France are now struggling with high levels of unemployment and are considering unpopular reforms to their social and health policies and to their more protective labour markets. The IPPR authors argue that the UK's 'Anglo-social model', combining US economic dynamism with Scandinavian social equity, is less exposed to economic instability and high unemployment and better equipped to meet rising expectations of public services. Yet the balance of advantage is not as one sided as it is often portrayed. Both Germany and France have higher standards of social care than the UK, while productivity, trade and investment in Germany are far higher than in the UK, for example, and France's GDP remains higher than the UK's (though its growth rate is slower). The lure of the US model, with lower taxes but marginal welfare policies, is greater in the UK than in continental Europe. Moreover, the current government strategy relies on high levels of investment that will ultimately demand either higher taxes or cutbacks in provision. At the Treasury, Gordon Brown fears that either way the government may lose the support of 'Middle England', a crucial political constituency, who may either vote against the government in protest against higher taxation, or turn away from under-funded and failing public education and health services.

The need to keep the middle classes on board is a major, though unexpressed and often unseen, driver of the government's reform programme. Tony Blair shares Brown's fears and his reforms are largely aimed at the middle classes and their votes in key marginal seats. This is why health and education are top of his agenda. Polly Toynbee wrote vividly about Blair's ambitions in the *Guardian*:

> This is a man in a hurry. His city academies are rolling out – the most expensive schools in the poorest places. The NHS is shortly to break new frontiers when money follows each electronically recorded patient . . . all this is to save the welfare state by ensuring buy-in from the middle cases, the original Blair project and still his theme tune. . . . There will be no public acknowledgement – nor much private concern – about Britain's gross inequality, the prime cause of

educational failure and social disorder. Blair is happy to talk of pulling up the poorest but refuses point blank to discuss any question relating to wealth, greed or the need for a fairer share of rewards . . . he points to his government's credentials on the minimum wage, tax credits and the phenomenal extra funding of the NHS and schools. Talk of inequality would only frighten the middle classes. The trick has been to do all this while keeping them on-side. What purpose would be served? Not enough has been done in his eight years. The underlying reason for remorseless social disadvantage remains a silent subject in Blair politics.[16]

The challenges of class, poverty and deprivation do remain unresolved and the government's regeneration programmes are small scale and smack of tokenism. More recently migration has presented new and sharp challenges which the government evades (and makes worse) by adopting a posture of being tough on illegal immigration and asylum seeking. Yet as Toynbee and David Walker have documented, real, but slow and covert, progress has been made towards social justice since 1997.[17] The government deserves credit for having placed public services at the head of the political agenda. Blair and Brown have not only made extra funding available for most services, but they have also introduced a vital emphasis on outcomes. Serious attempts are being made, for example, to lift children of poor families out of deprivation through Sure Start and expanded nursery care.

Target-setting is a feature of good management everywhere; people have a right to expect the same standards of service everywhere rather than a postcode lottery. But the 'Anglo-social' welfare state is anchored in the highly centralist British state under a core executive that is over-powerful and unrepresentative. The executive dominates the two other arms of government – Parliament and the judiciary – and its policies and actions are largely unchallenged.[18] The government's top-down and highly centralised managerialism leaves little room for public service users and local providers to shape services at the point of delivery and refine targets accordingly. The centre dominates and has demoralised local government, once the hub of local public services, and has re-distributed services and functions to a plethora of unelected bodies, or quangos. Local authorities are reduced to being mere administrative cyphers and their electoral legitimacy is draining away. The introduction of devolved administrations in London, Northern Ireland (though devolution there is suspended), Scotland and Wales in Blair's first term did begin to disperse power from the centre, and the Human Rights Act began a process of empowering citizens against the state. But there remains an urgent need to disperse power far more widely: both to protect local democracy from the centre and from unaccountable public bodies locally, and to empower citizens more strongly against the state and corporate power. The current state of affairs violates a core principle of democracy and thus social justice – namely, that of equality of citizenship, which depends on effective equality in the exercise of democratic decision-making.[19]

Voice and choice

There is some recognition of the need for reform to decentralise power and to empower citizens in the Prime Minister's 'choice and voice' strategy for the public service. Neither choice nor voice are necessarily incompatible with equity, as some argue, but Tony Blair's objective in introducing such concepts into public services is plainly motivated by his desire to win over the middle classes. As it stands, the strategy is incomplete and flawed. It tends to privilege those who are used to choosing and making their voices heard – that is, the middle classes, who have historically also benefited dispro-portionately from public services. The strategy derives from the Major government's Citizen's Charter in the 1990s, which attempted to introduce and make known minimum standards to 'empower' users of public services nationally and locally. At the time, this initiative was decried as mere 'consumerism' and a diversion from principles of common citizenship. But independent auditing of the charter by bodies such as the National Consumer Council agreed that it did contribute to improving services and making it easier for service users in the NHS, social services, housing and so on to complain. It also encouraged providers to give the public clear information and to take their complaints seriously. The charter did not give people economic and social rights as such; but on the other hand, its non-legal nature made it flexible and versatile in practice. The main gains, however, were probably in the areas of consumer information and customer relations rather than redress.

The present government has given the idea of choice a more prominent role in setting standards and making services more responsive. In March 1999, ministers published a White Paper on modernising government which contained the commitment to make public services more 'responsive', declaring, 'People are exercising choice and demanding higher quality. In the private sector, service standards and service delivery have improved as a result. People are now rightly demanding a better service not just from the private sector but from the public sector too.'[20]

In a speech in 2001, the Prime Minister said that 'the key to reform is re-designing the services around the user – the patient, the pupil, the passenger, the victim of crime'. He said further that the aim was 'choice with equity' – 'choice and consumer power are the route to greater social justice, not social division'.

The trouble is that the various users – a patient, pupil, a homeless family, a disabled person – are neither equal in resources or need nor equally empowered by this simple idea. Britain is fundamentally divided by social class and ethnic disadvantage, with levels of poverty, inequality and deprivation that still rank among the highest in western Europe. Inequalities in resources and the ability and confidence to participate reflect these divisions. In 2004/5, the Public Administration Select Committee (PASC) examined how far the mechanisms of choice and voice gave service users in health-care, education and social housing 'more power and control over the services they use' and identified a need to ensure that the mechanisms actually delivered, 'especially for those who are less articulate and more vulnerable and hence have a greater dependency on effective public services'.[21] This recommendation presents the government with a challenge that it seems unlikely to meet. As we have stated above, choice and voice offer more to the advantaged than the disadvantaged; and at best they make services more responsive, not users more powerful.

Some witnesses to the PASC were forthright about the significance of power and control – rather than 'choice' – for the people they served or represented. MPs asked Peter Hay, strategic director of Birmingham's social care and health directorate, what vulnerable people in social care wanted and valued. He replied:

> Being more in charge . . . I am not sure it is necessarily choice, but certainly control is the important bit. Most users talk about being more in control of the arrangements in their lives rather than making a choice, because most of them would choose not to be in that situation.[22]

Take, for example, the idea of parental choice between schools. This is essentially a false choice, for it is schools who choose their pupils, not parents who choose their children's schools. Further, it is well known that house prices rise in the catchment areas of popular schools, areas that are usually already advantaged. Witnesses to the PASC pointed out that other inequalities affected the choice of secondary schools . The National Audit Office (NAO) stated:

> Nationally the impact of a mother being from a black or other minority ethnic community was to decrease the likelihood of being offered a favourite school by half. Non-employed lone parents were twice as likely to express dissatisfaction with the outcome of the school application process as dual employed couples.

A Birmingham head teacher found that 'choice itself perpetuates or exacerbates inequality if there are not checks and measures in a system where people do not have equal power in the choosing'. Dave Prentis, general secretary of UNISON, the public sector trade union, warned, 'What has emerged is a picture of increasing social polarisation.'

The point is that people do not exercise 'equal power in the choosing'. For example, the committee examined experiments in 'choice-based lettings' in social housing. These schemes make for efficiencies, savings and shorter void times (when properties lie vacant) in social housing, and they empower people to the limited extent that they can apparently choose the home that they would like to move into. But while applicants can choose a property, they cannot necessarily have it, especially in areas where there is a high level of demand for social housing. The most that can be said is that they choose to be considered for a property. And of course we are discussing a situation in which they are very likely to be priced out of any choice at all in the private ownership or rented market.

As for 'voice', the government is finding it hard to escape from the long-established ruling tradition in this country. Traditionally, governments rule 'by consent' and are not enthusiastic (for good reasons as well as bad) about the idea that citizens might wish to participate in their governance. By and large, local authorities are equally ill at ease with any such notion. At central and local level, there has been an increasing willingness to consult, and the Blair governments have made real progress in this respect. But ever since the Labour government's well-meaning Skeffington report on public participation planning at the end of the 1960s, governments have intermittently tried and failed to progress towards participation, especially among disadvantaged communities with successive area-based schemes. Thus it is no surprise that the PASC has found that the government was equivocal 'about its intentions of engaging the users of local services', after examining its schemes to involve the public in the running of foundation hospitals and the Sure Start local projects for early-years services for children and their parents. Ministers seem to have lost their initial enthusiasm for the role of the elected boards of foundation hospitals, which were supposed to bring 'far greater local ownership and involvement of patients, the public and staff'. The establishment of the boards was marked by caution in the way that the 'electorates' were constructed and the role of the boards defined. The Healthcare Commission, yet another creation in the hydra-headed New Labour state, has now taken over responsibilities for generating controlled participation in the running of the NHS. Its new annual 'health check' is designed to involve both Patient and Public Involvement Forums and Overview and Scrutiny Committees.

Community boards, composed of representatives of parents, professionals and others working in small and recognisable areas, were part of the original design for the Sure Start scheme and some centres became 'vital centres of neighbourhood life'.[23] But the government's later plans for Sure Start involved the effective abolition of these boards and the transfer of much of their work to more remote local authorities. Similarly, the £2 billion New Deal for Communities, the flagship programme for regeneration in poor areas, began with high hopes for involving residents in the local renewal schemes, special elections being held in some areas with relatively high levels of turnout. But residents proved to be slower moving than the Office of the Deputy Prime Minister (ODPM) and government regional offices, anxious for demonstrable results, liked, and the emphasis shifted to stronger local and regional government direction. The elections also proved too expensive.

In public housing, voice has turned out to be a nuisance to government ministers and officials, who know better than council tenants what is best for them. On the one hand, tenants are given a vote on plans for the future ownership or management of their estates; on the other, if they choose to remain with their local council, they are penalised, as the government denies the council precious funds for improving and modernising their homes.

Even in their less ambitious manifestations – recording user satisfaction, handling complaints and offering redress – official voice mechanisms were judged by the MPs on the PASC to be 'far from satisfactory'. They argued that more care and imagination were required to make such mechanisms more effective and recommended the establishment of a public satisfaction index.

Government by targets

For all the talk of 'new localism' and responsive services, the government's shifting mix of targets, programmes, inspection and exhortation adds up to a command strategy – not just 'Tony wants' (as in the Whitehall vernacular), but 'Gordon wants' and 'John [Prescott] wants', to which the bureaucratic chain of command below responds. This is a top-down strategy, dominated and directed by a core executive within a highly centralised state. The desire of both 10 Downing Street and the Treasury to dictate reform and impose standards is dramatised by the politics of the relationship between the Prime Minister and Chancellor. Whatever the state of that relationship may be, the power of their respective demands is immense. The Treasury's public service agreements (PSAs) with departments dictate strategy and targets across the whole spectrum of government activity (in which the Prime Minister's Delivery Unit has also played a part since 2001) while No. 10 edicts on the Prime Minister's reform agendas are reinforced by bilateral meetings between No. 10's envoys ('young people with laptops', snorted a former minister) and ministers and their advisers, and hosts of emails. The Prime Minister, his deputy and the Chancellor dominate the network of domestic Cabinet committees, the engine-rooms of direction and change. Below Whitehall, quangos at all levels have taken over the delivery of many public services from local authorities. The health, benefits and employment services are national state enterprises. Local authorities are supposed to hold the ring at local level, but have been drained of resources and initiative by the overweening centre.

PSAs form the body of the government's strategy for public services. These agreements set targets across the whole range of government and have done much to improve the coherence, accountability and transparency of government policies and actions. The original deluge of targets and centralist diktats has been refined and the process is constantly changing. Broadly, PSAs are the responsibility of the Treasury and Prime Minister's Delivery Unit and are agreed periodically with government departments (and a few local authorities). They are shaped by the government's priorities in public services, the areas of policy for which departments are responsible, and the resources which the Treasury is prepared to invest in those areas. This is an ad hoc process which responds more to political pressures than to a framework of economic and social needs. One of the Treasury's aims is to reconcile middle-income taxpayers to the government's investments in public services. There is no overall framework that takes account of the social and economic needs or rights of the population, against which the government's priorities could be measured. They are concerned with waiting times for treatment on the NHS, for example, but do not question the adequacy of benefit levels for the unemployed.

There is, in short, no clear strategy to entrench social reform. Yet such a framework, encompassing strategy and priorities agreed outside as well as within Whitehall, is necessary if Britain is to create the social justice that is the avowed aim of the present government. The government could – and should – create and publish its own framework. But such a framework already exists, in the form of the ICESCR; and the government could employ, or adapt, this framework whether or not it incorporated the covenant into British law.

Meanwhile, the government can neglect economic and social needs that are in fact desperate so as to concentrate resources on services or needs that are higher up the political agenda. Housing is a case in point. As we shall see in Chapter 9, the government has failed to invest in providing urgently needed affordable housing, or even to ensure a high level of house-building. It is only belatedly trying to remedy a situation that has gone from bad to worse under its stewardship. The PSAs set fine-sounding strategic priorities and performance targets for the ODPM in housing, for example:

- achieving a better balance between housing availability and the demand for housing, including improving affordability, in all English regions;
- by 2010, bringing all social housing into a decent condition with most of this improvement taking place in deprived areas;
- increasing the proportion of vulnerable households in the private sector, including families with children, who live in homes that are in decent condition.

However, not only were the resources and political will necessary to deliver on such targets missing, even the threshold for 'decent condition' fell short of what is desirable. The select committee which oversees the ODPM found that the Decent Homes Standard was 'too basic' and applied to too few areas of the country.[24] The government replied that it expected landlords to improve properties to a higher standard and the regulator for registered social landlords said that they were doing so. But the National Consumer Council felt that the 'the ODPM has over-estimated the extent to which the market is likely to raise above these standards. In most situations the demand for housing exceeds supply. There are not pressures there.' The ODPM select committee pointed out further that funding was only 'geared' towards providing the basic level, 'so it is unclear how further investments are meant to be funded'; and if social landlords were unable to bring their stock up to higher standards, social housing by 2010 was still likely to be seen 'as the poor relation with a degree of stigma attached'.

Select committees can of course examine PSAs, as the ODPM committee has, and the government is admirably open about publishing its successes and failures in achieving the targets set; New Labour, according to Polly Toynbee and David Walker, deserves to be known as 'the most scrupulously self-monitoring government ever'.[25] But there is no rigorous overall analysis of the programme by a body independent of the government, and Treasury officials have been hostile to the idea that the NAO, the natural body to take on validating the whole process, might do so, even though several select committees have recommended that it should. The government's targets are set nationally after negotiations within Whitehall and with at least half an eye on potential electoral repercussions. There is a case, as we acknowledge above, for key national targets, standards and entitlements, backed by spending plans to fulfil them. But there is also, as two Fabian authors argue, a case 'for more local ownership of many targets (for example, school improvement targets) grounded in particular circumstances and needs, and nourishing a performance culture that involves something more than responding to eternal demands, with all the gaming, cheating and perverse consequences associated with this'.[26]

The PASC has pressed the government to build 'greater local autonomy' and 'de-centralised political accountability' into the target regime, and the government itself has acknowledged the need for 'constrained discretion' at local level:

> Greater discretion provides local service providers with more opportunities to innovate, design and develop services around the needs and priorities of their communities . . . it is likely that many public services will be more effectively governed by regional, or local,

bodies with better knowledge about providers' performance and the needs of the communities they serve.[27]

There is a clear need to decentralise in the interests of efficient and focused public services, and to allow local providers to set their own targets within an overall framework. Local schools could for example decide targets that met local needs involving school governors, parents and the local education authority. Yet as the latest democratic audit, *Democracy under Blair*, has shown, the government is most reluctant to share power, distrusts local authorities and looks to appointed public bodies to provide many local services.[28] So much of whatever shift towards local providers takes place will simply involve bodies without any direct accountability to their users or communities.

The PASC report on targets does go further, arguing that service users should be consulted along with service providers, local councillors and others 'at the sharp end of service delivery', and complaining that far too little attention is paid to the interests and needs of the users: 'The government says a great deal about strengthening the focus on users, but there is very little serious attempt to involve them in the measurement culture.'[29]

Influence on government

But consultation, desirable though it is if well done, is a bridge too near. As the IPPR's Social Justice collection argues, progress towards social justice should embrace 'democratic pluralism' and a guaranteed dispersion of power. Its authors share a view that social justice demands an equality of citizenship which gives people an effective and equal role in the exercise of democratic decision-making, and they propose a new constitutional settlement that enshrines the powers and funding of devolved administrations and local authorities. As David Miller argues, an important aspect of equal citizenship is the right to influence government. But only about a third of people think that they could have an influence on the way the country is run if they got involved in politics. Most citizens in Britain want more influence on government between elections but feel that they don't have anywhere near enough. And those that do are most likely to have social skills, educational background, professional or social position or industrial muscle. Those who do not are most likely to be poor, less well educated and in need.

The UN review of social justice in the UK

A UN committee has published an independent and authoritative review of Britain's progress towards social justice, which argues that the adoption of a charter or bill of economic and social rights could provide a clear and comprehensive framework for judging the state's progress on social justice while at the same time empowering individual people in need to engage more confidently in shaping and defining public services and benefits. This review was published in May 2002 by the UN Committee on Economic, Social and Cultural Rights, after its expert members had considered a government report on compliance with the ICESCR. The covenant sets out rights to an adequate standard of living, to the highest attainable standard of health, to protections of and in work, to shelter, social security and education, to partaking in cultural life and to benefits from scientific progress (see Chapter 2 and Appendix 1 for a full list of protected rights). Thus it provides a comprehensive framework, as it were, of targets focused on the needs and entitlements of individual citizens. Besides the report, the committee considered submissions from a range of non-governmental organisations and took oral evidence from government officials. Its concluding observations remain a valuable overall guide to progress on economic and social rights in the UK. We go on to describe the UN committee's comments and recommendations in full in Chapters 2 and 5; here we provide a short summary.

The UN committee began with praise for the enactment of the Human Rights Act in 1998, incorporating the European Convention on Human Rights – largely civil and political rights – into UK law (see Chapter 4); the establishment of the Northern Ireland Human Rights Commission; the New Deal employment programme; and other measures taken to reduce homelessness, rough sleeping and school exclusions undertaken since its third report in 1997. The committee also commended the adoption of the Care Standards Act 2000, establishing the National Care Standards Commission for England and the Care Inspectorate for Wales (and setting national minimum standards for the independent health sector to reflect those in the NHS); and welcomed the adoption of new cell standards in prisons (which halved overcrowding in cells) and the expansion of educational activities for prisoners.

The committee regretted that the British government still refused to incorporate the ICESCR in British law, pointing out that, having ratified the covenant, the UK was legally obliged to comply with its provisions and give them full effect in the domestic legal order. It expressed further regret that the UK has not yet prepared a national human rights plan of action, as recommended in the 1993 Vienna Declaration, and urged the government to do so. The committee then listed specific 'causes of concern': the existence of de facto discrimination; the inadequacies of the national minimum wage; the absence of a legally protected right to strike; the incidence of domestic violence; persistent and considerable poverty, homeless-ness, poor quality housing and 'fuel poverty'; the introduction of tuition fees and student loans in higher education; and segregated schools in Northern Ireland. The committee urged the government to incorporate the ICESCR into UK law, and further recommended that it 'review and strengthen its institutional arrangements' to ensure that its obligations under the covenant are taken into account, at an early stage, in formulating legislation and policies on issues such as poverty reduction, social welfare, housing, health and education. The committee also issued a series of detailed recommendations. Meanwhile, the *Daily Telegraph* rebuked the committee for the 'breathtaking effrontery' with which it had 'chosen to lecture the United Kingdom on the way in which we run our affairs'.[30]

2

Britain's international rights obligations*

What are the UK's international obligations on socio-economic rights? How are such rights supposed to be made available to citizens of this and other countries? What are the obligations with which the UK should comply and what standards are set? What is the attitude of British governments to such obligations and standards? These obligations and the rights which attach to them − as defined in international law − mark out the parameters of this audit. We begin here by briefly explaining the development of international law on economic, social and cultural rights. We then go on to describe in detail the obligations and standards set by the International Covenant on Economic, Social and Cultural Rights and the conventions of the International Labour Organization (ILO); the different mechanisms by which compliance is monitored; and how far the UK is bound by them.

Progress on socio-economic rights

The foundation stone of international human rights protection is the International Bill of Rights, which comprises the Universal Declaration on Human Rights (UDHR), the International Covenant on Economic, Social and Cultural Rights (ICESCR) and the International Covenant on Civil and Political Rights (ICCPR). The UDHR gives broad expression to civil, political, economic, social and cultural rights − all on an equal footing. It recognises a central range of economic, social and cultural rights. For example, Article 25.1 states:

*In collaboration with Judith Mesquita.

Everyone has the right to a standard of living adequate for the health and well-being of himself and of his family, including food, clothing, housing and medical care and necessary social services, and the right to security in the event of unemployment, sickness, disability, widowhood, old age or other lack of livelihood in circumstances beyond his control.

Article 26 recognises the right to education, and Article 23 establishes rights to and in work. The United Nations has always adhered in theory to the position that, as expressed at the World Conference on Human Rights in 1993, all human rights are 'universal, indivisible and interdependent and inter-related. The international community must treat human rights globally in a fair and equal manner on the same footing, and with the same emphasis.' But in practice individual governments and the international community have for years neglected economic, social and cultural rights and have placed far more emphasis on civil and political rights.

The twin UN covenants, the ICCPR and the ICESCR, elaborate respectively on the civil and political rights and the economic, social and cultural rights contained in the UDHR, and each establishes sets of legal obligations to protect these rights in the states that ratify them. Apart from the ICESCR, Britain has ratified five other major UN treaties which reinforce protections of socio-economic rights for particular groups – namely, the Convention Relating to the Status of Refugees (1951); the International Convention on the Elimination of All Forms of Racial Discrimination (CERD, 1965); the Convention on the Elimination of All Forms of Discrimination against Women (CEDAW, 1979); and the Convention on the Rights of the Child (CRC, 1989). Britain also subscribes to the wide-ranging protections of labour rights enshrined in the treaties of the ILO. Regional treaties protecting economic, social and cultural rights have also been drawn up and adopted in Europe, the Americas and Africa, paralleling those at the international level. Within Europe, the Council of Europe's European Social Charter and the European Union's Social Chapter provide important socio-economic protections (see Chapter 3).

The original intention of the international community was to draft a single international human rights covenant, but divisions between the west and the Soviet bloc compromised this objective and resulted in the creation of the two International Covenants. Broadly, the western states held that civil and political rights were more important and that human rights should be monitored at the international level. The eastern bloc states held that economic, social and cultural rights were more important, and they were hostile to establishing an international mechanism for monitoring human rights treaties. The international community has agreed to adhere, at least in theory, to the united position that all rights are indivisible and must be treated on an equal footing. In pursuit of this position, the other international and regional instruments on economic, social and cultural rights have been agreed and widely adopted. But in practice individual governments and the international community neglected socio-economic rights for years and placed far more emphasis on civil and political rights. From the outset, the UN Human Rights Committee, composed of independent experts, was set up to monitor compliance with the ICCPR and to monitor states' reports on their progress. In 1966, the UN General Assembly adopted an Optional Protocol to the ICCPR, enabling the committee to receive complaints alleging violations of rights set forth in the covenant. In contrast, a UN political body, the Economic and Social Council, was initially given the task of monitoring progress on the ICESCR. The current expert monitoring agency, the Committee on Economic, Social and Cultural Rights, was appointed only in 1984 and did not meet until 1987. There is still no Optional Protocol enabling the committee to receive and respond to individual complaints (although there is increasing support internationally for such a protocol; see below).

Further, the Commission on Human Rights, the world's largest inter-governmental human rights forum, focused its attention on the promotion and protection of civil and political rights through its procedures for addressing human rights violations, considering situations confidentially and appointing working groups or special rapporteurs to investigate human rights issues. Only recently has the commission addressed economic, social and cultural rights in a systematic way. It has now adopted various resolutions on socio-economic rights issues and appointed special rapporteurs on the rights to education (1998), food (2000), adequate housing (2000) and health (2002), as well as on other themes closely associated with such rights, such as extreme poverty (1998), the right to development (1998) and structural adjustment policies and foreign debt (2000).[2] Thus a new resolve to address economic, social and cultural rights is growing, not only at a global level, but also at a regional level throughout the world. In 1998, the Economic and Social Council insisted:

> In general, legally binding international human rights standards should operate directly and immediately within the domestic legal system of each State party, thereby enabling individuals to seek enforcement of their right before national courts and tribunals . . . Although the precise method by which Covenant rights are given effect in national law is a matter for each State party to decide, the means used should be appropriate in the sense of producing results which are consistent with the full discharge of its obligations by the State party.[3]

The British 'way of doing things'

However, political circles in the UK are opposed to any idea of incorporating the International Covenant on Economic, Social and Cultural Rights into British law. Such an idea does not fit into the world view of a political class which signs international human rights treaties as a matter of international good will and is satisfied that the 'British way of doing things' is superior so far as issues of democracy and human rights are concerned. Thus the UK government obstinately agrees to disagree with the UN Committee on Economic, Social and Cultural Rights, the expert body that monitors compliance with the covenant, on the need to incorporate the covenant into British law. The government is also one of the critics of an optional protocol to the ICESCR, now being discussed by a UN working group, which would give individual citizens a right of complaint to the committee. The government scarcely bothers even to publicise the obligations imposed by the covenant or the reports of the expert UN committee on UK compliance with those obligations. The committee's reviews generate little domestic discussion and have been largely ignored by the media – but not entirely. As we have mentioned, the *Daily Telegraph*, not necessarily representative of attitudes towards socio-economic rights or the work of the UN in British civil society, fulminated about the 'breathtaking effrontery' with which the committee 'has chosen to lecture the United Kingdom on the way in which we run our affairs'.[4] However, scrutiny is increasing, notably on account of the efforts of non-governmental organisations and charities, such as JUSTICE and Oxfam, and the Joint Committee on Human Rights (JCHR) (a parliamentary committee on which MPs and peers sit together), which published a report on Britain's obligations under the covenant after examining the UN committee's concluding observations in 2004.[5]

The UK government's official view was reiterated in evidence to the UN committee at its latest two five-yearly reviews in 1997 and 2002 and was set out clearly for the JCHR's own review.[6] For the government, Bill Rammell, then parliamentary under-secretary at the Foreign and Commonwealth Office, explained why the government was not willing to incorporate the UN covenant into British law or to give legal force to socio-economic rights. He described socio-economic rights as 'principles and objectives, rather than legal obligations', arguing that they represented issues 'for which there is no absolute standard and are rightly the business of governments and their electorates through general elections to determine what standard we should achieve'. He foresaw profound and adverse consequences should the courts look at issues such as the right to food or housing:

> For example, if the court took a decision on health, in terms of the adequate standard, and you had recently had a party that had been elected on a platform to private education expenditure, I think people would ask serious questions and have concerns about the process that was being undertaken.

He added that the wording of some articles in the ICESCR was 'sufficiently loose and imprecise' that, if incorporated, then 'the courts would end up making policy decisions that are properly the responsibility of government'. Questions about the allocation of resources between policy areas belonged within 'our governmental and political structure that is properly a matter for government and the general electorate rather than the courts'.[7]

Britain's international obligations

The ICESCR provides the central protections for economic, social and cultural rights under international human rights law. As we state above, Britain has ratified the covenant, along with five other major UN treaties, which reinforce protections of socio-economic rights for particular groups, and key conventions of the ILO, which are designed to protect important labour rights. The socio-economic rights that these instruments are designed to protect have a significant part to play in the lives of British people, and ought to be fully recognised in law along with the civil and political rights that are legally protected in the UK. The fact is that civil and political rights and economic, social and cultural rights are interdependent and indivisible. People in this country (and around the world) need both together to live satisfactory and autonomous lives: socio-economic rights are essential building blocks for people to realise the civil and political rights which secure democracy. Compliance with the ICESCR receives scant political or social scrutiny at a domestic level in the UK. Yet it protects rights which are vital to the everyday lives of British people:

- equality between men and women (Article 3);
- the right to work (Article 6);
- the right to fair conditions of employment (Article 7);
- the right to form and join trade unions (Article 8);
- the right to social security (Article 9);
- the right to protection of the family (Article 10);
- the right to an adequate standard of living (including the right to food, clothing and housing) (Article 11);
- the right to health (Article 12);
- the right to education (Article 13);
- the right to culture (Article 15).

These rights are to be guaranteed in accordance with the principles of non-discrimination (Article 2.2) and progressive realisation (Article 2.1). (See Appendix A for the text of the covenant.)

The ICESCR, as an international treaty, is binding on the UK in international law only. The UN committee that monitors it has moral authority only, but it does help to focus attention on socio-economic rights in the UK through its regular reviews. The government is obliged to submit a state report on its compliance with the covenant and non-governmental organisations increasingly also give evidence to the committee. Government officials then give evidence at a committee hearing and are interrogated by its members. The committee then adopts and publishes its concluding observations, which include positive remarks, criticisms and recommendations. The UK ratified the convention in 1976 (just six months after it had entered into force), and has since submitted four reports on its compliance with the treaty, most recently in 2002.

This brief audit uses as its framework the norms and obligations on socio-economic rights as defined in the ICESCR and interpreted by the monitoring committee of experts. We do not examine cultural rights to the same degree. Traditionally, countries like the UK, which are hostile to socio-economic rights or which have a poor record of compliance, argue that they are framed in terms that are too broad and ill defined to impose legal obligations. Thus, they demand, what does a right to health or adequate shelter imply, especially when health-care and housing standards vary so considerably between countries and regions? In contrast, they point out that a civil and political right, such as the right not to be tortured or discriminated against, is more clear cut and innately more amenable to definition.

In reality, such arguments are not inspired by genuine difficulties, for example, in deciding upon the appropriate standards for housing in a western European state such as the UK. British political and official circles are simply unwilling to have the domestic political and economic policies which shape the provision and standards of housing and access to housing – to take the same example – subjected to human rights criteria, especially if set by external bodies, and made enforceable by individual citizens through the courts.

In fact, while much remains to be done, an emerging body of

jurisprudence and related documentation now exists which more closely defines the scope of socio-economic rights and helps bust some of the myths surrounding their application. It is possible to begin to define the UK's obligations as set out in the ICESCR, as the UN Committee on Economic, Social and Cultural Rights showed in its concluding observations on the UK's record only four years ago, in May 2002 (we summarise these findings in Chapter 1 and more fully in Chapter 5). It would of course be desirable to go further and draw up actual case law, but in the absence of a complaints mechanism, no formal body of case law can exist. However, the committee's observations on the reports of other states, general comments and statements together constitute an authoritative interpretation of the covenant. Philip Alston, a former chairman of the committee, and others have argued persuasively that its general comments provide 'jurisprudential insights' and carry 'significant legal weight'.[8]

In theory also the ICESCR should exert some influence on the British courts, at least in so far as they can interpret legislation in a manner consistent with its obligations. However, in practice, the courts have shown little direct reliance on the socio-economic rights set out in the covenant. The JCHR concluded in 2004 that the ICESCR has 'a very limited impact in our domestic law'. However, the committee's report argues that the UK, in ratifying the covenant, has made a commitment, binding in international law, to abide by its terms. 'This requires government, Parliament and the courts to make efforts to ensure the fullest possible compliance with the terms of the Covenant'.[9] However, as we shall see later in this chapter, UK governments are quite prepared to ignore such international commitments, and even to denounce the terms of such treaties the UK has ratified.

Cross-cutting obligations

Each socio-economic right that we briefly examine in the rest of this audit comprises a specific body of norms and varying obligations. However, there are a number of cross-cutting norms and obligations, which form the overall scaffolding for the protection of socio-economic rights; and we consider them in turn here. The ICESCR, like all human rights treaties, imposes three types of obligation on states that ratify it:

- the obligation to *respect* the rights set out requires states to refrain from interfering directly or indirectly with them;
- the obligation to *protect* requires states to take measures to prevent third parties from interfering with the social, economic and cultural rights it contains;
- the obligation to *fulfil* requires states to adopt appropriate legislative, administrative, budgetary, judicial, promotional and other measures towards the full realisation of such rights. Under this obligation the governments of all states that have ratified the covenant should also take positive measures that enable and assist individuals and communities to enjoy their socio-economic rights, and to provide a right where individuals or communities are unable to realise the right themselves due to circumstances beyond their control.[10]

Non-discrimination and equal treatment

Non-discrimination and equal treatment are among the most fundamental principles of international human rights law. In the ICESCR, Article 2.2 prohibits discrimination on grounds of race, colour, sex, language, religion, political or other opinion, national or social origin, property, birth or other status. Article 3 obliges states to undertake to ensure the equal right of men and women to enjoy the rights set out in the covenant. While the covenant defines specific grounds of discrimination, the reference to 'other status' implies that the grounds actually set out are illustrative; and in 2000 the UN committee added physical or mental disability, health status (including HIV/AIDS) and sexual orientation to the list in its general comments.

International human rights law also encourages affirmative action to promote the equal enjoyment of human rights among all people and groups. For example, the CEDAW states:

States Parties shall take in all fields, in particular in the political, social, economic and cultural fields, all appropriate measures, including legislation, to ensure the full development and advancement of women, for the purpose of guaranteeing them the exercise and enjoyment of human rights and fundamental freedoms on a basis of equality with men.

Obligations – immediate and progressive

Exactly how should ordinary citizens in the UK benefit from the government's obligations under the ICESCR? First, it obliges British governments to use the maximum resources available to realise fully and progressively over time the economic, social and cultural rights that it protects, through legislation and other means. Article 2.1 of the covenant sets out the key obligations to which the United Kingdom is signed up, stating:

Each State Party to the present Covenant undertakes to take steps, individually and through international assistance and co-operation, especially economic and technical, *to the maximum of its available resources, with a view to achieving progressively the full realisation of the rights recognised in the present Covenant by all appropriate means*, including particularly the adoption of legislative measures [emphasis added].

Only a few key obligations, including the guarantee that British citizens can exercise their covenant rights free from discrimination, are thus of immediate effect. The covenant does not seek to guarantee to citizens of the UK (or other signatory states) immediate access to the generality of the rights it contains, such as for example a homeless person's right to be re-housed. The government is, however, bound to realise such a right for its citizens progressively over time.

Many countries interpret Article 2.1 as a permissive statement. However, the Committee on Economic, Social and Cultural Rights has made it clear that the article isn't an escape clause. In General Comment 3, issued in December 1990, the committee insisted that while states may seek to realise covenant rights progressively, 'steps towards that goal must be taken within a reasonably short time after the Covenant's entry into force for the States concerned'. Moreover, these steps should be 'deliberate, concrete and targeted as clearly as possible towards meeting the obligations recognised in the Covenant'.

In ratifying the covenant, the UK has accepted a central obligation to give effect to the rights therein 'by all appropriate means, including the adoption of legislative measures' (Article 2.1). The flexibility introduced by the phrase 'by all appropriate means' is designed to allow for the differences in legal and administrative systems among states; and the UN committee considers that the phrase covers administrative, financial, educational and social measures. Hardly surprisingly, a government's budget, spending programmes and policies, controls on corporate and individual conduct, and educational initiatives all have a role to play in securing the economic, social and cultural rights of citizens. Article 2.1, however, clearly recognises that legislative measures are necessary and sometimes indispensable and should thus play a central role, as the committee has noted.

However, Britain is obliged to go further. British citizens should be able to seek a remedy, or redress, when they are denied socio-economic rights to which they are entitled under the covenant. One way of doing this would be to incorporate the covenant into British law. The government has set its face against this. But regardless of incorporation, the UN committee insists that socio-economic rights must be justiciable in any state that has ratified the covenant: 'The Covenant norms must be recognised in appropriate ways within the domestic legal order, appropriate means of redress, or remedies, must be available to any aggrieved individual or group, and appropriate means of ensuring governmental accountability must be put in place.'[11] In other words, the British government should give people effective means of redress or remedies when their socio-economic rights under the covenant are violated – and, moreover, it must also be accountable for its policies.

This right to an effective remedy need not involve a judicial remedy through the courts. The UN committee has stated that 'among the measures which might be considered appropriate, in addition to legislation, is the provision of judicial remedies with respect to rights which may, in accordance with the national legal system, be considered justiciable'. In some cases, the committee has said that quasi-judicial or administrative mechanisms may provide adequate redress. The committee has also noted in General Comment 3 in 1990 that provisions under Articles 2, 3, 7, 8, 10, 13 and 15, covering non-discrimination, equality between men and women, trade union activity, protection of young people and their education, 'seem to be capable of immediate application by judicial and other organs in many national legal systems'.

The British government still holds the view, contrary to the position of the Committee on Economic, Social and Cultural Rights, that the socio-economic rights contained in the ICESCR are not justiciable, as Bill Rammell argued in evidence to the JCHR (see above), as did Lord Goldsmith in the negotiations over the EU Charter of Fundamental Rights (see Chapter 3). Britain's periodic reports to the committee state explicitly that the UK authorities regard economic and social rights as 'programmatic objectives rather than legal obligations'. A British official in the delegation reporting to the committee in 2002 also informed its expert members that 'the rights contained within this treaty are non-justiciable and . . . it is not within the remit of British magistrates to interpret its provisions'.[12] Thus socio-economic rights are met 'programmatically', and incompletely, as Chapters 6 to 11 show, by way of legislation; and their provision is not impartially monitored against human rights standards, apart from periodic reviews by the UN committee. Yet the complaint mechanisms associated with the CEDAW, the European Social Charter, the African Charter on Human and People's Rights and the American Convention on Human Rights provide evidence of the justiciability of socio-economic rights and of their enforcement through the courts; as do socio-economic cases from South Africa at the domestic level.

Delivery of economic, social and cultural rights

What does all this mean for ordinary citizens in the UK? First, according to the Committee on Economic, Social and Cultural

Rights, Britain is obliged, as a signatory state, to ensure that economic, social and cultural rights here are available, accessible, acceptable and of good quality. In general comments on the rights to adequate food, education, health and water, the committee defines these criteria within a general framework which allows for differences in exactly how they should apply. In general, the international experts say:

- the relevant goods, services and facilities must be *available* in sufficient quantity within a country;
- they must be *accessible* – that is, supplied free from discrimination, within safe physical reach and affordable;
- they must be culturally and ethically *acceptable*;
- they must be scientifically appropriate and of good quality.

Secondly, citizens of the UK should be given a say in policies, an opportunity to express preferences and influence in the ways rights are implemented, monitored and assessed. Such opportunities to participate in the delivery of socio-economic rights are a recognised human right in themselves.[13] These rights are of little value and even meaningless without participation. But what does this mean in practice? The processes should be accountable;[14] but while democratic arrangements are an essential component of the right to participate, they are not always sufficient. Special arrangements may be needed to give people living in marginal groups or social exclusion the capacity to participate effectively. Yet, as we have seen, British governments do not accept the validity of international human rights instruments so far as their domestic responsibilities are concerned, and have in the past even denounced them; and ruling traditions are not geared towards participation that goes beyond consultation.

Human rights standards at work

Well before ratifying the major UN socio-economic treaties and the European Social Charter, the UK was a founder member of the ILO in 1919. The ILO, which is the only surviving major creation of the Treaty of Versailles, became the first specialist agency of the UN in 1946.

The ILO formulates international labour standards through its conventions and recommendations, setting minimum standards for the right to organise, freedom of association, collective bargaining and other work-related issues. There are 185 ILO conventions, the first six dating back to 1919, and all but twenty-seven are still in force. Britain has ratified eighty-three ILO conventions, including, together with other EU countries, the core ILO conventions – no. 87 (1948), Freedom of Association and Protection of the Right to Organise; no. 98 (1949), The Right to Organise and Collective Bargaining; no. 100 (1951), Equal Remuneration; and no. 111 (1958), Discrimination (Employment and Occupation).

Under Article 22 of the ILO constitution, Britain is obliged to report back on its observance of all conventions that it is signed up to. Britain's reports (like those of other signatories) are monitored by two ILO bodies. The Committee of Experts on the Application of Conventions and Recommendations undertakes a juridical examination of state reports in closed session and makes observations on any discrepancies between a state's laws and practice and the requirements of ILO conventions (perhaps after asking for more information). On the diplomatic front, the Conference Committee on Standards (made up of state, employer and trade union representatives) meets at the ILO's annual International Labour Conference and discusses more serious cases raised by the committee in open session. This is a political forum that can take into account issues of policy. The conference adopts a final report. There is also an extensive complaints system. Individual states may submit complaints against each other and the ILO governing body will appoint a commission of inquiry to investigate. Employer organisations and trade unions are increasingly making representations that their government is not complying with its obligations and a tripartite committee considers their case (complaints by individuals are not admissible). The ILO can apply no sanctions, as with all international human rights bodies, other than to 'name and shame'.

British Conservative governments in the 1980s and 1990s were shameless. For ten years they refused to ratify ILO conventions and denounced others. In pursuit of their legislation restricting trade union power, they took a very narrow view of ILO Conventions 87 and 98, despite concerns expressed by the TUC and ILO supervisory bodies. The most notable violation of ILO obligations was Margaret Thatcher's decision in 1984 to ban trade union membership at GCHQ, the government 'listening' centre. Labour ministers after 1997 criticised the Conservative governments for their breaches of international labour standards, claimed that they took their ILO obligations 'very seriously', restored trade union membership to workers at GCHQ and ratified two core ILO conventions. They presented the Employment Relations Act 1999 as a response to ILO criticisms, but it made only partial compliance with Britain's obligations and was soon challenged in the 1999 report of the ILO Committee of Experts. As Chapter 11 makes clear, breaches of ILO conventions are likely to continue under New Labour.

International assistance and co-operation

Britain also has international obligations towards realising or protecting socio-economic rights in other countries under Article 2.1's provisions for 'international assistance and co-operation'. The UN Committee on Economic, Social and Cultural Rights has elaborated the dimensions of these obligations in its general comments, beginning with a general injunction in 2000 on covenant states, including Britain, to respect economic, social and cultural rights in other countries and to prevent third parties from violating them.[15] Countries with available resources, especially developed countries such as Britain, should also enable access to services, goods and facilities essential to economic, social and cultural rights and provide adequate aid. They are also requested to ensure that they give due attention to these rights in international agreements and tailor their actions as part of international organisations such as the World Bank, the International Monetary Fund and the World Trade Organization not only to respect economic, social and cultural rights but also to ensure that their agreements and policies take greater account of them. In its concluding observations in 2002 on Britain's latest periodic report, the committee encouraged the UK government, as a member of international financial institutions, in particular the International Monetary Fund and the World Bank, to do all it can to ensure that the policies and decisions of those organisations are in conformity with the obligations of States parties under the Covenant, in particular with the obligations . . . concerning international assistance and co-operation.

3

European protection of socio-economic rights

It is through Europe that the United Kingdom has made most progress towards protecting socio-economic rights at home. One of the consequences of joining the then European Economic Community in 1973 was that the UK also signed up to economic and then gradually social rights under what has become known as the 'first pillar' of the community. But the UK also ratified two instruments of the Council of Europe – the European Convention on Human Rights in 1951 and the European Social Charter in 1962 – which indirectly in the first case and directly in the second seek to protect economic and social rights. The European Union Social Chapter and the Community Charter of Fundamental Social Rights – not to be confused with the EU Charter of Fundamental Rights – have further added to the panoply of socio-economic protections. In this chapter we describe the overlapping effects of the obligations under these various European initiatives and how and where they may be enforced.

European Community law

European Community law has transformed the protection of economic and social rights in the UK, especially in employment. The first and greatest impact of EU law was in the areas of sex discrimination and equal pay, but it has subsequently pervaded nearly every aspect of employment.[1] EU law is particularly crucial in terms of employment rights – the EU is the only region in the world in which workers' rights are legally embedded, though only for nationals of the member states, or those with 'parasitic' rights (i.e. in the UK at present only workers of UK nationality plus those few non-nationals with 'parasitic' rights, though this is starting to change and broaden out). Membership of the EU carries with it obligations to implement in UK law the requirements of EU treaties, regulations, directives and decisions and to submit to the jurisdiction of the European Court of Justice (ECJ) as the final arbiter of EU law. Legislation decided at EU level can take three forms: *regulations* are directly applicable in member states and are most likely to have a direct impact on UK legislation; *directives* require member states to ensure that their national legal frameworks comply with their aims (and may not therefore necessarily lead to changes in UK legislation); *decisions* are addressed to and binding upon particular member states, corporate bodies and 'natural persons' (like regulations, they take immediate effect, but they do not have general application).

Thus the UK is obliged by law to comply with a wide range of EU regulations and directives, promoting inter alia socio-economic rights on equality, health, maternity pay, safety at work and pensions. British governments cannot ignore these obligations, as they do under most of the international human rights treaties that they have ratified. Community laws, such as regulations, apply directly, render inapplicable existing UK laws that are incompatible, and prevent Parliament from adopting any new conflicting measures. This doctrine is an essential part of the theory of community supremacy.[2]

Those EC legislative acts that are not directly applicable, i.e. directives, may be and often are enforced in tribunals and the courts in the UK in accordance with the ECJ doctrine of 'direct effect'. As member states cannot always be relied upon to implement directives promptly or properly, 'direct effect' can ensure that they can have effect in a member state from the date set for implementation, even if the member state fails to pass legislation or it is incorrect. This doctrine has been put to use to enforce, for example, the EU Equal Treatment Directive in sex discrimination cases in the UK.[3]

Socio-economic EU law is constantly evolving and taking effect in the UK. For example, until recently, the impact of EU law on discrimination was confined to sex discrimination, but the Amsterdam treaty of 1997 empowered the EU to take action against discrimination on grounds of 'sex, racial or ethnic origin, religion or belief, disability, age or sexual orientation'. Two EU directives, the Employment and Race Directives, were introduced in 2000 requiring the UK and other member states to legislate by 2003 or 2006 (in the case of age and sexual orientation). The Race Directive was implemented by the Race Relations Act (Amendment) Regulations 2003 (see Chapter 6).

The influence of the EU on economic and social rights in the UK is not confined to legislation. Social exclusion is seen in the UK as a quintessentially New Labour idea. In fact, the Social Exclusion Unit was set up in 1997 as part of a joint EU strategy against poverty and social exclusion, which the UK signed up to in the Amsterdam treaty. At the Lisbon summit in 2000, the UK agreed to the target of eradicating poverty in the EU by 2010. The European Commission requires member states to submit action plans on social exclusion and will over time continue to provide a practical measure of progress in the UK by comparison with policies and progress in other EU states. This emphasis on action is long overdue in the UK, as the Rowntree Inquiry into Income and Wealth argued: 'Policy-makers should be concerned with the way in which the living standards of a substantial minority of the population have lagged behind since the late 1970s. Not only is this a problem for those directly affected, it also damages the social fabric and so affects us all.'[4]

The European Convention on Human Rights

The most prominent European human rights instrument is the Council of Europe's European Convention on Human Rights (ECHR), which was ratified by the UK in 1951 and was finally incorporated into British law by the Human Rights Act 1998. The convention protects civil and political rights, but since human rights are in truth indivisible, the Human Rights Act has increasingly been used to argue for and protect social and economic rights. For example, the right to life (under Article 2 of the ECHR), the prohibition of torture and inhuman or degrading treatment or punishment (under Article 3) and the right to respect for family life, privacy and home (Article 8) have been used in the European Court of Human Rights and the British courts to protect socio-economic rights (see further Chapter 4). Moreover, some civil and political rights protected by the ECHR may equally be considered as economic, social or cultural, such as labour rights (under Article 11, on freedom of association and assembly) and the right to an education (under Optional Protocol 1, Article 2). But it is not the only treaty of the Council of Europe that the UK has ratified. Britain was the first nation to ratify the European Social Charter (ESC), as it was the first to ratify the ECHR.

The European Social Charter

The European Social Charter was signed in Turin in 1961 and was ratified by the UK the following year. The signatory governments in 1961 resolved to 'make every effort in common to improve the standard of living and to promote the social well-being of both their urban and rural populations by means of appropriate institutions and action'. The main supervisory body is the European Committee of Social Rights (though other bodies play a supervisory role). The committee is a body of distinguished jurists. The ESC came into force in 1965 and a number of important protocols have been added since, introducing (among other measures) a collective complaints procedure. A revised ESC was opened for signature in 1996 and came into force in 1999. Conservative governments refused to sign the protocols and the current government has held aloof from the revised charter.

The charter is a more substantial and detailed instrument than the International Covenant on Economic, Social and Cultural Rights, but a state ratifying the ESC is not required to accept all its terms. The UK has signed sixty of its seventy-two provisions, the lowest rate of acceptance of all EU member states bar Denmark. The influence of the two versions has grown over time in the EU and the revised charter was one of the inspirations for framing the EU Charter of Fundamental Rights (see below). But their influence in the UK has been limited. Much Conservative government legislation in the 1980s and 1990s did not comply even with the UK's commitments under the charter and the Conservatives went so far as to denounce three of the ESC obligations between 1987 and 1989. Labour governments under Tony Blair have been less openly hostile but have been reluctant to improve this country's record. The academic lawyer Keith Ewing has pointed out that the UK has not only one of the lowest levels of acceptance of charter obligations, but also 'one of the poorest records of compliance'. He has also criticised human rights lawyers in the UK for having 'woefully neglected' the ESC (and International Labour Organisation conventions; see below).[5] In the sixteenth (and latest) cycle of supervision, the Social Rights Committee of the Council of Europe examined forty-three of the sixty-seven obligations by which the UK is bound. The committee found that the UK is in breach of sixteen obligations examined and in compliance with twenty-three; it was unable to comment on another four obligations because it had not been given adequate information. The Institute of Employment Rights (IER) gave evidence to the Joint Committee on Human Rights identifying major breaches of employment rights in detail, and pointed out that victims of these violations were not able to take their complaints to the Social Rights Committee because the UK continued to refuse to ratify the collective complaints protocol. The IER commented: 'It is unacceptable not only to deny the right to ventilate social rights abuses in an international forum. It is also unacceptable that there is no forum in domestic law to challenge the violation of fundamental social rights.' The institute argued that the charter should be incorporated into British law, 'using the Human Rights Act as a template'.[6]

The EU Social Chapter

The EU Social Chapter forms part of the 1991 Maastricht treaty. The Social Chapter, unlike the Social Charter, can generate binding legislation and is potentially an important source of social and employment legislation for workers. However, a significant body of economic and social rights already existed in EU law, which had been developed from the economic rights contained in the original

1957 Treaty of Rome (as amended by the Single European Act 1986). The Social Chapter has proved a greater source of anxiety and even outrage to British governments than of additional socio-economic rights for British workers. The number of legal instruments adopted under it has been relatively small.

The Social Chapter (also known as the Community Charter of Fundamental Social Rights) was proposed at the Madrid summit in June 1989 to establish a set of socio-economic rights. Margaret Thatcher denounced it as a 'socialist charter' and at Maastricht, John Major spoke strongly against the Social Chapter, which embodied the original 1989 charter and required member states to adopt common social policies to implement the Community Social Charter. After heated debate Major persuaded the other eleven member state leaders to make the Social Chapter an optional clause, allowing member states to adopt it individually. On this basis, the UK opted out of the Social Chapter while ratifying the Maastricht treaty.

In 1997, the Labour government finally signed up to the Community Charter of Fundamental Social Rights, enshrining in British law core workplace rights, such as four weeks' paid holiday, obligatory consultation rights, pension rights for part-time workers, protection for workers in take-overs, and anti-discrimination measures. Wider provisions for social security and the rights of elderly and disabled people are left to member states under the principle of subsidiarity. Labour had profound misgivings about signing up to 'social Europe', fearing that such provisions could destroy the competitive advantage that Britain gained in the 1980s and 1990s and make the UK (and Europe) a less attractive place for foreign countries to invest in. These misgivings emerged strongly in the Blair government's approach to the idea of an EU Charter of Fundamental Rights.

The EU Charter of Fundamental Rights

The current government was hostile to the idea of an EU Charter of Fundamental Rights from the moment at which the European Council, meeting in Cologne, assigned the task of drafting it to a convention led by Valéry Giscard d'Estaing. The Charter was proclaimed at the EU Nice summit in December 2000 though its legal status is still to be determined. Strictly speaking, the Charter does not form part of the EU treaty framework as it has not been subject to ratification by the member states. However, the ECJ has begun to make reference to the document in developing its own jurisprudence on fundamental rights in EC law, so it has become de facto an important legal document.

The charter aimed to bring together 'modern' economic and social rights with the more recognised civil and political rights in a single document, making visible the 'common values' of the EU. However, the idea was confused from its very origin. It was seen variously as a comprehensive code of rights for the EU, as a means of mending gaps in the protection of civil and political rights or of making socio-economic rights legally enforceable, as a political or rhetorical tool for promoting common EU values, or as (in the words of a report by the House of Lords EU Select Committee in May 2000) 'a declaratory Charter' that might clarify the obligations of EU institutions.[7] In response to the select committee's report the government described the charter as a useful device 'for making rights more visible to the people'.

The inclusion of socio-economic rights in the draft charter was the most controversial element in the UK. Most witnesses to the Lords EU committee in 1999–2000 took the view that the charter should extend beyond civil and political rights, the International Commission of Jurists arguing:

> The greatest number of attacks on the dignity of the individual is witnessed in the social sphere . . . the Europe of human rights will always be incomplete if the social dimension is missing. The inclusion of economic and social rights in the EU Charter can and must contribute to prevent such inadequacy.

But the Confederation of British Industry and others were alarmed at such notions, arguing that socio-economic provisions should be in the form of aspirations, not rights. The Lords committee took the view that their inclusion ran the danger of enlarging the competence of the union 'by the back door' and that the ECJ might give them legal effect. Their report said that it was impracticable to make socio-economic rights justiciable at the EU level 'unless and until they are generally recognised at national level' and recommended that the non-binding nature of socio-economic rights should be made apparent on the face of the charter.[8]

Lord Goldsmith, then the UK representative on the EU convention that went on to frame the charter, and Jack Straw, the then Foreign Secretary, argued strongly against including enforceable socio-economic rights in the final document. At the foreign ministers' negotiations on the European Constitution in Brussels in May 2004, Jack Straw stated that he was willing to give the charter legal force only if it were made clear in the treaty on the constitution that the charter would not introduce new national socio-economic rights that would allow trade unions and other organisations to challenge UK law in the ECJ. In a speech to the CBI on 18 May 2004, Straw said that he would not allow the charter to 'upset the balance of Britain's industrial relations policy'. The government had put 'the interests of business at the heart of our negotiating position' on the treaty.[9]

Other member states were no more willing to adopt a charter that justified interference in their social security and housing regimes and created ideas of new entitlements or guarantees. Goldsmith spoke for more than the UK at the convention in arguing that the economic and social rights contained in the charter were merely 'principles' that would be realised as enforceable rights only 'to the extent that they are implemented by national law, or in those areas where there is competence, by Community law'.[10] He asserted that economic and social rights differed from other human rights because they were 'usually not justiciable'; and they were recognised and given effect in different ways by the member states, who were primarily responsible for legislating in these areas. Goldsmith relates that he 'fought very hard' to qualify the right of 'every worker' to protection against unfair dismissal by adding the rider that it should be in accordance with community law and 'national laws and practices' (which, in the UK, deny workers in their first year protection from unfair dismissal).[11]

Thus the charter, whatever its ultimate legal status, will offer the British and European people only tantalising glimpses of rights that are at once visible and out of reach.[12] As Lord Lester, who wanted the charter to make the protections of the European Convention more effective within the EU, remarked of the earlier 2000 draft, 'its declarations are couched in the ambiguous language of political compromise'.[13] Its affirmation of indivisible rights is false. The charter contains an incomplete list that distinguishes between enforceable rights, many of which are conditional, and generally unenforceable principles that are neither 'rights' nor 'fundamental'. For the EU institutions the charter would create an obligation to promote each of the rights set out, but deny them the capacity to extend their powers or competence to secure its objectives. It fails either to effect citizens' or workers' social rights or to guarantee social entitlements. It is hard to determine how real Straw's fears were and how far he was playing to the gallery, but while the charter may well remind member states of their obligations under international treaties, it certainly adds no new obligations.

Thus the charter proclaimed solidarity and indivisible European values but left the parameters of existing EU social law intact. The two previous social charters – the Community Social Charter (CSC) and the European Social Charter (ESC) – were to remain in being along with other international treaty obligations. But the Charter of Fundamental Rights took pains to ensure that member states could individually maintain their autonomy in domestic affairs by giving them no additional force across the EU and making them subject to the 'powers and tasks' of the EU in accordance with the principle of subsidiarity. The drafting convention was insistent on stressing the 'visibility' of the CSC and the ESC, but decided to exclude the right to work, the right to fair pay, and the right to housing from the Charter of Fundamental Rights, even though all three rights are in the ESC and the right to fair pay is part of the CSC. These rights fall within areas that touch closely on national sovereignty and sensitivities.

Meanwhile, attempts to secure ratification of the European Constitution have been stalled. The constitution is intended to be a new consolidating treaty for the EU, replacing all existing treaties and the 'three-pillar' structure with a single entity. If agreed, it will reform areas of substantive law and policy, and will incorporate the Charter of Fundamental Rights to be a legally binding document (as opposed to merely a politically persuasive one). However, the constitution may not enter into force until all member states have ratified it; the 'no' votes in France and the Netherlands in 2005 put a stop to its progress, and in June that year the European Council of Ministers declared a 'period of reflection' and agreed that any further developments should be re-visited in the first half of 2006.

In other words, Europe is moving only slowly and reluctantly towards recognised socio-economic rights, and the UK is in the rear of what progress exists. The rhetoric of indivisible rights is contained within strict limits on EU competence and deference to national discretion. In other words, certain economic and social rights are insufficiently fundamental to merit protection. But it is the custom in continental Europe to express aspirations initially in such rhetoric and then to keep them in sight. So the charter may yet contribute towards raising the status of economic and social rights in the EU's legal order and represent a 'shift in ethic' whereby economic and social rights are recognised and potentially integrated into the legal and political spheres.[14] After all, the Community Social Chapter is non-binding, but it has also inspired EU social legislation.

4

Socio-economic rights in court*

On 15 September 2003 Bill Rammell, then a junior minister at the Foreign and Commonwealth Office, gave evidence to the Joint Committee on Human Rights (JCHR) on the question of incorporating the International Covenant on Economic, Social and Cultural Rights (ICESCR) into UK law. Rammell spoke strongly against incorporation, on democratic and practical grounds (see Chapter 2 for discussion of his arguments), finally remarking that he did not believe 'that incorporation . . . would improve on the existing legal framework'.[2] But how well does 'the existing legal framework' manage to recognise and protect the full range of economic, social and cultural rights? Is it accurate to suggest that there is a legal framework that does so? If so, how effective is it? And how do judges interpret their own responsibilities when it comes to protecting socio-economic rights?

The existing legal framework

There certainly is no 'legal framework' that gives systematic protection to economic, social and cultural rights in the UK. European Union laws guaranteeing economic and social rights are binding in Britain and, as we saw in Chapter 3, the European Court of Justice (ECJ) is the final arbiter on their effect in this country. Britain's other international socio-economic obligations have only a marginal impact. Although the ICESCR matters formally, it has little effect in practice. This is because treaties such as that one, the

*In collaboration with Ellie Palmer.

European Social Charter and the International Labour Organization (ILO) conventions, mentioned in Chapter 2, have not been incorporated into British law through legislation and so do not have legal force – although there are some exceptions to this general rule. Thus, broadly, the courts are supposed to assume that Parliament does not intend to pass laws that are incompatible with the UK's international treaty obligations, including those that arise under human rights treaties, such as the ICESCR. They have therefore interpreted legislation in a manner consistent with those obligations, even if there is no obvious ambiguity in the legislation. Similarly, where there is a gap in the common law, the courts are supposed to try and make compatible decisions; and they should generally also seek to review the exercise of discretion by public bodies and to consider the demands of public policy generally in the light of these international obligations.

However, in practice, as Sandra Fredman, the academic lawyer, has noted, there has been little direct reliance on the socio-economic rights set out in the ICESCR or the European Social Charter. Indeed, she writes, in asylum cases where litigants have unsuccessfully attempted to rely on these rights, the courts have ruled that socio-economic rights guaranteed under the covenant are 'third category' and weaker than traditional civil and political rights.[3] The JCHR also concluded in 2004 that the ICESCR has 'a very limited impact in our domestic law'.[4] However, the JCHR report argues that the UK, in ratifying the covenant, has made a commitment, binding in inter-national law, to abide by its terms. 'This requires government, Parliament and the courts to make efforts to ensure the fullest possible compliance with the terms of the Covenant.'[5] Nevertheless, as we saw in Chapter 2, UK governments are quite prepared to ignore such international commitments, and even to denounce the terms of such treaties as the UK has ratified.

There is no external guardian of the full range of economic and social rights, as there is in the civil and political realm, where the European Court of Human Rights (ECHR) acts as a final court for individual citizens who believe that their rights have been violated and the UK courts have failed them. The ECJ acts as the final court of appeal on employment and other rights guaranteed by the EU.

Rights under the European Social Charter are subject to legal enforcement through a system of 'collective complaints' – but the UK government has refused to sign a 1995 additional protocol which set up the complaints system. Instead, the UN Committee on Economic, Social and Cultural Rights and the European Committee of Social Rights merely have an oversight role over progress on the rights that they monitor and cannot hear appeals from aggrieved citizens. The government is obliged to submit regular reports to these monitoring bodies on the UK's compliance with their requirements. In turn, the oversight bodies hold hearings at which the government and others give evidence and issue their periodic reports (see Chapter 5). The ILO Committee of Experts also monitors compliance with the UK's obligations under the ILO, but, as we have seen, their reports have only a limited impact upon government policies and laws (see Chapter 2).

Legislative protection of socio-economic rights

Bill Rammell presumably had Britain's extensive range of social legislation in mind when he expressed his satisfaction with the existing 'legal framework'. For, while most socio-economic rights have no direct legal protection in the UK, this is not to say that such rights are wholly unprotected. They are not protected as rights, but their substance is guaranteed under duties imposed on public bodies. Thus legislation on housing, education, health-care, employment relations, discrimination, social care, disability and related matters does impose obligations on local authorities and other public bodies which coincide with significant aspects of socio-economic rights. In addition the courts may judicially review the policies and actions of public bodies under this legislation. Furthermore, there is specific legislation, much of it inspired by EU directives, protecting citizens from discrimination on grounds of race, sex, religion and belief (but not yet age and sexual orientation) in employment and guaranteeing rights of access to social services, education and social security. As we saw in Chapter 2, citizens who experience discrimination in the EU sphere of influence have enforceable legal rights.

We go on below to consider in some detail cases in which the courts have adjudicated upon socio-economic rights through judicial review of the policies and actions of public bodies under domestic legislation. In effect, therefore, the courts are often unwillingly, and not expressly, adjudicating upon rights guaranteed under the ICESCR and the European Social Charter, but only in the context of their obligations to give effect to EU law, their general obligations in English public law, and their new obligations under the Human Rights Act (HRA). Thus the level to which covenant rights are protected is established in the first instance by government and Parliament, and secondarily by use of the considerable discretion that legislation normally gives to the public bodies responsible for social provision. This means that anyone who falls outside the provision made under the legislation has no overriding socio-economic right on which they can call, apart from whatever protection may be found under the HRA. As the JCHR observes, 'marginalised groups or individuals, who fall outside of the scope of the legislation' may be left vulnerable, 'since they cannot challenge the limitations of the legislation in protecting their economic, social or cultural rights'.[6] For example, an asylum seeker deprived of benefits under the Nationality, Immigration and Asylum Act 2002 cannot claim redress from the courts on the grounds that their rights to social security under Article 9 of the ICESCR have been violated. Nor could a claimant go to court under Article 9 to challenge the level of benefit they receive because they consider it to be insufficient to live on. As the JCHR commented, 'where Covenant rights are protected through legislation, therefore, the level to which these rights are protected is for Parliament and the executive to determine'.[7]

The protection of the Human Rights Act

While socio-economic rights are for the most part protected only through domestic legislation, the Human Rights Act 1998 does offer opportunities to make up for the limitations and gaps in legislation through the courts. The twin categories of civil and political rights and economic, social and cultural rights are indivisible and overlap.

The protections of the European Convention on Human Rights (which the HRA, as we have seen, imports into UK law) extend into the economic and social sphere, with particular regard to the right to life (Article 2), protection against degrading and inhuman treatment (Article 3) and respect for family and private life (Article 8). Thus though the HRA is primarily concerned with civil and political rights, it also affords some indirect protection for the economic and social rights guaranteed in the ICESCR, the European Social Charter and ILO conventions. Its parent human rights instrument, the European Convention,

- protects the rights of trade unions and their members through the right to freedom of association, guaranteed under Article 11;
- gives minimum protection to the economic right to an adequate standard of living under Article 3, which guarantees freedom from inhuman and degrading treatment and does therefore at least offer minimal protection against the effects of utter destitution (see below);
- may protect rights to adequate and competent health-care and treatment through Article 2 (the right to life) and Article 8 (rights to privacy, personal autonomy and physical integrity); and
- guarantees access to education under the First Protocol (which has been incorporated into British law under the HRA).

But though there is little ostensible protection of socio-economic rights, it is clear that the ECHR judiciary at Strasbourg has adopted a 'dynamic approach' to interpreting rights under the convention that has, as Ellie Palmer writes, 'opened avenues for the protection of vulnerable individuals in respect of claims to receive a standard of protection consistent with human dignity, and respect for their psychological and physical integrity'.[8] She argues that the Strasbourg judiciary, although variable, has become more willing to develop positive obligations under the European Convention for people in need, recognising embryonic duties to make public health provision as part of the right to life under Article 2, to ensure medical care or welfare for vulnerable individuals under Article 3 (protection against inhuman or degrading treatment), and secure welfare housing for people with disabilities under Article 8 (respect for family and private life).[9]

However, the ECHR has not developed the potential use of Article 2, on the right to life, to construct a general 'social right' which would impose positive obligations on states to take measures to protect people's lives more broadly. It is Articles 3 and 8 that have allowed the court to protect the human dignity and personal integrity of vulnerable claimants. For example, it is now broadly established that where individuals are at risk of degradation and suffering, even if this is caused by non-state actors, European governments may be found guilty of violations of Article 3 if they fail to take positive steps to protect them. Furthermore, although the essential object of Article 8 is to protect people from arbitrary action by the authorities, that is, a negative duty, the court has derived positive obligations from it. Article 8 cannot be stretched to give a right to a home as such, but it can be used to consider housing needs in so far as they bear upon family and personal life. So, for example, the court stated, in the case of a disabled Italian man who was evicted and then hospitalised, that while the article does not create a right to a home, 'a refusal of the authorities to provide assistance [in respect of accommodation after eviction] to an individual suffering from a severe disease might in certain circumstances raise an issue under Article 8'.[10] Furthermore, examining the legality of the forced eviction of a gypsy from a local authority caravan site in the UK in 2004, the court warned that although it left a margin of discretion 'to national authorities' in cases where resources were involved, their decisions were subject to its review 'for conformity with the requirements of the Convention'.[11]

Socio-economic issues in the British courts

The HRA enables the courts to apply the human rights standards of the ECHR to the executive and administrative decisions of authorities and bodies performing public functions at all levels of government in the UK.[12] British courts give a wide margin of discretion to public authorities in cases involving resources in the UK. The doctrine of judicial deference to the executive remains a central determinant of their conduct. They are reluctant to trespass on the domain of the executive, being acutely sensitive to the proposition that public resources are scarce and being aware that to insist on re-housing, hospital treatment or other public service in any one case will have budgetary repercussions that may affect the rights of others. Moreover, they are inhibited by their own lack of knowledge and expertise from examining the validity of the policy decisions of government and public bodies. These constraints remain in place in their exercise of judicial review, and most especially in their treatment of socio-economic cases. They do not regard challenges that raise issues of resource allocation as 'non-justiciable' for that reason alone, but as soon as the resource issue raises its head, they have tended to resort to deference and pay less attention to countervailing human rights than to public resources. Therefore, not only have the courts generally given public authorities wide scope in interpreting the usually discretionary statutory obligations for the delivery of services or facilities, but they have often even avoided enforcing mandatory obligations where lack of resources has been the reason for refusals.

As we have shown above, the HRA does offer opportunities for judicial intervention in certain socio-economic issues. Moreover, since the HRA binds the courts themselves to act compatibly with convention rights, they are obliged to do so while developing the common law. Further, under Section 2 of the HRA, all the courts (and tribunals) must take account of the decisions of the ECHR at Strasbourg. While they are not legally bound by the European Court's jurisprudence, prudence alone means that they ought not to ignore it, if only to achieve one of the primary objects of the HRA – namely, to bring rights home and to limit further recourse to Strasbourg. Thus the courts have been required since 2000 (when the HRA came into force) to scrutinise legislation and the common law for conformity with convention rights, and they may make orders and grant relief or remedies to people whose rights have been violated.

The HRA has also had a more profound constitutional impact. By importing the rights granted by the ECHR and requiring courts to take account of Strasbourg case law, such as the case of *Connors* (see note 10), the Act has in principle shifted the balance of judicial scrutiny and reasoning from a traditional textual approach to the wider Strasbourg test of proportionality[13] and the use of the European Convention as a background for restraint on government conduct. The Act is also re-shaping the traditional boundaries between the courts, Parliament and the government and public authorities. It has long been a fundamental tenet of the British constitutional settlement that the courts and executive are bound by the doctrine of the separation of powers and that they do not accordingly transgress into their separate domains. It is in this sense that the courts show deference to the executive. However, several judges have now argued that the Act has created a new balance of power, giving the courts a function of constitutional review across old boundaries.

A brief historical overview

The expansion of judicial review from the 1970s onwards seemed to offer the prospect of the courts intervening to secure some economic and social entitlements, but in practice there was scarcely any advance. Homelessness and immigration cases bulked large in the judicial review caseload, but few prospered. There were hardly any social security, health-care or family cases. In 1983, the Child Poverty Action Group reported, for example, that its 'test case strategy' in the 1970s, focusing on benefit and homelessness cases, encountered 'judicial hostility' and 'procedural and institutional inadequacies'.[14] In two important 1980s cases, the House of Lords ruled that the courts should subject cases involving governmental social and economic policies to a low level of scrutiny, and that in general the courts were procedurally ill equipped to deal with such issues and were not in a position to test the validity of policy decisions.[15] In the 1980s and early 1990s, the courts acquiesced in the Conservative government's disengagement on welfare and social issues that involved economic and social rights, denying for example appeals from homeless persons, and upholding refusals of benefits and cuts in local authority social services. In 1994, the Equal Opportunities Commission did win a case on women's employment rights that brought wide gains for women workers (*R. v. Employment Secretary ex parte EOC*), but this case depended on the superiority of positive EU employment laws over UK law.

The later 1990s brought politically sensitive challenges on community care, health treatment and education, where the courts found for the plaintiffs (see Appendix B). But judicial review generally remained limited to making the exercise of executive discretion comply with standards of 'reasonable' process, legality and procedural propriety; and the courts generally adopted a formalistic approach that leant heavily on statute rather than the more open and balanced scrutiny of the proportionality test developed in Strasbourg for the review of government conduct. It is important to stress that the ECHR, like the UK courts, seeks to hold a balance between the protection of fundamental individual rights and the needs and resources of the whole community. But it requires a wider and more nuanced test than that applied traditionally in the UK courts. It seeks to ensure that limitations of protected individual rights are imposed only if they are prescribed by law, intended to achieve a legitimate objective and necessary in a democratic society. In the next section of this chapter, we consider how far the UK courts are becoming willing to use the wider proportionality test to review the validity of the policies of government and public bodies to protect socio-economic rights, to review the decisions and policies of the government and public bodies, and to resolve the tensions between rights and resources.

Judicial decision-making in socio-economic cases
Most economic, social and cultural rights may not be protected as such in British law, but human rights organisations and individuals have shown themselves increasingly ready to test the extent to which the courts will hold the government and public bodies to account for failing to provide satisfactory access to health, education, housing and welfare services or to press the claims of marginal groups or individuals for more priority in the allocation of scarce resources. There is no principle in English law which prevents the courts from intervening in politically sensitive disputes over issues of resource allocation. But the obstacles to success – notions of constitutional propriety, procedural limitations and concern for the difficulties of public bodies – are great, as we have pointed out above.

Appendix B illustrates the continuing legal see-saw between the needs and rights of individual people and state resources. The *Barry* case in 1997 (names or initials in italics refer to cases discussed in Appendix B) concerned the withdrawal by Gloucester City Council of laundry and cleaning services to an elderly immobile man because the council did not have the resources to continue meeting his needs. The House of Lords narrowly decided that a local authority could take into account its own resources when assessing a disabled person's need and deciding how to meet them, even though the 1970 Chronically Sick and Disabled Persons Act created an apparently mandatory obligation on councils to provide disabled people with the facilities they required. Otherwise, the Law Lords said, the Act would make the council liable to an open-ended budgetary commitment. But they added that once an authority had decided what arrangements were necessary to meet a particular disabled person's needs, then they owed a duty to the person to continue those arrangements or reassess his circumstances.

In light of the *Barry* case, local authorities across the country began to renege on other community care duties on grounds of lack of resources. But the courts gradually began to toughen up the protection for welfare rights in cases that followed. First, they gave substance to the rule that authorities had to provide arrangements for applicants that they had themselves assessed to be necessary under welfare legislation (see *Blanchard*); and then insisted that authorities should carry out proper individual assessments of need rather than simply follow blanket policies and could not pre-empt such assessments (see *Tandy*; *Tammadge*; *A, D and G*).

In *Tandy*, a wholly different panel of Law Lords than in *Barry* refused 'to downgrade duties to discretions over which the courts could have very little real control' and ordered that the council was under a duty to provide home tuition to the sick child and could not implement a blanket resource-driven policy. The lower courts then became more willing to recognise mandatory obligations which overrode resource questions (for example, see *Mohammed* and *Kujtim*). Yet *Tandy* was no breakthrough for a human rights approach. The court's reasoning was based entirely on traditional statutory interpretation, not a more fundamental human rights approach. Further, the impact of the decision on resources was likely to be negligible, since only two other children had been affected by the council's policy (though the resources implications of decisions that followed were greater).

On resources, the courts have accepted that new and stringent 'cost-effective' policies might lead to less generous provision for individual users than was deemed necessary either originally or on review and may well still be necessary from an individual's or group's point of view. But they have shown themselves ready to examine individual 'care plans' to ensure that claims of greater efficiency aren't entirely masking reductions in arrangements that users require. They are also ready to give precedence to the needs of individual users over blanket policies in the interests of the wider community. The *Coughlan* case is an outstanding example. The Court of Appeal ordered a health authority to keep open a residential home they intended to close so that the authority would keep its promise to six disabled residents that it would remain their home 'for life'. The court decided that the closure decision was a breach of their 'legitimate expectations', a substantive and developing doctrine of English law that reflects the flexibility of judicial review at its best. The decision is also notable for clarifying the consultation process that authorities should adopt prior to closure decisions, and has led to a number of cases where local residents have been able to challenge closures. Before the HRA came into force in 2000, the decision also stressed the obligation on the authorities to respect people's family and private life under Article 8 of the ECHR while consulting the public on policy decisions. But the resource implications in this case were limited and the power of the idea of 'legitimate expectations' meant that the court could justify its intervention without having openly to substitute its decision for that of the authority.

Homelessness: a triumph of resources over needs
Since the enactment of the HRA, a series of homelessness cases has revealed the precarious nature of the courts' decisions in the *Tandy* and *Kujtim* cases[16] and has demonstrated the uncertain course that the courts are steering between confronting the failures of public policy and concern for the funding predicaments of public authorities. These cases (*Mrs A, G* and *W*) also show how reluctant judges are to

exercise their new powers of constitutional review in welfare cases. The courts turned down appeals from these vulnerable families against the decisions in three London boroughs to refuse them accommodation under Section 17 of the Children Act and their cases were finally determined by the House of Lords in 2003. At heart the refusals were inspired by the desperate shortage of housing in inner London. Vulnerable families such as these had no prospect of being rehoused off housing waiting lists in the ordinary way and came to social services departments for emergency accommodation. Social services had for years provided accommodation for children in desperate need with their families so that they could keep families together. But Lambeth, like other councils, was refusing to provide emergency accommodation for such desperate families together, offering only to rehouse children separately, a policy which effectively forced vulnerable families to find their own remedies rather than lose their children.

The most distressing of these cases was that of *Mrs A*, a single parent who actually already lived in a council flat with three children under the age of eight, two of whom were autistic and severely disruptive. But the flat was damp and in disrepair and conditions there were 'appalling'. The two autistic children used to climb out of the flat and run off and so were at risk from a nearby road. A social services assessment recognised the need for an urgent transfer to suitable permanent accommodation away from the road and with a secure garden or play area. But Mrs A had little prospect of actually being rehoused.

It was argued for all the families that the authorities were under a mandatory duty to meet their needs for accommodation; and specifically for Mrs A that the social services assessment triggered such a duty. The House of Lords ultimately held that the 1989 Act set out duties of a general nature, which were not intended to be enforceable on behalf of individuals. These duties were owed to all the children in need in a local authority's area, and not to each child in need. Lord Justice Nicholls explained that the more specific the duty, the more absolute it became; the more general, the more 'freedom' a public authority had. The Law Lords were very sympathetic to the 'seemingly intractable problem' of local authorities' lack of resources and the 'multifarious demands' upon them; did not wish to 'divert funds and manpower' away from other significant social services; were moved by the potential consequences of providing immediate accommodation for all the families in housing need; and were concerned about the danger of such families jumping the queue in areas of desperate housing shortage. However, they ruled against local social services departments adopting near-universal policies of refusing to provide accommodation for parents and children together.

The flexible interpretation of the duty under the Children Act is tantamount to denying that any duty at all exists, but the court showed itself to be primarily concerned about the possibility of disrupting the local housing waiting lists. It was decided therefore that the only duty on the local authorities was to give intelligible and adequate reasons for refusing accommodation; and for the House of Lords, it was enough to point to the general pressure and competition for resources, without considering the impact on the individual families.

These cases echoed an outstanding case from the late 1980s. Children were forced to stay at home in the London borough of Tower Hamlets because there were not 'sufficient' primary school places. But Lord Woolf ruled that the duty of the secretary of state to provide places in schools could not be enforced for the benefit of individual children; it was rather a 'target duty' owed to the public at large. In Mrs A's case, no attempt was made to argue that the council was under a positive duty under Article 8 of the ECHR to provide for the housing needs of vulnerable people suffering from a disability. Yet in a case shortly before Mrs A's, Mr Justice Sullivan had concluded that the abject failure to provide for the needs of a severely disabled adult within a reasonable period (the *Bernard* case) constituted a clear breach of Article 8. Enfield Borough Council had a positive duty under Article 8 to provide suitable housing so that Mrs Bernard could maintain her physical and psychological integrity.[17]

The *Donoghue* case, which arose very shortly after the HRA came into force, also showed that the courts were moved more by the needs of the authorities than by those of vulnerable people in need, even if children were involved. Ms Donoghue was a pregnant single parent with three young children who was officially designated as being 'intentionally homeless'. She sought the protection of Article 8 against eviction from emergency accommodation by a housing association and failed. The fact that four children would ultimately share the desperation of homeless conditions with their mother, or might well be separated from her, did not weigh very strongly against the interests of a housing association in the midst of a severe shortage of rented accommodation for poor households in the UK. None of the other international conventions ratified by the UK which give protection to the rights of children were considered, including Article 9 of the UN Convention on the Rights of the Child: 'State parties shall ensure that a child shall not be separated from his or her parents against their will, except when competent authorities subject to judicial review determine, in accordance with applicable law and procedures that such separation is necessary for the best interests of the child.'

The charity Shelter argued at the Court of Appeal that the authority's position could not be justified in terms of a 'pressing social need' as required under the European Convention, especially in Ms Donoghue's case, where her immediate need was to continue in temporary accommodation, which would not therefore disrupt the local housing waiting list. However, Lord Woolf concluded that the court had to pay considerable attention to Parliament's intention in the Housing Act 1988 to give preference to the needs of people who are dependent on social housing as a whole over intentionally homeless people. There was no principled debate over the intentions of Article 8; no attempt to find a balance between individual rights under Article 8 and the right of the landlord to repossess the accommodation; no recognition of the need to read the Act's provisions compatibly with the European Convention.

Tolling 'the bell of tight resources'

The courts are inhibited not only by their sensitivity to the scarcity of resources, but also by a usually parallel concern not to substitute their judgments for those of the authorities. The well-known case of *Child B* illustrates this reluctance to second-guess authorities and the tensions to which it gives rise. Child B was a young girl dying of leukaemia who was refused a potentially life-saving treatment on the grounds that the cost would not reflect an efficient use of resources, given that the prospect of success was small and the health authority had to fund treatments for other patients. Mr Justice Laws in the divisional court accepted that it was, at first instance, for the health authority to decide how scarce resources should be distributed, but the court had a secondary duty to ensure that only those infringements of the right to life of a ten-year-old girl that were substantially in the public interest could be justified. He ruled that in view of the limited evidence of a clear policy of priorities, the health authority was interfering with Child B's right to life on grounds that were not substantial enough. He accepted that the court should not make orders on health-care priorities (unless it had *some* understanding of the likely effects for other patients). But he then added: 'Where the question is whether the life of a ten-year-old child might be saved, by however slim a chance, the responsible authorities . . . must do more than toll the bell of tight resources.'

It is a phrase that has gone down in judicial history, but the decision was short lived. Yet his insistence on the need for close scrutiny in cases in which convention rights are engaged has the makings of a human rights approach, the more so because he also insisted that the exercise of executive discretion should be transparent and demonstrably fair – reflecting the valuable new common law principle that authorities should give reasons for their decisions. Yet the Court of Appeal at once shut the door on the idea that the courts might perform an evaluative role distinct from that of the executive. The appeal judges decided unanimously that the courts were not in a position to assess the correctness of an administrative decision and refused to accept Laws's view that the authority's reasons for refusing treatment were not clear enough, in another historic phrase:

Difficult and agonising judgments have to be made as to how a limited budget is best allocated to the maximum advantage of the maximum number of patients. This is not a judgment that the court can make . . . it is not something that a health authority such as this authority can be fairly criticised for not advancing before the court.

In general, it is reasonable to conclude that the courts are unwilling to upset government and administrative decisions; that they are very sensitive to arguments about scarce resources; and that their interventions are restricted to issues of process rather than policy. If people were given socio-economic rights, the courts could begin to review policies within the wider perspective of the principle of 'progressive realisation', a principle which we argue offers an escape from the rigidities of the their current impasse (see Chapter 5).

Destitution and asylum support

The judiciary has always wavered over the issue of whether human rights include the right to a minimum standard of living. Every now and then a judge does issue a strong statement in support of this proposition, as Lord Hoffman famously did in the case *Matthews v. Ministry of Defence* in 2003:

> Human rights are the rights essential to the life and dignity of the individual in a democratic society. The exact limits of such rights are debatable and although there is not much trace of economic rights in the fifty-year-old convention [the ECHR], I think it is well arguable that human rights include the right to a minimum standard of living, without which many of the other rights would be a mockery.

But the government's policies to deter asylum seekers threw into sharp relief Hoffman's view of the issue of destitution and a state's duty to protect people against living in inhuman and degrading conditions. The European Court has long interpreted Article 3 of the Convention, which prohibits torture and inhuman and degrading treatment, positively by ruling that the failure to make social provision for vulnerable people in acute need constitutes a violation of the article. In 2002, the government enacted the Nationality, Immigration and Asylum Act, which under Section 55 requires asylum seekers to seek benefits as soon as 'reasonably practicable' upon entry to the UK. Otherwise they are denied all benefits while also being prohibited from seeking work (without special permission from the government).[18]

The government's policy caused widespread misery among 'failed' asylum seekers, who were reduced to sleeping rough and begging in their thousands, were usually unable to get medical treatment or even attend to basic hygiene, and were being placed at risk of crime and prostitution. They often sought charitable assistance and shelter that was in very short supply. We describe the case of Wayoka *Limbuela*, a leading applicant for judicial relief, in Appendix B. Hugh Tristram, who advised asylum seekers for the Refugee Council, described their conditions to the Court of Appeal. A council day centre open on weekdays from 9.30 a.m. to 5.30 p.m. (2 p.m. to 5.30 p.m on Wednesdays) offered asylum seekers some meals during those times, but had no sleeping accommodation and was closed in the evenings and at weekends. The centre had just four showers and no separate hand-basins. Tristram explained:

Many [asylum-seekers] sleep outside our offices, in doorways, in the gardens of a local church and sometimes in telephone boxes (the only place where they are able to keep dry). They do not have enough blankets and clothing to keep them warm. They are often lonely, frightened and feel humiliated and distressed . . . Staff have seen the condition of asylum-seekers visibly deteriorating after periods of rough sleeping . . . On one occasion I had to tell a group of three homeless asylum-seekers to leave the building on a Friday evening during a torrential downpour with nothing more than a blanket each, a food parcel . . . and a list of day centres. When I saw them the following Monday their condition had deteriorated considerably, their clothes were filthy, they had started to smell, and they had been unable to find any of the centres listed. Other clients have become depressed and have threatened suicide; one was sectioned after she was found lying across a railway track. Their story is not exceptional – we see people in this situation on a daily basis.[19]

Asylum seekers appealed to the courts in their hundreds. In October 2003, a judge complained that a quarter of the cases lodged at the administrative court were those of destitute asylum seekers – some 800 cases in all.

The lower courts came to contradictory rulings, some judges upholding appeals from asylum seekers under Article 3, others turning them down. Basically, it was agreed that withholding support to a destitute person did not amount to inhuman or degrading treatment in itself; what mattered was how severe that person's deprivation was, as measured by the Strasbourg court in the Diane Pretty case. This case sets a high threshold. In short, 'ill treatment' should attain a minimum level of severity and involve actual bodily injury or intense physical or mental suffering. Treatment that humiliates or debases an individual, diminishing his or her human dignity or arousing feelings of fear, anguish or inferiority capable of breaking an individual's moral and physical resistance, may count as 'degrading'. Suffering which flows from illness, physical or mental, may be covered where it is, or risks being, exacerbated by treatment for which the authorities can be held responsible.

What seems to have divided the courts was the question of whether they should find that the government was in breach of Article 3 if destitute asylum seekers sleeping rough were at risk of 'inhuman and degrading' conditions, or if they had first to suffer the degrading effects of destitution or the consequences of having no home and no income were aggravated by illness or some other factor. In March 2003, and then again in September, the Court of Appeal ruled that it was not unlawful for the government to refuse support 'unless and until it is clear that charitable support has not been provided and the individual is incapable of fending for himself', and then again, that Article 3 did not come into play until the asylum seeker's predicament 'had reached or was verging on the inhuman or degrading'. So for example the living conditions of T, an asylum seeker obliged to sleep rough at Heathrow airport after being denied benefits and prohibited from working, were not in breach of Article 3: 'He had shelter, sanitary facilities and some money for food. He was not entirely well physically, but not so unwell as to need immediate treatment.'[20]

Commenting on this case, Eric Metcalfe, legal director of JUSTICE, argued that the notion of 'inhuman or degrading' treatment under Article 3 was insufficient to address the full range of human rights issues that appear to arise from such forms of destitution. There is more to respect for human rights than simply ensuring the absence of torture, or inhuman or degrading treatment, he wrote, and such cases were not a failing in the case law surrounding Article 3 . . . so much as a continuing failure of UK law *in general* to recognise economic, social and cultural rights such as the right to work, the right to shelter, and the right to social security as independent and free-standing human rights.[21]

However, the Court of Appeal and then the House of Lords, hearing conjoined appeals from Limbuela and two other asylum seekers, finally ruled against the 'wait and see' approach. Limbuela had temporarily found and been evicted from emergency shelter and the courts accepted that he did not have access to overnight accommodation and his chances of securing food and other necessary facilities were remote. Thus his circumstances were sufficient to meet the Pretty standard of deprivation. The Appeal Court observed that if the government's appeals against decisions favourable to the asylum seekers were upheld, then around 600 of them denied support would have to rely on charitable support that was simply not available. Thus the courts, setting aside their customary deference to the executive, considered how far European Convention rights should protect people's most basic socio-economic entitlements and subjected UK legislation involving considerable resource questions to scrutiny in accordance with the standards set out at Strasbourg – something they were unwilling to do in the case of primary welfare schemes.

Yet the wheels of misfortune continue to turn. The House of Lords and the Court of Appeal ruled in two cases involving failed asylum seekers suffering from HIV/AIDS in 2005 that the two women, referred to as ZT and N, should be returned to Zimbabwe and Uganda, their respective countries of origin, where their effective treatment would cease.[22] The judgments amounted to a sentence of death and the courts were aware of the 'acute dilemmas posed by persons with no right to remain in this country who, however, face illness and death if they are expelled'. Lord Nicholls explained in the case of N:

As the Strasbourg jurisprudence confirms, Article 3 cannot be interpreted as requiring contracting states to admit and treat AIDS sufferers from all over the world for the rest of their lives. Nor, by the like token, is Article 3 to be interpreted as requiring contracting states to give an extended right to remain to would-be immigrants who have received medical treatment while their applications are being considered. If their applications are refused, the improvement in their medical condition brought about by this interim medical treatment, and the prospect of serious or fatal relapse on expulsion, cannot make expulsion inhuman treatment for the purposes of Article 3. It would be strange if the humane treatment of a would-be immigrant while his immigration application is being considered were to place him in a better position for the purposes of Article 3 than a person who never reached this country at all . . . No one could fail to be moved by the appellant's situation. But those acting on her behalf are seeking to press the obligations arising under the European Convention too far.

In another asylum test case in January 2006, a destitute mother of three failed to persuade the High Court that the government's policy of refusing welfare and housing support to force women in her position to leave the UK was unlawful. The Refugee Council and Refugee Action reported that a pilot scheme targeting 116 failed asylum-seeking families was driving them 'underground' to avoid having their children taken into care, and in court the mother's lawyer warned that the scheme put the children at risk of trafficking, sexual exploitation, illegal working and other abuse.[23] But the judge ruled that the policy was not incompatible with the ECHR and refused permission to seek judicial review, stating that 'the question whether the policy is desirable is for Parliament, not for the courts'.

The standard of judicial review in socio-economic cases
The judiciary has broadly decided that it should discard the traditional Wednesbury test (which asks whether an official decision is utterly irrational)[24] in cases where European Convention rights are engaged and apply instead the more rigorous proportionality test. Thus in a much-cited speech in 2001, Lord Steyn dismissed an earlier Court of Appeal decision as being too close to Wednesbury review and considered that courts were now obliged to assess the actual balance which a public authority had struck and to consider how much weight an authority gave to competing interests and issues.[25]

The limitation of human rights must meet a pressing need within democratic society and must be proportionate to the legitimate aim being pursued. But other judges have rowed back on this robust attitude to their responsibilities, and especially in socio-economic cases. Thus for example in another famous speech, Lord Hope said that the courts would in some ECHR cases have to recognise that

> difficult choices might have to be made by the executive or the legislature between the rights of the individual and the needs of society. In some circumstances it will be appropriate for the courts to recognise there is an area of judgment within which the judiciary will defer on democratic grounds to the considered opinion of the elected body.[26]

Hope explained that it would be easier for the courts to recognise 'discretionary areas of judgment' where the issues in front of them 'involved questions of social or economic policy, [particularly] where the rights are of high constitutional importance or are of a kind where the courts are especially well placed to assess the need for protection'. Doubts have been raised about the constitutional propriety of such a doctrine, but it is most confidently defended in the broad area of socio-economic policy, on the customary grounds that the courts do not have the institutional capacity of expertise to make judgments in these areas. So where, for example, commentators have expressed concerns about areas of discretion in the national security context, they have accepted deferential margins of discretion in complex cases of resource allocation.[27]

Nevertheless, the argument is ongoing. Not only are human rights indivisible and too multi-faceted to be placed in watertight categories of this kind. As Lord Steyn made clear, the very idea of constitutional review dictates that all cases involving European Convention rights should be analysed in the same way. Thus, as the eminent constitutional lawyer Murray Hunt argues in a recent collection, 'proportionality is not so much a test or a standard as a whole new type of approach to adjudication' and 'a major landmark on the road to a true culture of justification implicit in *all* human rights adjudication' [emphasis added].[28] Other judges have qualified Hope's position. For example in a recent speech, Lord Justice Simon Brown, while agreeing that a high degree of deference was owed to Parliament, took the view that the courts could not subjugate their role as guardians of human rights to the authority of Parliament and must interfere where 'Parliament has over-stepped the limits of what is justifiable'.[29]

Human rights watchdogs

An important influence on the attitudes of the judiciary to their role in adjudicating upon human rights is the parliamentary Joint Committee on Human Rights (JCHR), which monitors progress on the HRA and subjects all legislation to human rights scrutiny. It has been suggested, for example, that the willingness of Mr Justice Collins to challenge the Home Secretary in an early test case on the refusal of benefits to asylum seekers (see above) may well derive from a robust JCHR report on the Immigration and Asylum Bill in 2002[30] which warned that it was difficult to envisage a case where an asylum seeker could be made destitute without violating either Article 3 or Article 8 of the European Convention.

Be that as it may, the judges do not act in isolation. They are very sensitive to opinion, both that of the general public and more specialist views. There is no question but that the committee plays a crucial part in ensuring that UK legislation is compatible with the ECHR. Its work also serves to make evident that Parliament too has a responsibility to protect human rights, and indeed to emphasise the collaborative nature of human rights protection. Its reports have highlighted various civil liberties and socio-economic concerns, for example on the compatibility of intended mental health and homelessness legislation with European and international human rights norms, as well as now bringing important human rights instruments, such as the ICESCR, into the parliamentary and political domain. Thus the committee's reports may exert a cumulative influence upon the conduct of the courts.

Further, various public bodies and agencies are charged with protecting and promoting various aspects of socio-economic rights nationwide. Chief among them are the Commission for Racial

Eqality, the Disability Rights Commission and the Equal Opportunities Commission (which the government intends to merge); the Children's Commissioners in England, Scotland, Northern Ireland and Wales; both a human rights commission and an equality commission in Northern Ireland; the Health and Safety Commission and Executive (and their Northern Ireland equivalent); and the Social Security Advisory Committee. There is also an active non-governmental sector comprising of bodies like the Child Poverty Action Group, JUSTICE, Mind, Oxfam and Shelter, many of which combined to give evidence to the UN Committee on Economic, Social and Cultural Rights in 2002. Most of these bodies, official and non-official, are aware of the human rights dimensions of their work and some actively pursue case work, but they could have much more influence upon the social and political environment in which the judiciary and Parliament operate if they made the human rights element explicit in all their activities and publications. Plainly also, if Britain did incorporate socio-economic rights into UK law, the task of protecting vulnerable people against violations of their rights would be greatly facilitated (e.g. the Terrence Higgins Trust, seeking to defend asylum seekers with HIV/AIDS, was not able to argue the case on the basis of a general right to health in British law) and the range of cases that these bodies take on would be broadened.

5

Making socio-economic rights work

Resistance in the political classes to introducing economic, social and cultural rights into the United Kingdom derives in the first instance essentially from a fundamentalist attachment to the doctrine of parliamentary sovereignty, and secondly from a profound misunderstanding of the nature of the international regime for protecting and achieving socio-economic rights. There are of course other obstacles, material and ideological. For example, industry is fiercely opposed to giving workers further employment rights and, as we have seen, has the backing of a government that is determined to maintain a 'flexible' labour market.

But here we deal first with the belief that the judiciary ought not to intervene in matters of social and welfare policy. We then demonstrate that the modern regime of socio-economic rights gives the courts a limited, but constructive, role in their realisation without necessarily bringing the executive and judiciary into conflict on political issues. It is about time that policy-makers in this country gave as much attention to the emancipatory role that enforceable socio-economic rights could perform in empowering citizens, acting individually or together, as they do to their potential to divide the courts and the executive. Both arms of governance would do well to regard the protection and enhancement of human rights across the board as a collaborative exercise in which they have complementary responsibilities to respond to citizens' needs. There is a compelling case for a systematic approach to improving the well-being of British citizens within a legal framework of socio-economic rights. We recognise in Chapter 1 above, and in Chapters 6 to 11 that follow, that the current government has made considerable progress in advancing the socio-economic well-being of the British people. Yet current arrangements – in the UK as in other western European nations – leave substantial minorities of people poor, disadvantaged, often homeless and desperate; they fail to protect ethnic minorities, people with disabilities and women from discrimination in their lives and careers; and they allow other social and economic injustices. We will argue the case in this chapter for enforceable socio-economic rights as a way forward – but not as a panacea. New laws and the courts cannot alone bring about social justice. The prevalence of de facto discrimination, despite the widening expanse of anti-discrimination laws, shows that all too clearly.

Keeping the courts at bay

In Britain we live in a parliamentary, not a popular, democracy. The doctrine of parliamentary sovereignty places the 'Crown in Parliament' at the apex of the state, not 'the people'; and in modern times, for 'Crown' read the political executive. Elected governments sit in Parliament and no formal separation between the executive and legislature exists; the judiciary is separate, but subordinate, to a Parliament in which the executive normally holds sway. The main task of the courts is to hold the executive accountable to the rule of law and to ensure that it neither exceeds the powers it is given through legislation nor violates the common law.[1] Traditionally, the protection of human rights, commonly known as civil liberties, rested primarily not with the courts and rights inscribed in the law or the constitution, but on the sovereignty of a Parliament able to make and unmake laws as it saw fit – a precarious pillar for liberty.[2] The Human Rights Act 1998 has changed much of that, but it may yet be repealed.

The political executive has found it hard enough to stomach the courts' interventions to protect civil and political rights under the new Act. The idea that they might also protect socio-economic rights is harder still to digest. The separation of powers in the UK is constitutionally imperfect, but it exists very strongly in conventional political thinking; and public services, welfare and social justice are regarded as the proper domain of the executive and Parliament, on which the courts should not trespass. As we have seen in previous chapters, government ministers and judges alike are ready to repulse any idea of introducing enforceable economic and social rights, employing arguments that derive from this basic position. It is held that elected governments have the democratic mandate to determine the substance of social and welfare provision in the UK by legislation; only they can properly decide how this provision should be organised and funded. The boundaries of the judiciary are thus defined by the remits of the executive and Parliament. It is argued that the courts are not competent to inquire into social and economic questions, nor equipped to take political decisions, on for example budgetary priorities, nor resourced to determine policies in education or health where the executive has access to professional expertise lacking in the courts. Moreover, unelected judges ought not to interfere in individual cases, as these will often involve them in making decisions that re-distribute resources and disturb government budgetary allocations for which they have no democratic legitimacy.

There is of course much truth in the arguments advanced above. We agree with the view that it is not appropriate for the courts to engage in large-scale redistribution of resources or to second-guess government policies in detail. But there is a way of making socio-economic rights justiciable across the board that avoids this danger, as we explain in the next sections of this chapter. But it is also important to recognise that these arguments fail entirely to come to terms with the overriding need to recognise the central place that human rights occupy in the protection of the dignity and well-being of citizens in modern democracies. The interdependence of democratic arrangements and human rights is now widely, and rightly, recognised around a world which bears constant witness to often gross violations of human life and dignity and which has sought since 1948 to protect on a universal basis individual people and communities from such violations. Democratic governments possess and exercise considerable powers of state. Human rights safeguards are designed not only to protect people against abuse or neglect by the state, but also to make use of a state's powers to protect people's dignity and well-being against abuse by any other organisation or individual. These safeguards must be grounded in the rule of law if they are to have any effect. For example, the constitution of South Africa – which we take as a model in this chapter – describes its Bill of Rights as the 'cornerstone of democracy in South Africa' and compels the state to 'respect, protect, promote and fulfil the rights in the Bill of Rights'. Meanwhile, the electoral system in the United Kingdom fails to represent the political choices even of those who vote and privileges select 'Middle England' groups at the expense of the needs of other, often poor, members of society, thus undermining the democratic credentials of both government and Parliament.[3]

Britain has been committed to human rights in varying degrees over time through common law, domestic legislation and international and European human rights instruments. The rule of law requires no more of British governments, and also no less, that they should translate these commitments into reality; and it is the role of the courts to ensure that they do. But the authorities in Britain have long been reluctant to give their human rights commitments the force of law. The traditional insistence that the courts have no place in the ordering of society by government has been so strong in the UK that governments from 1950 onwards have continually rejected proposals that Britain should give legal force at home to the positive civil and political rights that its civil servants and lawyers had assisted in framing for the rest of Europe in the European Convention on Human Rights (ECHR). The Human Rights Act (HRA) does now, as we have seen, offer limited protection to social and economic rights alongside civil and political rights (see Chapter 4). The courts have therefore been obliged reluctantly to consider issues that they believe are the prerogative of elected governments. But ministers and judges are unanimous that to go any further and create full economic and social rights would introduce anarchy in social and welfare policies and bring the courts into political conflict with the executive. Yet as we have argued in Chapter 3, socio-economic rights are essential for all the people in this country to share in the country's prosperity and to exercise the civil and political rights that are now recognised politically and legally.[4]

The significance of progressive realisation of rights

A major misunderstanding – and often enough, crude ignorance – of the sophisticated international regime for protecting socio-economic rights lies at the heart of some of the arguments against incorporating such rights in this country. There is a distinct difference between the thrust of the international covenants and regional conventions and instruments protecting civil and political rights, and that of the International Covenant on Economic, Social and Cultural Rights (ICESCR) and its derivatives. Because the civil order of societies such as the UK is more developed than their social order, the resource issues underlying civil and political rights are settled and taken for granted: resourcing the governing institutions, the courts, criminal justice, prisons, elections and so on takes place almost out of sight. Thus civil and political rights instruments, such as the ECHR, rarely involve the courts in major resource questions but rather raise issues demanding immediate compliance and redress; and the critics seem all to assume that the courts would determine complaints of violations of economic and social rights on the same basic case-by-case and immediate model that applies in general to civil and political rights.

But the ICESCR recognises that socio-economic rights fall into two categories: rights to housing, health, education etc., which generally require substantial state investment over the long run; and rights which are more closely related to civil and political rights, such as trade union and employment rights, which may require scarcely any state funding. Rights of the first type usually demand resources for their realisation and raise political issues of distribution. The ICESCR therefore guarantees 'the progressive realisation' of such rights, expressly recognising that such socio-economic rights raise complex political and resource issues and will usually take more time to realise than civil and political rights protected under its sister International Covenant for Civil and Political Rights and the ECHR – which is why it seeks to ensure that they are progressively rather than immediately realised. On the other hand, it is possible and appropriate for individual economic and social rights cases to be resolved on their immediate merits, especially where resources issues are not salient. For example, the UN Committee on Economic, Social and Cultural Rights has indicated that some socio-economic rights are capable of immediate enforcement. Among them are:

- the guarantee of non-discrimination in access to socio-economic rights (Article 2(2), ICESCR);
- the equal rights of women and men (Article 3);
- equal remuneration for work of equal value without distinction of any kind (Article 7(a)(i));
- the right to strike (Article 8);
- the right of everyone to form and join trade unions, and the right of trade unions to establish and join national and international trade union organisations and to function freely (Article 8);
- the right not to be evicted without due process of law (part of the right to housing under Article 11);
- the right to protection against forced marriage (Article 10.1).

The UN committee also prioritises certain socio-economic rights with major resource implications, especially those involving children. Thus it singles out special measures of protection and assistance for children (Article 10(3)) and compulsory primary education available to all (Article 13(2)) as capable of immediate realisation.

It is important also to recognise that the articles in the ICESCR that seek to protect rights such as the right to adequate housing or the right to work are actually bundles of rights, containing broad rights and specific entitlements and protections. For example, the right to housing includes broad provisions on the accessibility and condition of housing alongside rules governing security of tenure and evictions. It would therefore also be possible immediately to challenge violations of these more specific measures if the ICESCR were in force in the UK.

We should make it clear that resistance to the intervention of the courts in economic and social decisions involving major resources is a common phenomenon around the world. Politicians and judges alike in other countries regard these as political decisions and do not wish judges to become too involved for the very reasons that the political establishment in the UK advances. Such caution is evident in the decisions and practice of the courts in South Africa, where economic and social rights are inscribed in the constitution. The ICESCR takes full cognisance of this common position. Precisely because economic and social rights normally involve the availability and allocation of resources, and require expert evaluation that the courts lack, the ICESCR sets out, as we have indicated in Chapter 2, a process of broader appraisal that allows the courts to look behind an individual case and assess whether the authorities are on their way to realising the right in question progressively in the light of their 'maximum resources' – the principle of progressive realisation.

In other words, the ICESCR, if incorporated into British law, would introduce a 'broad form' of judicial review so far as the more substantial economic, social and cultural rights were concerned, as opposed to a 'strong form', with judges themselves making policy decisions and trade-offs, determining precisely what level of social support is constitutionally required, and issuing court injunctions and applying immediate remedies and damages in individual cases.[5] We use the term 'broad form' to signify the distinction from the more immediate effect that judicial review can entail. But the review itself – a human rights review – should at the same time be stronger than judicial review has customarily been, more stringent and open, drawing far more on the facts, requiring public authorities fully to explain their decisions and inquiring into the human rights merits of decisions rather than just the decision-making process. As we have seen in Chapter 4, the courts are making uncertain progress towards this deeper, human rights type of review.

The arguments of government politicians such as Lord Goldsmith and Bill Rammell against creating justiciable socio-economic rights (see Chapters 2 and 3) are founded on the idea that they all involve major resource questions and would all command a 'strong form' of judicial review. In fact, under the ICESCR, those that involved resources would almost all qualify for a 'broad form' of review, except in exceptional circumstances.[6] It is incumbent on all those who wish Britain to recognise socio-economic rights in law to clarify these points and so ensure that the argument does not take place on false premises. Non-governmental organisations, including some of those that have given evidence to the UN Committee, could do more to promote the ICESCR's framework for protecting socio-economic rights, not least by making explicit use of the obligations and standards it imposes in their reports and lobbying activities.

The government's 'weak' view of its obligations

Ministers like to have their cake and eat it. On the one hand, they argue against enforceable socio-economic rights on the false premise that the courts would be involved in 'strong' and immediate judicial review of resource questions. On the other, they argue, as Bill Rammell, then a minister at the Foreign and Commonwealth Office, did in oral evidence to the Joint Committee on Human Rights (JCHR), that the principle of progressive realisation 'backs up' the government's view that the rights set out in the ICESCR 'constitute principles and objectives' that need not be implemented immediately (see further Chapter 2). The JCHR properly objected to his invoking the principle to support the view that the rights were merely aspirational policy objectives, which did not impose precise obligations on states.[7] The MPs and peers on the committee found that his interpretation under-stated the obligations under the covenant in two ways. First, as we point out above, the rights that do not raise resource questions do impose immediate obligations. Secondly, 'the principle of progressive realisation . . . serves in a number of respects, not to weaken, but to strengthen and specify the state's obligations'. The committee's report agrees that the covenant does envisage an incremental approach, but states that it also requires states to do considerably more than support the covenant rights as 'principles and objectives':

> The requirement of progressive realisation is by no means a weak obligation, in particular for a wealthy state. It requires states to 'take steps' with immediate and continued effect, towards the protection of each of the Covenant rights. Such steps should be 'deliberate, concrete and targeted'. Progressive realisation requires a clear programme or plan of action for the progressive implementation of each of the Covenant rights.[8]

The committee also stressed that the covenant obliges govern-ments to protect rights 'to the maximum of available resources', quoting the UN International Committee's General Comment No. 3:

> In order for a State party to be able to attribute its failure to meet at least its minimum core obligations to a lack of available resources it must demonstrate that every effort has been made to use all resources that are at its disposition in an effort to satisfy, as a matter of priority, those minimum obligations.

Further, as the committee pointed out, the principle of progressive realisation also requires that there should be no retrogression in the protection of economic social and cultural rights. Governments are bound to justify any retrograde measures; and except in exceptional circumstances, they should refrain from diminishing the protection of covenant rights through legislation, changes in policy or withdrawal of funds. New legislation should comply with covenant rights and should seek to implement a positive obligation to fulfil these socio-economic rights.

Moreover, as the JCHR report notes, the government would also be bound to draw up a plan of action for realising socio-economic rights that takes into account the concluding observations of the International Committee (see below) along with the Committee's general comments, on which we draw for this chapter. In fact, as of now, the government variously neglects or regards them with disdain. Rammell's evidence clearly shows how little regard the government has for the International Committee's observations as well as how little understanding ministers have of the strict obliga-tions that the principle of progressive realisation imposes on their government. The JCHR expressed the view that the ICESCR should provide a framework and 'additional impetus' for government policy and that the obligations of progressive and non-discriminatory realisation of covenant rights required 'continued and measurable progress; safeguards against retrogression; clear targets and bench-marks for poverty reduction; and the equal treatment of vulnerable groups'.[9]

Participation in economic, social and cultural rights

We have concentrated on the legal aspects of socio-economic rights, but they also have a democratic dimension. If the ICESCR were introduced into British law, citizens of the UK would be given a say in policies; an opportunity to express preferences; influence on the ways rights are implemented, monitored and assessed; and civil society and interested NGOs could join Parliament in scrutinising government progress. The opportunity to participate in the delivery of socio-economic rights is a recognised human right in itself.[10] These rights are of less value and even meaningless without participation. Yet, in practice, this principle represents almost as large a challenge to the 'British way of doing things' as does the concept of justiciable socio-economic rights. Once again, Bill Rammell under-estimated what the covenant asks of his government in his evidence to the JCHR. He said that, 'if you go through each of the Articles and areas of responsibility under the Covenant', the government's public service agreements (PSAs) put robust targets in place for 'progressively enhancing and realising' covenant rights. Quite apart from the fact that the Treasury paid no heed to the covenant in the planning for PSAs, Treasury officials have always been hostile to any idea of independent evaluation of the PSA targets process. It is true that there was a measure of public debate of the Comprehensive Spending Review that set PSAs in place, but there was scarcely any participation from outside (or often even within) government in framing them.

It is true that the British state is ready enough to go through the motions of consultation, but it has always been half hearted about allowing people to participate in making decisions and policies, for good as well as bad reasons. Jack Straw once described Britain as an executive democracy, by which he meant that the political executive aims generally at best to secure the consent of the public for its actions and policies; and wherever public participation is involved, it is usually designed to win that consent rather than to share power. Where government policies affect ordinary people, ministers do not shrink from bludgeoning those polices through, as they are doing for example with their plans to press public housing out of local authority control: tenants who agree to outsourcing their homes are rewarded with funds for their improvement; those who vote against are punished by being denied funding.

The existing structures to secure accountability through Parliament are formal and weak. In theory, the public nature and formal procedures of the legislative process, on which the UK relies heavily in providing for social and welfare measures, should open up new policy moves to informed opinion and public scrutiny and amendment. In practice, governments can usually shoehorn new measures through without full-scale public or even parliamentary debate (though at the time of writing, education and welfare policies are coming under intense pressure from the government's own back benches). The increasing reliance on private and voluntary providers and services is also an important area of concern, as their work is often protected from public disclosure under rigid contracts which may also deny redress to those whose socio-economic rights are being infringed. Overall, existing democratic arrangements would have to be greatly strengthened, but that would not be enough to comply with the ICESCR. It envisages that special arrangements would probably be required to give marginal or excluded people and their communities the capacity to participate effectively. In some respects, the government has recently moved in this direction, with its policies for the regeneration of deprived neighbourhoods, but seems to have lost patience with communities who don't necessarily act with sufficient despatch.

If the covenant were in force in the UK, the government would also be obliged to give people effective means of redress or remedy when their socio-economic rights under the covenant were violated – which in effect would give ordinary people a grasp on policy-making. The courts often act as open forums on the rights and wrongs of government policy and assist in shaping debates on important issues. The covenant doesn't necessarily seek to make redress available only through the courts, but allows for quasi-judicial or administrative tribunals and mechanisms to rule on complaints and to provide redress.[11] However, the courts would become the main arena in which questions of compliance with socio-economic rights would be resolved. People would only be able to realise a few such rights with immediate effect – for example, freedom from discrimination in respect of socio-economic rights, protection of trade union rights etc. (see below). They would have the opportunity to challenge government or local policies in respect of the generality of protected socio-economic rights, but would be less sure of immediate redress. However, the government would be bound to realise such rights for them progressively over time and, as the JCHR has pointed out, would have to take 'deliberate, concrete and targeted steps' towards doing so 'within a reasonably short time'. The judiciary would of course have to adapt to the new broader responsibilities (see page 89 below).

Progressive realisation of socio-economic rights in action

For the first time governments would have to draw up their social and economic policies within a legal framework that obliged them to make purposeful progress towards satisfying everyone's socio-economic rights and needs, and empowered people to call them to account when they failed. To take an example, government neglect of the housing needs of poorer people from the 1980s onwards could well have triggered 'broad' judicial review were the ICESCR incorporated into British law. British citizens ought anyway to have been involved in framing housing policies at local and national levels; but in any event, they would have been able to seek a remedy, or redress, if they were denied housing appropriate to their needs. It would then be up to the courts to examine their particular needs and to consider more broadly whether the right to housing was being progressively realised. The Grootboom case in 2000 in South Africa, where socio-economic rights are protected under the constitution, gives an example of what could happen.[12]

Mrs Grootboom and her family were among hundreds of illegal squatters who were forcibly evicted from council land earmarked for low-cost housing. Their shacks and belongings were destroyed. The High Court ordered the government to provide them with basic shelter and the case went on appeal to the Constitutional Court. The South African constitution requires the state to adopt and implement a comprehensive housing programme. The court made it clear that it was not for the judiciary to second-guess the government on its housing policies but rather to assess whether its measures represented 'reasonable' progress towards satisfying the housing rights of South Africans. The constitution required the court to consider not only the government's legislation but also the supporting policies, programmes and budgets, in considering how reasonable its housing measures were. The resources at the state's disposal were an important factor; the court did not expect the state to spend more than it could afford. The court found that the state's housing programme was a major achievement and a systematic response to a pressing social need. The overall programme aimed to realise access to housing for all. However, the court also found that the government had neglected the short-term needs of people such as Mrs Grootboom and the other squatters. There was no provision, in national, provincial or local policy, to rescue people in desperate need. But the housing measures required under the constitution had to include measures to 'provide relief for people who have no access to land, no roof over their heads, and who are living in intolerable conditions or crisis situations'.

The court handed down two orders. The first order enforced a settlement between the local authority and Grootboom community giving them basic shelter and services, sanitation and running water; at the same time, the court stressed that its judgment must not be seen as an approval of 'land invasion' of the kind that had occurred in order to jump the housing queue. The second order declared that the state was obliged to 'devise and implement within its existing resources a comprehensive and coordinated programme progressively to realise the right of access to adequate housing'.

The Grootboom judgment is a useful precedent for our purposes, as it shows that even so broad an issue as national housing policy is justiciable. The case also demonstrates that a judicial process exists which allows the courts to come to a considered judgment without pre-empting the role of government, and without having expert knowledge of the practicalities of housing, land and the other social issues involved. The doctrine of reasonable progressive realisation also resolves the resources issue in individual cases, such as this, as the South African Constitutional Court was able to come to a judgment without necessarily privileging one individual or group at the expense of others who had been waiting longer for housing. In practice the judgments took a largely 'broad' form. The general order was declaratory with a socio-economic rights content, ruling that the existing plans for low-cost housing had to be adjusted to provide some housing opportunities for 'people in desperate need', though it did not set any time frames within which the state had to act. Further, the court would have found the government's housing programme acceptable had it promised to provide some housing for people in desperate need 'within a reasonably short time'. Existing plans did not hold out that prospect, but it would have been enough, according to the court, to have a programme that had some 'end in sight'. Under the court's order, the individual plaintiffs need not have received any relief at all; and the court also declined to supervise or oversee the implementation of its orders, leaving this role to the South African Human Rights Commission. This is not the draconian situation that opponents of justiciable socio-economic rights warn of.

However, the South African experience also shows that socio-economic rights can take a 'strong' form under the country's constitution.[13] In several cases, the Constitutional Court has intervened to modify government policies on drug treatments and pricing. In 2002, it reviewed the government's arguments for confining the dispensation of Nevirapine (a drug used to prevent mother-to-child transmission of HIV/AIDS) to only eighteen pilot sites (two in each of the country's nine provinces) and refusing it elsewhere. The government explained that the pilot sites were intended to monitor the safety of the drug and to assist in developing a national prevention programme. However, the Constitutional Court upheld the previous High Court order requiring the health authorities to make Nevirapine available to all pregnant women. It recognised that the government was better placed than the courts to formulate and implement policies on HIV/AIDS, including measures on mother-to-child transmission, but it had failed to adopt reasonable measures to achieve the progressive realisation of the right of access to health-care services.

The restriction policy was held to be rigid and unreasonable, denying mothers and their babies outside the pilot sites the opportunity of receiving a potentially life-saving drug that could be administered within the state's available resources. The court issued prescriptive orders removing the restrictions on the use of Nevirapine and expediting its use nationally (though it also gave the government discretion to adapt the orders if an equally appropriate or better alternative treatment became available). In short, the court showed little deference either to the government's justifications for the policy or to separation-of-powers barriers to its intervention: in fact, it took the view that the courts had the power to enter mandatory injunctions directing the government to develop policies that would lead to the 'progressive realisation' of socio-economic rights. The government has since complied with the court's decisions.[14]

It should be stressed that making socio-economic rights justiciable in South Africa is subject to the same kinds of tensions and debate as we have here in Britain. The courts are anxious not to pre-empt the prerogatives of a government elected under proportional representation (and so more representative than British governments), they are mindful of the resources issues which can lie behind their decisions and they rarely make full use of the powers at their disposal. For example, the Constitutional Court rejected the request of a 41-year-old terminally ill man suffering from chronic renal failure to compel the KwaZulu-Natal health authority to provide him with dialysis.[15] He argued that the authority was denying his right to life. However, as a diabetic suffering from chronic heart disease, he did not meet the criteria for dialysis treatment at the hospital, which could meet less than a third of the demand. Treatment was therefore limited to patients who were candidates for kidney transplants, not those who like him would require life-long dialysis. The court took the view, judged correct in the circumstances,[16] that rationing of the scarce resources available was not antithetical to the right to health, but integral to it. One judge, however, did lapse into the familiar view that some of the socio-economic rights in the constitution were aspirations rather than rights proper. More broadly, given the huge expanse of deprivation in South Africa, the courts alone cannot of course make socio-economic rights a reality for most South Africans.

Nevertheless, cautiously and even timidly, they are gradually making progress towards political as well as legal recognition of economic and social rights in their country.

Progress towards rights-based judicial decisions in the UK

It is evident that the judiciary would have substantially to adjust its thinking and processes to adjudicate upon socio-economic cases if economic, social and cultural rights were to be enacted in the UK or incorporated into British law. By and large, the courts do not like to inquire too deeply into the facts of the cases before them. They would therefore have to modify their reluctance to do so in cases where they had to rule on the broad question of whether or not the government was bringing about the progressive realisation of a socio-economic right. But they would also be required to approach their processes of evaluation more holistically than they have hitherto. The advent of the HRA has undoubtedly begun to shift judicial attitudes in a holistic direction, against a strong undertow of traditional and narrow statutory construction and deference to the executive. As we have seen in Chapter 4, the shifts towards a more positive human rights perspective have been slow and uncertain, subject to both advances and reverses, and the courts are profoundly cautious about venturing beyond the reach of statute.

The courts have traditionally undertaken a formalistic approach to the evaluation of public law issues. Prior to the HRA, they paid deference to the principle of parliamentary sovereignty and resisted developing a judicial role that would enable non-elected judges to engage in assessing decisions by the government or public authorities in accordance with human rights or other principles or standards not set out in statute law. The Act obliges them to go beyond statute, as it were, but they still tend towards a formalistic approach to the broad issues raised by questions of human rights and needs, and stick closer to the letter rather than the spirit when considering the broadly drafted provisions of human rights law. Until very recently, they have also preferred to adhere to the grounds for judicial review of government conduct enunciated by Lord Diplock in 1985 – procedural impropriety, illegality and irrationality – rather than the proportionality test developed in Strasbourg. Diplock's criteria are basic but narrow tests, especially that of irrationality, or 'unreasonableness', which, following the Wednesbury principle (after the leading judicial case), gives public authorities a very wide degree of latitude. The proportionality test, by contrast, demands a far more precise standard of scrutiny for the defence of human rights: namely, that any restriction of a protected human right must meet a 'recognised aim', must fulfil a pressing social need and must be proportionate to the objective of meeting that need.[17]

The courts have been shifting slowly and uncertainly, as we state above and in Chapter 4, towards a 'rights-based' approach to public law and developing principles and values for their appraisal of the authorities' compliance with the ECHR. But a crucial break from the past came in May 2000, when the House of Lords unequivocally determined in a case involving a prisoner's rights that the Strasbourg proportionality test was the appropriate standard where 'fundamental rights' were engaged.[18] The Law Lords took care to distinguish their decision from a recent Court of Appeal verdict in an immigration case couched in 'language reminiscent of the traditional *Wednesbury* ground of review',[19] and stressed that the courts had to assess the relative weight that a public authority had accorded to 'competing interests and considerations' in making its decision. All well and good? Not exactly. The courts have remained reluctant to let go of their traditional deference to the executive in public law and may be developing a partial 'margin of discretion' in which they give the government and public authorities more latitude on human rights, and particularly socio-economic rights (see Chapter 4).

It is not entirely clear where the balance of opinion currently lies. On the one hand, it is confidently expressed within legal circles that the courts do not have the institutional capacity or expertise to form judgments in areas of socio-economic policy where issues of resource allocations are involved. On the other hand, a number of judges have expressed the view that proportionality is not so much a test or a standard, but a wholly new approach to adjudication that must apply across the board in human rights cases.

Lifting the burden on the courts

The beauty of the concept of progressive realisation is that it removes the main obstacle to judicial review of socio-economic policy issues. Under human rights law as it stands in the UK, the courts are asked to decide single cases – a child refused expensive health care, a homeless mother denied emergency accommodation – that have knock-on budgetary consequences. The courts then feel driven to find arguments to justify ruling against the applicants in order to avoid interfering in the allocation of resources, even (as we have seen in Chapter 4) in cases where the public body concerned is under a mandatory duty to provide a service or facility. The concept of progressive realisation lifts that immediate burden from the courts and at the same time ensures that broad socio-economic policies come under informed scrutiny within an overall legal framework that requires the authorities to make basic economic and social rights available and accessible to all.

Consider, for example, the House of Lords hearing of the three homeless cases in London boroughs which we describe in detail in Chapter 4. The court upheld decisions by local authorities in London to deny them emergency accommodation although the case of one mother, Mrs A, at least was distressing in the extreme. In their concern not to meddle, the Law Lords ultimately held that the statutory duty to rehouse homeless families was of a general nature only that could not be enforced on behalf of individuals. The court was, as ever, moved by the potential consequences of providing immediate accommodation for all the families in housing need and disrupting the local housing waiting lists. The courts are thus at an admittedly self-imposed impasse. They are unwilling to enforce socio-economic rights in individual cases for fear of putting too much strain on public resources, and they then retreat to a vague 'target duty' on the authorities – a metaphor, as Mr Justice Sedley once called it – which merely requires authorities to aim at making provision but involves no sanction against failure. It is not clear how satisfactory the courts find this; they cannot relish the apparent inhumanity of leaving a mother such as Mrs A and her children in appalling and dangerous conditions indefinitely, especially as equivalent cases of unmet human need are likely to continue coming before them.

However, the principle of progressive realisation offers a constructive way out of the dilemma. It is not an alternative which will necessarily result in immediate or full redress for people in need, but at least it would ensure that the government and public bodies are pursuing positive policies designed to eradicate such need for all, and it would give the courts the opportunity to take into account the short-term needs of people in desperate straits, such as Mrs Grootboom and Mrs A, as well as unmet long-term goals. Quite what 'target duty' the courts would seek to impose on the authorities would have to be determined. Under the ICESCR, states are under 'a minimum core obligation to ensure the satisfaction of at least the very minimum essential levels of each of the rights'.[20] These are very basic provisions indeed. In a developed nation such as Britain, with the fifth largest economy in the world, the concept of a minimum core obligation will clearly be higher than for a developing nation; in general, socio-economic rights should be measured in comparative, not absolute, terms and other European nations should be taken as comparators. Britain's economy has been growing consistently for a decade and Britain is forecast to remain near the top in GDP internationally for decades to come. Any shortfalls in making a reality of socio-economic rights in their entirety ought to raise questions about whether 'the maximum of available resources' is being devoted to their realisation.

Britain's failures on economic and social rights

We have already described the 'Anglo-social' model of New Labour's welfare policies and paid tribute to the progress that has been made in restoring a measure of social justice in the UK (see Chapter 1). Yet that progress falls far short of this country's obligations under the ICESCR. Bill Rammell, who is now higher education minister, told the JCHR in oral evidence that the government's PSA targets in effect set robust targets for progressively 'enhancing and realising' covenant rights. As we have pointed out above, the government does not involve the public in the process of drafting and agreeing the PSAs – and Parliament is wholly on the margins of the process, as are most ministers. But public participation, especially that of vulnerable and marginal communities, is intrinsic to the process of realising covenant rights. Further, the whole programme, admirable as some of its aims may be, basically reflects the government's priorities, with no reference to the framework of economic and social rights set out in the covenant. As for accountability, that is left to the judgement of the Chancellor; and the Treasury is resolutely opposed to any idea of external evaluation of the success of the PSAs, even on their own terms.

By contrast, the ICESCR seeks to protect a universal set of economic, social and cultural rights in some detail and the International Committee has set about providing a valuable stock of standards and rules of interpretation. If the covenant is incorporated into domestic law, its rights then become enforceable – which would bring about a major advance for citizens in the UK. The UK's reporting obligations under the covenant, with a process of five-yearly external review by international experts, provides a strong external evaluation within a robust framework. The idea of a plan of action within that framework, monitored by the International Committee, is integral to the process of progressive realisation, and the UN committee strongly urged the government to prepare 'a national human rights plan of action' as recommended in the Vienna declaration following the 1993 UN World Conference on Human Rights.

Members of the JCHR pressed Rammell on this point, but he responded that such a plan would not be appropriate at present (and would anyway be a matter for the Department of Constitutional Affairs). Lord Falconer, secretary of state at the DCA, ducked the issue when he gave evidence to the JCHR in December 2003, suggesting that the government should consider the idea when the interdepartmental review of the UK's human rights obligations was complete (as it now is) and the new Commission for Equality and Human Rights was established (which it is not). There the idea lies, safe in the long grass.

Yet the idea could transform the government's cautious and almost secretive approach to social justice. The Committee on the

Administration of Justice (CAJ), the Northern Irish human rights watchdog, has suggested that in relation to key covenant rights, the government should

> have a plan which sets targets and timetables, and arises from an open, public, transparent and participative process wherein decision-makers have been held properly to account and alternatives have been actively considered . . . Only in this way can the government show that it is genuinely seeking to meet its obligations fully and to progressively realise its obligations.[21]

It is shocking that the government continues to fail to prepare a national plan on economic, social and cultural rights in the UK, especially given the range of 'serious concerns' that the UN Committee on Economic, Social and Cultural Rights has expressed in its last two sets of concluding observations in 1997 and 2002. These concerns show how far the UK is from meeting its obligations under the covenant. Table 5.1 sets out the principal concerns and recommendations of the UN committee, in both 1997 and 2002.

This is a formidable list of areas in which socio-economic rights are by any reckoning at risk of being infringed, even if it is possible to specify only one widely recognised violation of the covenant – the refusal fully to protect the right to strike. The following chapters review the state of economic and social rights in key policy areas – discrimination and equality, poverty, health, housing, education and work. In our view, Britain is failing to protect socio-economic rights in all these areas, and there must be a question whether the government's overall policy of accepting major inequalities within society makes its socio-economic injustices incurable, as the work of the social epidemiologist Richard Wilkinson suggests (see Charter 1).[22] Overall, at the very least, it is clear that the range of actual or potential violations is wide-ranging; in this chapter, we review the state of deprivation in the UK largely from the point of view of the International Committee.

Table 5.1: The Committee on Economic, Social and Cultural Rights'
concerns and recommendations

	1997	2002
Discrimination	Despite the protection of laws and elaborate machinery against protection, significant de facto discrimination continues to exist against women and blacks and other ethnic minorities. Women continue to occupy a significant lower percentage of managerial positions, particularly in the private sector, and a correspondingly higher percentage of lower-paid and part-time jobs. A substantially higher rate of unemployment persists among blacks and other ethnic minorities and disproportionately more occupy lower-paid jobs. The rate of unemployment among Catholics in Northern Ireland is alarming – twice that of Protestants – and is substantially higher than the national average. The government needs to take effective measures against these discriminations.	De facto discrimination persists against marginalised and vulnerable groups in society, especially ethnic minorities and people with disabilities, in housing, employment, education and other goods and services. The committee regretted the government's unwillingness to adopt a comprehensive Equality Act and urged the enactment of comprehensive legislation on equality and non-discrimination in United Kingdom law (in conformity with Articles 2.2 and 3 of the covenant).

	1997	2002
Pay		The national minimum wage is not set at a level that gives all workers an adequate standard of living (in accordance with Articles 7 (a) (ii) and 11 of the covenant); and its wage protection does not apply to workers under eighteen years of age and discriminates against workers aged between eighteen and twenty-two in giving them a lower minimum wage. The national minimum wage should be fixed at a level that provides an adequate standard of living and extended fully to younger workers.
Health	The committee called for immediate action to remedy the worsening waiting times for surgery on the NHS, which were then eighteen months or longer. The position called into question, the committee noted, whether the UK government was making its best efforts to satisfy Article 12 of the covenant.	

	1997	2002
Employment rights	The failure to incorporate the right to strike in domestic law violates Article 8 of the covenant. The right to strike should be incorporated in legislation. Employees participating in a lawful strike should not ipso facto be regarded as having breached an employment contract. The government should abolish the right of employers to differentiate between union and non-union members by giving pay rises to non-union employees – a practice which is also incompatible with Article 8.	The failure to incorporate the right to strike in domestic law violates Article 8 of the Covenant. The right to strike should be incorporated in legislation, as the committee recommended in 1997, and strike action should no longer entail the loss of employment.
Domestic violence	The committee noted with concern the serious incidence of domestic violence against women, estimated at 680,00 cases in 1995. The committee asked the government to report at the next CESCR review on its measures against domestic violence and their effectiveness.	The incidence of domestic violence has increased in recent years. The government should continue its efforts to combat domestic violence and ensure that there are sufficient refuge places to meet the needs of victims of domestic violence. Again, the committee asked for a report on the measures the government was taking to deal with the problem.

Children

The committee expressed concerns about the conditions for children in state care and about reports that the significant reduction in children's homes and increased resort to fostering has led to an increasing incidence of abuse in foster homes. The government should consider relying more on effectively supervised children's homes. The committee was alarmed that corporal punishment was practised in private schools and that the government did not intend to eliminate the practice.

The physical punishment of children in families should be prohibited (as recommended in 1995 by the UN Committee on the Rights of the Child).

Poverty

Despite the developed state of the UK economy, unacceptable levels of poverty exist among certain segments of the population, especially in Northern Ireland. The economic benefits of gains in prosperity are unevenly distributed and the gap between rich and poor has widened significantly. The committee found it disturbing that some one million people do not apply for social benefits to which

Considerable levels of poverty persist in the UK, as the committee observed in 1997, especially in certain parts of the country, such as Northern Ireland, and among certain sections of the population, such as ethnic minorities, people with disabilities and older people. Despite measures taken to combat poverty and social exclusion, the gap between the rich and poor has increased. The committee expressed

	1997	2002
	they are entitled, and that the government restricts access to free legal aid with respect to a number of economic and social rights. Social assistance should be more carefully targeted on the poorest groups and efforts should be made to improve take-up. More accessible legal aid for social and economic rights would facilitate take-up of these and other socio-economic benefits.	particular concern about the high levels of child poverty among certain groups of society and urged the government to address the problem of poverty and social exclusion as a matter of high priority, especially among marginalised and vulnerable groups and in particular regions, such as Northern Ireland.
Homelessnes	Homelessness remains a problem that is not adequately addressed in the UK. Vulnerable groups such as travellers and ethnic minorities do not receive sufficient protection against evictions. The committee asked for closer monitoring of homelessness and forced evictions in the government's report to the next CESCR review.	Homelessness persists, despite the committee's earlier concern, particularly among ethnic minorities; and a large number of the homeless are alcoholics or suffer from mental illness. The government should focus its efforts to combat homelessness on those groups who are disproportionately affected, such as ethnic minorities, and take measures to ensure that homeless persons suffering from serious health problems receive adequate health care.

	1997	2002
Housing conditions		Poor-quality housing and 'fuel poverty' continues to be a problem for a large number of families and individuals. The government should take immediate measures to improve the situation of the large number of families and individuals who live in poor housing conditions and give relief to people who are 'fuel poor'.
Higher education		The introduction of tuition fees and student loans in tertiary education is inconsistent with Article 13(2)(c) of the covenant and tends to worsen the position of students from less privileged backgrounds, who are already under-represented in tertiary education. The government should take effective measures to ensure that tuition fees and student loans do not have a negative impact upon such students.
School exclusions	About 13,000 children are permanently excluded from school. A disproportionate number of these children are of African-Caribbean	

origin. The committee recommended that defined criteria be adopted for school exclusions and asked for a report on government programmes for training excluded children.

| Northern Ireland schools | The educational structure in Northern Ireland continues to be heavily segregated on the basis of religion, though about 30 per cent of parents would prefer to send their children to integrated schools. Current government policy, which appears to consist of being willing to consider integrating existing Protestant or Catholic schools if it is the wish of the majority in a given school, is ineffective and is likely to preserve the status quo. | The educational structure in Northern Ireland continues to be heavily segregated on the basis of religion, despite the increased demand for integrated schools. The government should consider, as it had recommended in 1997, introducing measures in Northern Ireland to facilitate the establishment of additional integrated schools in areas where a significant number of parents have indicated their desire to have their children enrolled in such schools. |
| Human rights education | | Human rights education in schools, and for the judiciary, prosecutors, government officials, civil servants and others involved in implementing the covenant, does not give adequate attention to economic, social and cultural rights. |

The major areas in which UK governments are at risk of failing progressively to realise socio-economic rights are poverty, inequality and housing – which are also the areas of priority for the ICESCR; as the committee emphasised in its statement on poverty in 2001, poverty itself constitutes a denial of rights under the covenant. In its 2002 report, the committee urged the government to address poverty and social exclusion as a matter of high priority. The government's written evidence to the committee stated that it 'regards the fight against poverty and social exclusion as central to its entire programme', and emphasised recent falls in 'absolute poverty' and levels of child poverty. Yet as Chapter 7 shows, poverty levels remain disturbingly and damagingly high and disproportionately affect ethnic minorities, people with disabilities, children and women. The links between poverty, poor-quality housing and fuel poverty are persistent and appear ineradicable. There is an urgent need for a rights-based legal framework against which the government's progress on reducing poverty and its attendant evils and success in involving poor people themselves can be measured.

The government is also vulnerable on its record on equality and protection against discrimination. There is an urgent case for the creation of fully comprehensive legislation on equality and protection from discrimination, as the International Committee recommended. Further, such legislation needs to be 'free-standing', since at the moment the HRA protects people only against discrimination in relation to civil and political rights; otherwise, the UK will arguably be guilty of violations in this area. And yet the remedies are at hand. The ECHR, on which the HRA is based, actually establishes a 'free-standing' right of equality, but the government has not yet ratified it and thus it is not part of the HRA. The government says it supports in principle the inclusion of the right to equality in the ECHR, but fears that it might lead to an 'explosion of litigation'.[23] This is precisely the same objection that opponents of the HRA raised before it came into force, which never materialised. The government was for some years against the idea of introducing a Single Equality Act and the International Committee actually reported that it remained unwilling to do so. But it now has plans for an Equality Act, though it may be long delayed and it is not yet clear precisely how comprehensive it will be (see Chapter 6). The government intends first to establish the new Commission for Equality and Human Rights, and then to legislate, but as the JCHR argues, it would be better to give priority to a 'levelling up' Act and to place a positive duty on public authorities to promote equality across all relevant areas as a basis for the commission's work. In the meantime, the extensive nature of de facto discrimination in the UK against ethnic minorities, women and people with disabilities is shocking, and it occurs in key areas of life, employment, housing and education. A government which is as open to ideas of social engineering could do much to right the wrongs that take place daily. The JCHR comments that the level of inequality, especially for ethnic minorities and people with disabilities, is well documented and recognised by the government itself.

The government would seem to be in violation of the right to housing under Article 11 of the ICESCR across the board, from a basic right to shelter to the wider right to 'live somewhere in security, peace and dignity'. Here again, as Table 5.1 shows, the committee noted in its concluding observations in 2002 the persistence of homelessness in the UK, especially among vulnerable groups, and the high levels of alcoholism and mental illness among homeless people. And homelessness continued to rise after the committee's report (see Chapter 9). The government has put in place a legislative framework for re-housing the homeless and there are homelessness strategies and bodies in England, Scotland, Wales and Northern Ireland. But as Chapters 4 and 9 show, vulnerable families and individuals continue to suffer from damaging refusals of accommodation, and the courts refuse to intervene, even in the most distressing cases. Moreover, as evidence to the JCHR from ADT Fourth World, the Children's Law Centre and the Disability Rights Commission points out, the authorities' strategies and measures do not reach all marginalised groups affected by homelessness.[24] It is poverty that maroons vulnerable people in homelessness and insecurity, but, as Chapter 9 argues, the long-term neglect of affordable housing is a potent factor – and here the government certainly falls short of its duty of progressive realisation.

Three international human rights bodies have repeatedly identified

British law as incompatible with the right to strike: the International Committee, as above, the ILO Committee of Experts and the Council of Europe European Committee of Social Rights. The Institute of Employment Rights argues that Britain's employment laws are generally 'the most restrictive in Europe' and require drastic surgery if they are to meet international human rights standards. Chapter 11 describes the government's arguments for refusing to accept the view of the international bodies that protection against loss of employment is necessary in order to protect the right to strike. However, several trade unions have stated that they have desisted from strike action, or repudiated strike action by their members, to avoid the danger of dismissal for those members. It is our view that the current law places undue restrictions on the right to strike, as protected under international human rights instruments, and should be amended unambiguously to protect workers from dismissal after a strike. The narrow legal definition of 'trade dispute' outlaws secondary or 'sympathy strikes', and removes immunity for actions taken against a parent company which is the actual, but not the immediate, employer involved in a trade dispute. The Employment Relations Act 2004 amended the law allowing employers to discriminate between non-union and union members, about which the International Committee expressed concern, after the European Court found that the law breached the right to freedom of association under the ECHR.[25] However, the JCHR points out that the 2004 Act left some incompatibilities unremedied, particularly by failing to give trade unions, as well as employees, a right to redress where employers offered inducements to employees not to join the union.

The International Committee did welcome the introduction of a national minimum wage under the Labour government, but expressed concern that it was not set at a level that provided all workers with an adequate standard of living, did not apply to workers aged under eighteen and discriminated against workers aged between eighteen and twenty-two (see above). The government has responded to some of these concerns, raising the adult rate to £5.05 an hour from October 2005 and, twelve months earlier, introducing a minimum wage rate of £3 an hour for sixteen- and seventeen-year-old workers. But workers aged between eighteen and twenty-two still receive a lower rate (now £4.25 an hour). In March 2006 the Low Pay Commission published its annual report on the minimum wage;[26] the government has followed some of its recommendations and from October the rates will increase further, to £5.35 for adults, £4.45 for 18–22-year-olds and £3.30 for 16–17-year-olds.

The International Committee expressed concern about the high and growing incidence of domestic violence both in 1997 and 2002, and in evidence to the JCHR, the CAJ drew attention to the particularly high level of domestic violence in Northern Ireland. However, the government has since passed the Domestic Violence, Crime and Victims Act 2004 to strengthen protection against domestic violence, especially for children. Meanwhile, the concept of 'reasonable chastisement' continues to allow physical punishment of children to continue, though not as a defence against major assault, in contravention of the UN Convention on the Rights of the Child; new faster adoption procedures threaten poor families and mothers with the loss of their children; and state care continues to be an unsatisfactory start in life for many disadvantaged children. There are considerable doubts over the effects of the government's decision to introduce tuition fees and student loans in higher education, and the International Committee expressed its concern that the new policy had tended to worsen the position of students 'from less privileged backgrounds', who were already under-represented in higher education. It seems (as we write) that fewer young people are applying for university places and a larger drop is anticipated ahead of the introduction of £3,000 tuition fees. A survey of careers advisers reported early in 2006 that the new funding regime was damaging the government's attempts to attract more students from disadvantaged backgrounds, and that universities were failing to promote their bursary schemes for poorer students. Britain is required under the ICESCR to make higher education 'equally accessible to all, on the basis of capacity, and in particular by the progressive introduction of free education' (Article 13). The government must take seriously the obligation to progressively realise wider access to higher education as the actual outcomes of its policies become clearer over time. School exclusions have risen again after falling under government pressure and there are disquieting signs of discrimination against black pupils that require redressing. The punitive and under-funded mental health regime also requires sensitive attention. The needs of the mentally ill take second place to public fears aroused by a very few high-profile cases when mentally ill people released into the community have murdered or injured members of the public. The Mental Health Act Commission has reported severe funding shortages in mental health institutions and hospitals, which are run down and often dirty and neglected along with their inmates. A Healthcare Commission report on cleanliness found that mental hospitals performed particularly badly.[27]

What next?

The most powerful – and popular – way of guaranteeing socio-economic along with civil and political rights in the United Kingdom would be either to inscribe them in a new written constitution or to pass an indigenous Bill of Rights as part of a constitutional settlement. As we have seen, the majority of people in the UK are in favour of a Bill of Rights that protects both categories of human rights. But the authorities in Britain have shied away from unconditionally giving people socio-economic rights with constitutional protection. Thus the HRA is probably the best model for enacting economic, social and cultural rights in the UK. The Act, as we have seen, incorporates the civil and political rights protected in the ECHR into British law while maintaining the central doctrine of parliamentary sovereignty. The constitutional safeguards in the Act empower the courts to make a declaration of incompatibility for new legislation while giving them no power to strike down either primary or secondary legislation (though only when the parent Act protects incompatible secondary legislation). At the same time, ministers are obliged to declare the compatibility of draft legislation with the Act on introducing it into Parliament.

In the same way, the ICESCR or European Social Charter, or parts of them, could be set within a framework of domestic law in the UK. First, if it were the ICESCR that were incorporated, govern-ments would be obliged to use the maximum resources available to realise fully and progressively over time the economic, social and cultural rights that were protected, through legislation and other means; or, in the words of the covenant, 'to take steps, . . . especially economic and technical, *to the maximum of its available resources, with a view to achieving progressively the full realisation of the rights recognised in the present Covenant by all appropriate means*, including particularly the adoption of legislative measures [Article 2.1, ICESCR, emphasis added]'.

For ordinary citizens in the UK, this would mean that economic, social and cultural rights of good standard are being realised and made accessible over time (see Chapter 2). Citizens and governments would have to decide in partnership how they were organised and made available, but in general, the relevant goods, services and facilities must be affordable, available in sufficient quantity, supplied free from discrimination, within safe physical reach, and culturally and ethically acceptable. Socio-economic rights would become justiciable in their own right – that is to say, either individuals or communities who felt that any of these rights were being ignored or violated would be able to take their case to the courts, either for immediate resolution or for a 'broad', less immediate human rights form of review that evaluated thoroughly how far the government was seeking to realise those rights progressively over a reasonable period of time within the resources available. At the same time the government would be obliged to set out its plans for realising socio-economic rights in an open and participatory way.

Ultimately, of course, people's social and economic rights would not be determined within the courts. The distribution of society's resources is a matter for democratic debate and decision, not judicial arbitration; and the courts are properly mindful of public opinion. What is significant is that justiciable socio-economic rights would provide a human rights framework within which government, the courts and the public, especially those in need, could develop shared values, review policies and allocate resources. The political parties are sceptical about the willingness of the public to accept the costs of a more equal society – hence the government's reliance on 'stealth' taxes to fund improved public services. But there is much to build on. Polls show that the public regard living in an equal society as an important part of democracy.[28] A framework of socio-economic rights would give legitimacy and space to individuals and communities to argue their case, for example, for decent housing or educational opportunities. They would additionally be able to take their case to the courts for adjudication with the assistance of skilled advocates; and the courts would thus provide a forum for debate and resolution. Policy-making on economic and social rights these days is a narrowly based process in which individuals and communities in need are treated as recipients of services, not partners, and they rarely make their voices heard. Party political policies are shaped by electoral perceptions in the battle for the 'centre ground'[29] – not common ground – and deference to organised interests more than by need or social justice. By arming people with socio-economic rights, we enable them to make the case within British society not only for social justice, but for a healthier society for all.

6

Equality before the law?

The legal system guarantees equality and provides protection from discrimination in the UK in three ways: firstly, through common law; secondly, through the Human Rights Act 1998, which incorporates the European Convention of Human Rights into British law; and thirdly, through specific anti-discrimination laws. In the chapters which follow we deal with issues of discrimination and inequality as they arise and examine the evidence of discrimination and disadvantage in the key areas of income, health, housing, education and employment. This chapter sets out a brief overview of the legal framework for protection from discrimination.

1. Common-law protection of equality

It is clear that equality before the law is a central tenet of the common-law notion of the rule of law: 'it is inherent in the very notion of law, and in the integrity of the law's application, that like cases be treated alike over time'.[1] However, the common law is limited in the protection from discrimination that it is able to provide. Professor Jeffrey Jowell has explained that the common law's reach

> is limited because its primary concern is not with the content of the law but with its enforcement and application alone. The Rule of Law is satisfied as long as laws are applied or enforced equally, that is, even-handedly, free from bias and without irrational distinction. The rule of law requires formal equality which prohibits laws from being enforced unequally, but it does not require substantive equality. It

does not therefore prohibit unequal laws. It constrains, say, racially-biased enforcement of laws, but does not inhibit apartheid-style laws from being enacted.[2]

Jowell argues that the common-law principle of equality before the law is supplemented by a further constitutional principle that 'requires government not to treat people unequally without justification'.[3] Lord Hoffman, giving the judgment of the Privy Council in *Matadeen v. Pointu*, said that 'treating like cases alike and unlike cases differently is a general axiom of rational behaviour'.[4] However, even here equality is only one test of official action; other considerations or interests can defeat it. Thus, equality is not a free-standing entitlement in English law.[5] Relying on a common-law equality principle as a ground of judicial review will only assist in combating the 'most bizarre' or 'obviously unfair' cases of discrimination, while leaving untouched forms of discrimination which are 'not generally regarded as problematic'.[6]

2. Human Rights Act protection from discrimination

The protection of rights by common law is now reinforced by the Human Rights Act 1998 (HRA), which gives domestic effect to some of the rights contained in the European Convention on Human Rights (ECHR). One major contribution is the principle of non-discrimination, contained in Article 14, which provides that the exercise of convention rights and freedoms must be secured without discrimination on any of the following specifically enumerated grounds – sex, race, colour, language, religion, political or other opinion, national or social origin, association with a national minority, property, birth – or on the basis of 'other status'. The protection here is limited to the civil and political rights found in the ECHR. Article 14 is not a free-standing right to protection from discrimination; it is ancillary to other convention rights. Protocol 12 aims to ensure more comprehensive protection from discrimination under the convention by providing that the enjoyment of any rights set forth by law shall be secured without discrimination on any grounds, and that no one shall be discriminated against by any public authority on any grounds.[7] The UK government has so far refused to sign the protocol.[8] In its view, the protocol is 'too general and open ended' and 'it does not make clear whether "rights set forth in law" includes international law as well as national law'.[9]

The government is concerned that 'the European Court of Human Rights might hold that a right set out in an international agreement, but not incorporated into United Kingdom law, is covered by Protocol 12'.[10] The potential for Protocol 12 to make economic, social and cultural rights justiciable is a major underlying concern, especially since 'new rights are not necessarily cost free (*especially when they are economic, social and cultural rights*) and may affect the rights of others, as many rights have to be balanced against each other' (emphasis added).[11] Two eminent human rights lawyers, Lord Lester and Professor Sandra Fredman, have criticised the government's objections as unconvincing:

> The text of Protocol 12 is necessarily 'general and open ended' if it is to provide the free-standing rights against discrimination. It is no more general and open-ended than is the text of the free-standing rights against discrimination in the International Covenant on Civil and Political Rights, or of similar guarantees in the written constitutions of other Commonwealth and European countries. It is not clear why it matters to the government whether Protocol 12 applies to rights set forth by international law as well as by national law. The only relevant international law is the international law by which the states parties to Protocol 12 would already be bound.[12]

The HRA gives effect to ECHR rights in two ways. First, under Section 3 it holds that 'so far as it is possible to do so, primary and subordinate legislation must be read and given effect in a way which is compatible with' the convention's Article 14 on non-discrimination among other provisions. This interpretive obligation applies to both past and future legislation. Subordinate legislation is invalid and ineffective to the extent that it cannot be interpreted to be compatible with Article 14. If a compatible interpretation of primary legislation is impossible then the incompatible legislation must continue to be given effect.[13] The courts can issue a declaration of incompatibility, but it remains for Parliament to decide whether to amend the legislation so as to achieve compatibility. The potential within these provisions to protect against discrimination was seen in the case of *Mendoza v. Ghaidan*, where the Court of Appeal found that the HRA enabled it to read provisions in the Rent Act 1977 so that the words 'as his or her wife or husband' were taken to mean 'as if they were his or her wife or husband', thus ensuring the provisions avoided discrimination against same-sex cohabiting couples.[14]

Second, under the HRA it is unlawful for public authorities to act in a way which is incompatible with convention rights, unless such an act is the effect of primary legislation. Individuals or organisations directly affected by such unlawful acts can seek legal redress. This duty is limited to public authorities and so leaves private acts in important areas such as employment, housing and the provision of goods and services outside the scope of the HRA. For regulation of these areas, people must rely on specific anti-discrimination acts.

3. Anti-discrimination laws

It was the failure of common law to provide effective protection from discrimination that led to the enactment of specific anti-discrimination legislation. This legislation has developed in a piece-meal fashion, responding to immediate problems, to determined lobbying by groups seeking protection from discrimination or to the legal developments of the European Union. As a result of this patchwork approach, gaps and inconsistencies have developed.[15]

Until 2003 the legislation covered discrimination on the grounds of sex,[16] gender reassignment,[17] marriage,[18] colour, race, nationality or ethnic or national origins,[19] disability;[20] and in Northern Ireland, religious belief, political opinions[21] and membership of the Irish Traveller community.[22] There is also protection from unfavourable treatment on the grounds of trade union membership[23] and for part-time workers.[24] In 2003 the UK was required to implement the EU Race and Employment Directives. They created new definitions of indirect discrimination and made changes to the way in which the burden of proof operates in discrimination cases. Most significantly it required the extension of anti-discrimination legislation to cover religion or belief [25] and sexual orientation. [26] The EU also requires the government to introduce legislation prohibiting age discrimination by 2006. The need to implement the directives provided an ideal opportunity to create a single Equality Act that would rationalise the legislation, ensuring an equal level of protection for all grounds of discrimination and removing inconsistencies and anomalies. This opportunity was not taken; instead the government chose to do the minimum that was needed to implement the directives and passed them as secondary legislation under the European Communities Act.

However, in its 2005 general election manifesto Labour promised to introduce a Single Equality Act by the end of the present parliament. The Equalities Review and Discrimination Law Review set up in February 2005, along with the proposed Commission on Equality and Human Rights (CEHR), will influence this process (see further pages 121–3 below).

A single Equality Act is much needed. In persisting with the piecemeal approach to improvements in equality law, the government has added protections which only apply to those forms of discrimination covered by the EU directives which it introduced. The changes required by the Race Directive only apply in respect of race or ethnic or national origin. They will not apply to discrimination on the grounds of colour or nationality.

The scope of the existing legislation, that is the areas of activity in which the legislation prohibits discrimination, differs for each of the protected grounds. Employment is central to the EU framework of economic and social legislation and to the government's strategy for taking individuals out of poverty. It is not surprising therefore that the greatest degree of protection from discrimination is in the field of employment. As will be clear from the evidence below, sex, race and ethnicity, disability, religion and age are relevant variables for inequality in participation in the labour market and in income levels. While it is possible to show that these factors are important variables, it is more difficult to identify and quantify the extent to which discrimination in the labour market is a factor.

The Race Relations Act, the Sex Discrimination Act (SDA), the Disability Discrimination Act and the Fair Employment and Treatment Order (FETO) also cover discrimination in education, the provision of goods, services and facilities and the disposal and management of premises. This means that discrimination on the grounds of sexual orientation, gender reassignment and religion or belief (except against Jews and Sikhs, who are treated as a racial group, and for protection under the FETO in Northern Ireland) is allowed in education, property, housing and the provision of goods, services and facilities. The Equality Act 2006 sets out in part to correct some of these anomalies and make unlawful 'discrimination on the grounds of religion or belief' in these areas.[27] It also extends the definition of religious discrimination in anti-discrimination legislation to take in those of no belief. Following an amendment of the Bill at third reading in the House of Lords, Section 81 of the Equality Act allows the secretary of state to make regulations prohibiting discrimination on the grounds of sexual orientation in relation to the provision of goods, services and facilities. But this latter measure is only an enabling power and concerns exist that it may not lead to the introduction of thorough protection.

The effectiveness of the legislation in tackling discrimination is also curtailed by the exemptions and exclusions that apply even in areas of activity apparently covered by the legislation. The possibility of addressing discrimination by public bodies was significantly curtailed by the House of Lords' interpretation of Section 29 of the SDA in the case of *Amin*. They found that the anti-discrimination legislation only applied to acts done on behalf of the Crown which are 'at least similar to acts that could be done by private persons.'[28] This meant that the discrimination legislation did not apply to many of the core functions of public bodies. For example, the Act can apply to the police as an employer, as this was an act similar to something done in the private sector, but did not apply to actions by the police for which there was not private sector equivalent, for example arrest and stop and search activities. The need to bring public bodies within the ambit of the race relations law became imperative following the finding in the Stephen Lawrence inquiry report that 'institutional racism exists both in the Metropolitan Police Service and in other police services and other institutions country wide'.[29] The potential for the existence of institutional racism within public bodies was acknowledged by the then Home Secretary, Jack Straw:

> In my view, any long-established, white-dominated organisation is liable to have procedures, practices and a culture that tend to exclude or to disadvantage non-white people. The police service, in that respect, is little different from other parts of the criminal justice system – or from government departments, including the Home Office – and many other institutions.[30]

As well as being white dominated, these institutions also developed at a time when the predominant norms were based on a person being male, able bodied, Christian and heterosexual. The arguments that apply for the existence of institutional racism within public bodies also apply to these forms of institutional discrimination.

In response to the Stephen Lawrence inquiry report, the government passed the Race Relations (Amendment) Act 2000, which makes it unlawful for a public authority to discriminate on grounds of race in carrying out any functions.[31] A similar provision exists in Northern Ireland in relation to discrimination on the grounds of religious belief or political opinion.[32]

The government is attempting to extend anti-discrimination legislation further into the realm of public authorities. The Disability Discrimination Act 2005 prohibits public authorities, in carrying out their functions, from discriminating on the grounds of disability. The Equality Act 2006 extends this discrimination on the grounds of gender, and religion or belief. However, the JCHR expressed concern that the definition used of 'public authority' had exceptions and that it fell short of the wider meaning of 'public authority' contained in the HRA. The committee noted in particular, in relation to religion and belief, that 'any decision of a public authority to refuse entry clearance or leave to remain, or anything done in pursuance of such a decision, is exempt from duties of non-discrimination and harassment under the Bill'.[33]

Individual enforcement

In Great Britain, three commissions have been established to combat discrimination: the Commission for Racial Equality (CRE), the Equal Opportunities Commission (EOC) and the Disability Rights Commission (DRC). However, the current legal framework focuses on individual instances of discrimination and as a consequence individual cases have been at the sharp end of tackling discrimination. A single discrimination case can lead to changes across both public and private sectors. For example, high profile sexual harassment cases have led major employers to take sexual harassment more seriously and to develop policies to prevent and address such harassment. A successful discrimination case attracts widespread publicity that can impact beyond the individual instances. Thus one of the responsibilities of the commissions is to assist complainants to take their cases forward and to create wider awareness of the laws governing discrimination and the remedies that are available. Individual cases also inform the commissions where there are matters that warrant further attention, for example the extent of discrimination or harassment within a particular organisation or sector and/or the lack of clarity of one aspect of the law. Individual cases are clearly important to effectively tackling discrimination but they rely on the willingness of individuals to come forward and pursue a claim. The support available for individuals prepared to come forward and pursue a claim is therefore critical to the success of anti-discrimination legislation.

Individuals who face discrimination are able to seek redress through the judicial system. Cases of discrimination relating to work can be taken to an employment tribunal; all other cases are heard at a county or sheriff court. Individuals may receive advice and information about the law and also support for legal representation. In relation to both, individuals face significant barriers in gaining access to justice. Widely accessible legal aid is vital if discrimination law is to be effective. Many victims of discrimination are not financially eligible for legal aid; however, the nature of discrimination means that vulnerable groups are likely to be disproportionately financially eligible. Legal aid is available so that solicitors and law centres can provide advice and information to individuals who experience discrimination. However, the availability of specialist employment advice is not sufficient to meet demand.

Trade unions are another source of advice and information to their members. However, unionisation is often lowest in those sectors where the most vulnerable groups facing discrimination work. In relation to race, sex and disability discrimination advice and information is available from the individual commissions. At present there is no regulatory body providing advice and information for those bringing discrimination claims in on the grounds of sexual orientation and religion or belief. The absence of a single equality body and the lack of public funding for discrimination cases significantly reduces the ability of regulations prohibiting discrimination on the grounds of religion or belief or sexual orientation from having an impact. The government is funding advice and information to employers and employees about the new regulations; but, perversely, should an employee, having learnt of their new rights, wish to exercise them and bring a claim of discrimination, there is no public assistance available for representation before an employment tribunal.

It is inevitable in employment litigation that there will be inequality of arms between worker and employer. This inequality is magnified by the particular complexities and difficulties of discrimination cases, such as the need for expert evidence and statistical data to prove indirect discrimination. The availability of legal representation has a significant impact on the chances of a case succeeding. Research in relation to disability found that while an unrepresented client has only a 12 per cent chance of success, for clients with legal representation the chance of success increases to 28 per cent.[34] In England and Wales, legal aid is not available for actual legal representation before an employment tribunal, except in 'exceptional cases'. In the four years to 2004 only four cases received funding under this exception.[35] In Scotland there is limited legal aid for cases brought before a tribunal. This was thought to be necessary to ensure equality between the parties to meet the fair trial requirements of the ECHR.[36]

Support for legal representation from the commissions is limited. In 2002 the CRE received 1,300 applications for assistance; it gave full advice and assistance in 600 cases but provided full legal representation in only 81. In the absence of legal aid, individuals often represent themselves before a tribunal. Individuals bringing their own case may face the threat of a wasted costs order of up to £10,000 if it is found that their conduct was 'unreasonable', the case was 'misconceived' or they acted 'vexatiously'.

As mentioned above, individual case litigation can be a catalyst for change in discriminatory practices and policies. The ability to achieve this wider change is constrained where the employer offers an out-of-court settlement with a confidentiality clause. Such a clause, while providing necessary compensation to the worker, can operate to prevent changes in the discriminatory practices. The Legal Service Commission (LSC) requires a worker to accept a reasonable settlement, whether or not there is a confidentiality clause. In doing so, the LSC resolves the tension between the public goods of tackling discrimination and ensuring value for money in the use of legal aid in favour of the latter.

Remedies

A person who succeeds in a claim for discrimination is entitled to compensation for pecuniary and non-pecuniary losses that he or she may have suffered. The removal of the £11,000 limit on the level of compensation that can be awarded, following the European Court of Justice decision on the *Marshall (No.2)* case, has allowed claims by those in higher pay and middle and high management positions,[37] and the trend in award levels over the past decade has been upwards. In calculating the compensation, tribunals include an award for injury to feelings. In addition to these awards, tribunals in England, Wales and Northern Ireland can award aggravated damages to compensate the victim of the wrong for mental distress (injury to feelings) in circumstances in which the injury has been caused or increased by the manner in which the defendant committed the wrong, or by the defendant's conduct subsequent to the wrong. This focuses on the effect on the victim rather than on punishment and deterrence on the employer. At present it is not possible for tribunals to award exemplary damages, which aim to punish and deter the wrongdoer. A recommendation by the Law Commission to allow the award of such damages has been rejected by the government.[38]

In addition to awarding compensation, a tribunal can make

recommendations on actions to be taken to obviate or reduce the adverse effects of the discrimination on the applicant. In Northern Ireland, under Article 39(1)(d) of the FETO, a tribunal is able to make a recommendation that the 'respondent take within a specified period action appearing to the tribunal to be practicable for the purposes of obviating or reducing the adverse effect on a person other than the complainant of any unlawful discrimination to which the complaint relates'. In all other cases the ability to address discriminatory practices and policies beyond those affecting the individual applicant is restricted, as the tribunal cannot make general recommendations.

The recommendation must relate to improving the position of the applicant. Within this legislative framework the task of addressing wider discriminatory practices falls on the different commissions.

The powers of the commissions

In Northern Ireland there is a single equality body responsible for the enforcement of anti-discrimination legislation. In Britain there are plans for the creation of a single Commission for Equality and Human Rights to be in place by 2007/8 (CEHR, see pages 121–3 below). In the meantime strategic enforcement, investigations, research, advice and assistance remain the responsibility of the three existing commissions: the CRE, the EOC and the DRC. The remit of each of these commissions remains limited; neither sexual orientation nor religion or belief are within the remit of any of them. In designing the CEHR lessons must be learnt from the strengths and weaknesses of the current legislation and the powers and functions of the existing bodies.

One of the key powers given to the EOC and CRE was the power to conduct formal investigations.[39] Such investigations were originally envisaged as the key tool for tackling discriminatory practices. The legislation allows the commissions to carry out 'general' as well as 'named' investigations. A general investigation can be into a particular issue (pregnancy discrimination), or into a particular sector (financial services). A named investigation, by contrast, is carried out in relation to a particular individual, company, organisation or institution. Formal investigations provide an important tool with which to develop understanding of the nature and extent of discrimination. For the CEHR it will be important to allow such investigations beyond the grounds and areas in which discrimination is currently prohibited, as they will provide a mechanism by which to establish whether patterns of discrimination exist in areas not covered by the current legislation. The Equality Act 2006 gives the CEHR a broad remit in this respect (see below).

Judicial interpretation has severely limited the CRE's and the EOC's abilities to carry out named investigations. The CRE believed named-person investigations could be undertaken into the actions of a particular person or body where there was an actual allegation of discrimination and where there was no such allegation. However, the House of Lords in *Prestige*[40] held that a named-person investigation could not be purely exploratory. There could be no named investigation where there was no suspicion of a breach of anti-discrimination laws. The decision in *Hillingdon*[41] placed further constraints on named investigations: the Court of Appeal required the CRE to have sufficient evidence 'to raise in the minds of reasonable men . . . a suspicion that there may have been acts by the person named of . . . discrimination of the kind which it is proposed to investigate'. This required not only reasonable suspicion of discrimination but that the reasonable suspicion must be of the type of discrimination which is being investigated. The net effect of *Hillingdon* and *Prestige* was to make named formal investigations into sex and race discrimination almost impossible. By the time the DRC was created the problems with named formal investigations had become clear and the powers given to the commission appear to allow for non-accusatory named formal investigations. Only the FETO clearly allows named investigations to be undertaken without requiring a suspicion of wrongdoing.[42]

Where a formal investigation reveals that a person has committed or is committing unlawful discrimination, a commission is able to issue a non-discrimination notice (NDN). This notice allows the commission to demand that the discrimination be stopped and allows it to monitor steps that are taken to prevent further discrimination. However the commission cannot use the NDN to demand specific changes; it can only recommend changes. The CRE has since asked for the power to state in a NDN what changes in the respondent's practice are the minimum necessary.

In creating the DRC, lessons were learnt from the weaknesses of the NDN powers of the CRE and the EOC. The DRC is able to issue a NDN that not only includes a 'recommendation to the person concerned as to action which the Commission considers he could reasonably be expected to take' but also requires the recipient to propose an adequate action plan for dealing with discrimination. If the DRC is not satisfied with the action plan, it can request revision of the plan and can make recommendations as to what action the commission considers might be included in an adequate plan. Ultimately the DRC can challenge an unsatisfactory action plan in court and seek a court order detailing an adequate action plan. The DRC also has powers to enter into 'voluntary undertakings' in lieu of enforcement actions.

The proposed Commission for Equality and Human Rights

The government announced its intention to establish the Commission for Equality and Human Rights in October 2003, following recommendations from bodies including the JCHR. In May 2004 the government produced a White Paper entitled *Fairness for All*, upon which it received responses from various interested groups, and followed up with its conclusions in November 2004. The Equality Act, which provides the statutory basis for the CEHR, received Royal Assent in 2006. But will the commission enjoy the coherent legislative framework, powers and independence from government it needs to be effective?

One of the three key purposes of the CEHR is equality (alongside human rights and good relations between different groups). Amongst its fundamental duties as contained in the Act are that it should set out to ensure that 'people's ability to achieve their potential is not limited by prejudice or discrimination' and that 'each individual has an equal opportunity to participate in society'. The CEHR will be required to monitor the law, providing advice and recommendations to the government, and identify means of achieving progress towards social change. There will be between ten and fifteen commissioners as well as a chief executive, who will be an ex officio commissioner.

The commission will produce strategic plans at least every three years.

The CEHR will subsume the existing commissions and the powers it will possess will broadly reflect their present ones – though powers presently only in one equality strand will now exist for all. The CEHR will have a general authority to conduct research and publish its findings, as well as providing advice on the law. Investigating commissioners, charged with carrying out inquiries and enforcement, may be appointed. While some existing commissions are restricted to investigating only suspected violations of the law, the CEHR will work differently. It will conduct general inquiries, in the course of which, if a suspicion develops that the law has been broken, a separate investigation may be established. The CEHR may issue an 'unlawful act notice', describing the violation and requiring steps to stop it and prevent it from recurring – this appears to be a greater power than that of recommendation possessed by some of the existing commissions. The person believed to be in breach of legislation may be obliged to produce an action plan, or enter an agreement, without admitting liability. The proposed single commission, like the presently existing commissions, will be able to support legal action by individuals based on equality law, though it will not be able to support free-standing human rights cases, even those involving the non-discrimination provisions of Article 14 of the ECHR (see above).

One of the first tasks for the CEHR will be to make proposals on the introduction of a single Equality Act, as promised in Labour's 2005 manifesto. Yet it is arguable that it will be difficult for the CEHR to function as an effective body without the prior existence of a single Act, not least because of the complexity of current equality legislation, as well as the uneven coverage it provides. It may be, therefore, that the government has made a mistaken approach to the problem of inconsistent provision for equality. Lord Lester's Equality Bill of 2003 proposed both simultaneous provision for a single equality commission and a single Equality Act.

The JCHR expressed other doubts about the CEHR and its powers as set out in the Equality Act, although it generally welcomed the legislation as 'the most important legislative measure for the advancement of human rights in this country since the Human Rights Act'.[43] The JCHR recorded concern that the legislation creates a hierarchy of rights for the CEHR, in which civil and political rights under the European Convention are rated above other rights, including social and economic ones. It regretted that, while the CEHR would be able to institute or intervene in legal proceedings in its own name, it could not seek judicial review where it believed a public authority had acted in a way that could breach human rights under the ECHR. The commission is given no express duty or power to participate in UK reporting processes in relation to international human rights agreements – which the JCHR argued it should have.

Finally, the JCHR criticised the government for defining the CEHR as a non-departmental public body, rather than a more independent entity along the lines of the Electoral Commission or the National Audit Office. (Non-departmental bodies can be abolished by the government without the need for legislation and have lesser powers.) The Act provides for the secretary of state to appoint and dismiss the commissioners, the chairman and the deputy chairman; to approve the appointment of the chief executive and the terms and conditions of other commission staff; and to provide overall funding, including determining remuneration and allowances for commissioners. The annual report of the CEHR will not be made directly to Parliament, but to the secretary of state, who will lay the report before Parliament. Taken as a whole, the JCHR argued, these measures possibly betrayed a desire on the part of the government 'to retain an unhealthy degree of control over the Commission's activities'.[44]

Positive duties

Formal investigations and NDNs do not provide adequate mechanisms for tackling deep-rooted patterns of inequality and exclusion. Effectively tackling structural discrimination requires a move to legislation that creates positive duties to promote equality. There are limitations in what can be achieved by a legal framework that focuses only on providing redress for individual instances of discrimination. The academic lawyer Colm O'Cinneide has marshalled a coherent criticism of this approach which is widely shared. Such laws, he says, are 'fire-fighting': they 'focus on remedying individual acts of discrimination after the event, not on the elimination of structures and patterns of behaviour that perpetuate discriminatory practices . . . the remedies are limited to redressing retrospectively the immediate wrong, rather than removing discriminatory practices across an organisation'. Such a framework can create hostility towards an equality agenda. The threat of litigation creates a culture of 'passive compliance' aimed at avoiding liability rather than a proactive culture that supports equality. Furthermore, such legislation is

> capable only of targeting discriminatory acts that generate detectable consequences that negatively impact on specific individuals. This means that many forms of institutional discrimination will slip under the radar. This has the additional consequence that practices that amount to institutional discrimination are often made to appear acceptable, as they are outside the legally established definition of discrimination. Deeply rooted discriminatory practices benefit from the cloak of acceptability.[45]

In the great tradition of UK equality laws, there is now a slow, uneven and piecemeal introduction of positive duties. The Race Relations (Amendment) Act 2000 created a duty on public authorities to pay 'due regard' to the need to 'promote equality of opportunity and good relations between persons of different racial groups'.[46] The aim of the duty is to ensure that public authorities take positive steps to remove barriers to race equality and that race equality and good race relations are central considerations in their policy making, service delivery and employment practices. The 'general duty' is supplemented by 'specific duties' on designated public authorities, including a requirement to prepare and publish race equality schemes explaining how they will discharge their obligations. The CRE has a central role in the enforcement of these new duties. It can issue a compliance notice against a public authority that is failing to meet its specific duties. Compliance with the duties is also monitored by the audit inspectors. In an independent review of the impact of the duties, two thirds of public authorities reported that they had produced positive benefits.[47]

The Disability Discrimination Act 2005 places a duty on public authorities to promote equality on the grounds of disability. The Equality Act 2006 creates a duty on public authorities to 'have due regard to promote equality of opportunity between men and women'.[48]

Positive duties to promote equality on a broad range of grounds are a feature of the various pieces of devolution legislation. The National Assembly for Wales is under a duty to ensure that its business and functions are carried out with 'due regard' to the principle of equality of opportunity.[49] The Greater London Authority Act requires the London Assembly, the Mayor and specified public authorities to make appropriate arrangements with regard to the principle that there should be equality of opportunity for all. This is supplemented by a duty to promote equality of opportunity for all persons irrespective of their race, sex, disability, age, sexual orientation or religion, to eliminate unlawful discrimination, and to promote good relations between persons of different racial groups, religious beliefs and sexual orientation.[50] Under the Scotland Act, devolved institutions can promote and encourage equal opportunities. This is defined as 'the prevention, elimination or regulation of discrimination between persons on grounds of sex, marital status, on racial grounds, or on the grounds of disability, age, sexual orientation, language or social origin, or of other personal attributes, including beliefs or opinions'.[51] This has been characterised as an 'enabling power' rather than a positive duty.[52] The power to promote equal opportunities has been included in legislation concerning significant areas of social policy including health, housing and education.[53] However, a key weakness in the positive duties and powers in relation to the devolved institutions of Wales, London and Scotland is the absence of effective enforcement mechanisms. The successful use of the duties and powers in promoting equality has merely been the consequence of a favourable political climate.

Under the pressures of sectarian conflict, there is a more extensive duty in Northern Ireland, backed by more effective enforcement mechanisms. Section 75 of the Northern Ireland Act requires a public authority in carrying out its functions in Northern Ireland to have

due regard to the need to promote equality of opportunity:
- between persons of different religious belief, political opinion, racial group, age, marital status or sexual orientation;
- between men and women generally;
- between persons with disability and persons without;
- between persons with dependants and persons without.

The duty requires relevant public authorities to prepare equality schemes which must be approved by the Northern Ireland Equality Commission. The commission refers any scheme that it cannot approve to the Secretary of State for Northern Ireland, who can impose an alternative scheme on the authority if necessary. It also monitors compliance with schemes it has approved and investigates complaints about non-compliance from individuals. The equality schemes are required to set out the impact assessment, monitoring, consultation, training and information access arrangements, including the preparation of equality impact assessments, that the authority intends to take to implement the duty. The Section 75 duty has 'begun to generate real shifts in consultation, monitoring and policy assessment procedures . . . [it] has brought equality issues to the forefront of public authority concerns in Northern Ireland'.[54] The success of such procedural compliances will ultimately be judged on whether they secure changes in the substantive outcomes.

In Northern Ireland aspects of the positive duty extend beyond public authorities into the private sector. A key focus there has been the need to tackle discrimination and inequality in employment. To address this the FETO contains a duty on employers to secure 'fair participation' in employment for members of the Roman Catholic and the Protestant communities. While the FETO does not define fair participation, it is clear that it involves redressing imbalances and under-representation in employment between the two communities in Northern Ireland. Employers must monitor their workforce on the basis of religious affiliation and undertake a periodic review (once every three years) of their employment practices to determine whether members of each community are enjoying or are likely to enjoy fair participation in the employment of the firm. If necessary, employers must take affirmative action measures to secure fair participation.

7

Impoverished citizenship

In 2004 the Department for Work and Pensions proclaimed in its sixth annual report that 'winning the battle against poverty is a central aim of this Government'.[1] But the battle against poverty is one fought with limited armour. While the profile of poverty and social exclusion has been elevated under successive New Labour governments, the continuing absence of economic and social rights in law demonstrates that social justice is a stated ideal rather than a legal ambition. The expectation of an 'adequate standard of living' is a morally undisputed one, enshrined in the International Covenant on Economic, Social and Cultural Rights and numerous international and European human rights treaties, yet millions of people in the UK continue to live in poverty, with insufficient resources to enable them to participate as equal citizens.

People in poverty are vulnerable to falling below a level of adequacy, a position which impacts upon their individual well-being and quality of life as well as their ability to exercise full citizenship. The United Nations High Commission for Human Rights clearly identifies being in poverty in any society as a violation of human rights, defining poverty as 'a human condition characterised by the sustained or chronic deprivation of the resources, capabilities, choices, security and power necessary for the enjoyment of an adequate standard of living and other civil, cultural, economic, political and social rights'.[2]

The Council of Europe's Malta declaration of 2002 also states that poverty and social exclusion are factors that undermine the enjoyment of human rights and demands that progress must be made towards effective access to social rights for all, in particular for the most deprived and vulnerable. The declaration made was: 'Poverty and exclusion will be eliminated only when fundamental social rights will be legally binding.'[3] Poverty and social exclusion therefore are increasingly being seen as a denial of human rights, not only in a development context but also as a basis for challenging poverty in more affluent nations. For example, as argued in a recent draft for the Northern Ireland Bill of Rights, 'since poverty and social exclusion represent a fundamental denial of human dignity, the protection of social and economic rights is an integral part of the delivery of effective human rights'.[4]

A rights-based approach to poverty recognises the moral obligation of the 'non-poor' towards those in poverty as well as positioning people in poverty as legitimate claimants of entitlements.[5] Without the legal enforcement of such rights, however, people in poverty have few avenues by which to demand a better life for themselves and their families.

The status of economic and social rights in the UK

Although seemingly necessary, in order to protect the most vulnerable citizens, social and economic human rights are not given priority in the UK. Indeed, Jeff Kenner, the academic lawyer, notes that, when contrasted with civil and political rights,

> many economic and social rights, such as rights to housing or social assistance, are often not regarded as 'rights' at all, or at least not *fundamental rights*, but rather as mere policies or programmes capable of progressive realisation and non-justiciable in the sense that they are deemed incapable of being invoked in a court of law or applied by judges.[6]

With the exception of some economic rights, largely stemming from EU directives, few social and economic rights are enforceable in UK domestic law. Those that do exist largely relate to paid work and working conditions: for instance, the right to equal pay, a limit on working times and more recently, extended maternity and paternity rights and flexible working practices.[7] In effect, then, the economic and social rights that do exist offer greater protection to the 'working citizen' rather than those outside paid employment, usually the poorest citizens. One enforceable social right and obvious exception to this is entitlement to social security benefits. But entitlement to benefits is subject to strict guidelines and benefits have increasingly become means tested. Social and economic rights have been upheld by British courts in some areas of housing, health and education but decisions in favour of such rights are made on an individual basis rather than stemming from a legally protected and enforceable foundation. Anti-discriminatory legislation also affords protection to some groups vulnerable to poverty, such as disabled people, women and people from ethnic minorities, but no socio-economic rights exist to offer protection against the discrimination emanating from poverty itself.

The UK government has some legal obligations in relation to human rights, including social and economic rights, being party to the various international and European human rights covenants and declarations set out in Chapter 2, and along with other signatory states, the UK is obliged to achieve progressive realisation of such rights. The right to an adequate standard of living for health and well-being, to food, clothing, housing, medical care, social services and social protection is enshrined in these human rights treaties. The UK has also signed up to a number of International Labour Organization conventions covering rights at work.

However, while the principle of economic and social rights can be found in these international treaties, their protection is restricted in national law because such social rights are not inscribed in the UK at constitutional level. In reality, their absence in domestic law means that little protection exists against the violation of economic and social rights for UK citizens. One reason given for the non-implementation of economic and social rights is that they are not justiciable. In effect, though, many civil and political rights, such as freedom of expression, are just as open to interpretation as is the social right of 'adequacy in living standards'.[8]

Nevertheless, despite the lacunae of social and economic rights in UK law, some developments can be identified which may allow for the realisation of rights or, at the very least, widen the space for a social rights discourse. One such development has been the EU Charter of Fundamental Rights (which includes some European Social Charter rights as well as civil and political rights; see Chapter 3). However, although formally and jointly adopted in 2000 by the European Council, the European Parliament and the European Commission and incorporated into the draft constitutional treaty, it is not legally binding and places no obligations upon member states. Indeed, the UK government is at pains to make clear that while it encourages recognition of the charter and the European Convention on Human Rights (ECHR), its recognition is subject to 'special rules of interpretation and application. The package will ensure that citizens' basic rights and liberties are fully in legal view at EU level, without disturbing the primary responsibilities of the Member States.'[9] Clearly, this is not a warm embrace of the potential to realise social and economic rights in domestic law. The charter, however, has been seen as an important move, by virtue of the inclusion of social and economic rights alongside civil and political rights within the same document.[10]

Another development, which may go some way towards the achievement of socio-economic rights, is the endorsement of the Human Rights Act 1998 (HRA). The HRA came into force in the UK in 2000, providing a framework for the operation of the ECHR within UK law. The Act does not make the ECHR part of domestic law as such but it does enable individuals to enforce convention rights and freedoms against public authorities through the domestic courts.[11] While the HRA primarily attends to civil and political rights, some provisions in the Act can be invoked to defend economic and social rights relating to housing, education and health-care rationing (see Chapter 4).[12] In addition, the HRA may provide the court with the impetus towards a more extensive interpretation of rights.

A further opportunity to promote the necessity of economic and social rights appears in the proposed Bill of Rights for Northern Ireland (2001), updated in 2004. The Bill incorporates a number of social and economic rights covering paid work, housing, education and living standards.[13] The Northern Ireland Human Rights

Commission argues that government, as well as the judiciary, has a positive role to play as an advocate of economic and social rights. There was, however, some criticism over the prominence of economic and social rights in the proposed Bill, specifically because, if introduced, Northern Ireland would be out of line with the rest of the UK in protecting socio-economic rights.[14] While there may be opposition from some quarters, it is certainly the case that there is very strong public support in Northern Ireland for the inclusion of social and economic rights in a Bill of Rights for the province.

The inclusion of economic and social rights in domestic law would be an endorsement of the importance of such rights and could bring about cultural change, promoting a more 'rights-aware' populace. This may have particular significance for people experiencing poverty and social exclusion, in terms not only of improved material circumstances but also of how they are viewed in society – as people whose rights are violated rather than as 'failures' or 'victims'. Also, as noted by the Committee on Economic, Social and Cultural Rights in 2001, the application of a rights framework reinforces some of the features of current anti-poverty strategies: 'Anti-poverty policies are more likely to be effective, sustainable, inclusive, equitable and meaningful to those living in poverty if they are based upon international human rights.'[15]

At present people experiencing poverty or social exclusion have little means of redress;[16] they literally have no 'right' to stand up and demand a better quality of life. The incorporation of social and economic rights in law would grant a higher protection against the daily violations that people in poverty are subjected to and go some way to ensuring adequacy in living and working standards for all citizens.

The next section outlines the experience of poverty in the UK and illustrates the extent to which people in poverty still lack the necessities for an adequate standard of living, a condition that impacts on their ability to participate as equal citizens.

Excluded from an adequate standard of living

Although the UK has one of the richest economies in the world, its affluence has not prevented people in poverty going without essentials such as food, adequate shelter, heating and equal access to mainstream services and activities. The Poverty and Social Exclusion Survey (2000), which asked a representative sample of the population what household items and activities they considered that everyone should be 'able to afford and which they should not have to do without', found:

- 27.7 per cent of individuals lacked at least two socially perceived necessities;
- Around 9.5 million people could not afford to keep their homes adequately heated, free from damp or in a decent state of decoration;
- Almost 7.5 million people were unable to engage in social activities considered necessary, such as visiting friends and family or attending weddings and funerals, because of lack of money.[17]

A similar and more recent poverty and social exclusion survey, conducted in Northern Ireland between 2002 and 2003, found that one third of households lacked three or more items considered 'necessary'.[18] As well as going without, poorer households spend proportionately more of their income on basic essentials, such as food, housing and power needs.[19]

The missing essentials of life

Money

At the core of poverty is the lack of an adequate income – whether from low-paid work or insufficient benefits. The Family Budget Unit's assessment of a low cost but acceptable (LCA) budget has shown that families in paid work can meet the requirements of a basic budget, but those without work (on jobseeker's allowance or income support) fall short of a liveable budget by nearly £10 a week for a couple and around £7 a week for a lone-parent family.[20] It remains the case that many benefit payments are well below the government's own headline indicator for poverty (households below 60 per cent of national median income). Benefit levels are also substantially lower than general earnings. In 2005, the basic income support payment (for a person over 25) was £56.20 a week, around an eighth of median weekly earnings.[21]

In recent years, improvements in benefit levels for families with dependent children and pensioners have increased their income levels. By April 2003, out-of-work benefits for families with two or more dependent children and for pensioner couples had risen by around 15 per cent, relative to earnings, when compared with 1998.[22] Changes in tax credits have also brought about a rise in incomes, but despite their assumed success in combating poverty, only a fifth of tax credit recipients in 2003/4 were no longer on a low income because of tax credits received.[23] Adults of working age without children, who comprise half of all adults dependent on benefits, have seen falling benefit levels and poverty rates for this group are now higher than in 1997.[24] There is also concern that the very poorest have been left behind.[25] While some low-income households have benefited from recent changes in the tax and benefit systems, around a fifth of the population of Great Britain were living on poverty-level incomes in 2004/5.[26]

Non-take-up of benefits leaves many people on even lower incomes; and for some types of household, non-take-up has increased since 1997. For example, the number of pensioner households entitled to but not claiming council tax benefit rose from 30 per cent in 1997/8 to 40 per cent in 2003/4.[27] In the same year, two thirds of pensioners who were entitled to minimum income guarantee (MIG) – additional benefit specifically aimed at the poorest pensioners – but did not receive it lived in low income households, compared to around two fifths of pensioners in receipt of the MIG. The new pension credit, which replaced the MIG scheme in 2003, is also plagued by low take-up; around one and a half million households entitled to pension credit fail to claim.

Table 7.1 shows percentage take-up of various benefits and the amount, totalling between £5,400 million and £9,310 million, left unclaimed in 2003/4.

Table 7.1: Take-up of benefits, 2002/3

Benefit	Take-up by caseload*	
Total unclaimed		
(£ million)		
Income support	85%–95%	270–970
Minimum income guarantee	63%–74%	800–1,520
Housing benefit	84%–90%	760–1,400
Council tax benefit	65%–71%	880–1,200
Jobseeker's allowance (income based)	55%–70%	590–1,170

*Caseload take-up compares the number of benefit recipients (annual average) with the number who would be receiving it if everyone took up their entitlement.

Source: *Income Related Benefits: Estimates of Take-Up in 2002/2003* (Department for Work and Pensions, 2005)

Food

Benefit and tax credit levels are still set without reference to the cost of living, meaning that for most people who depend on them a healthy diet is unaffordable.[28] Fluctuations in household income, such as the loss of free school meals in the school holidays, can directly impact upon a family's food budget and result in 'unacceptable levels of poverty and social exclusion'.[29] Resourceful ways of saving money on food, such as eating at the homes of friends and family, is one strategy that may be employed but ultimately people in poverty may simply go without.[30] At the very least, poverty often means economising by cutting back on provisions, eating less or buying budget-priced, poorer-quality food. Such cut-backs can lead to a reliance on 'cheap calories', often from processed foodstuffs with high fat and sugar content and consequent damaging effects on health.[31] People on a low income have an increased risk of diet-related diseases, such as cancer and coronary heart disease, partly due to inadequate access to nutritious foods, a phenomenon known as food poverty.[32] Insufficient income to purchase food has led to the emergence of food redistribution schemes throughout the industrialised world, supplying surplus or donated food to people in food poverty. It is estimated that at least eight million free meals are re-distributed every year from surplus food stocks to poor households in the UK.[33]

Fuel

Another budgeting strategy made by poorer households is to cut back on money spent on heating. In England a household is considered 'fuel poor' if its members (often just a single person) must spend more than 10 per cent of the household income on fuel just to maintain a satisfactory heating regime.[34] An estimated 2.25 million households are estimated to be fuel poor.[35] Fuel poverty damages people's quality of life and health, with an increased risk of illness and of death in winter. Many older people cannot afford to insulate or heat their home sufficiently, contributing to the 31,600 excess deaths in England and Wales during the winter of 2004-5,[36] a greater number than many European countries with colder winter temperatures.[37]

The government has set a target to eradicate fuel poverty for vulnerable households in stages and to eliminate it altogether by 2018.[38] Partial success has been achieved through the government's Warm Front scheme, which provides grants for insulation and heating to people in receipt of benefits who live in privately rented and owner-occupied homes. Winter fuel payments for those over sixty, a direct annual payment to help supplement low-income pensioner households, has also reduced fuel poverty but significant increases in fuel costs are halting progress. It is anticipated that the government will need to increase spending substantially on its fuel poverty programmes by more than half in England if the 2010 target of eradicating fuel poverty amongst vulnerable households is to be met.

Education

While education is a basic right, enshrined in numerous international treaties, children from poorer backgrounds are much less likely to have a successful education, disadvantaging them in the workplace and increasing their susceptibility to poverty in adult life. Nearly 90 per cent of 'failing schools' are located in deprived areas and have a large proportion of pupils eligible for free school meals,[39] entitlement to which can be used as a proxy for poverty. There is a considerable gap between the performance of children in receipt of free school meals and others. For example, eleven-year-old pupils in receipt of free school meals are twice as likely not to achieve basic standards in literacy and numeracy as other eleven-year-old pupils.[40] Children living in poverty are also much less likely than wealthier children to obtain GCSEs or to continue in education, training or employment.[41] Poorer parents may struggle with costs associated with school, such as uniforms and school trips;[42] the impact for children in poverty may be an experience of exclusion and stigma during their formative years at school, as they miss out on key activities because of lack of money.

Health

Massive inequalities in access to health services and outcomes exist between the social classes in the UK. The chances of ill health and mortality are increased at all stages of the life cycle for people in poverty. Infant mortality is twice as high for babies born to parents in the unskilled manual class than in the professional class; and children in the bottom social class are five times more likely to die from accidental causes and fifteen times more likely to be killed in a house fire than children in the highest social class.[43] Incidence of coronary heart disease and cancer also disproportionately affects lower socio-economic groups. Life expectancy in some poorer areas of the UK is more than ten years lower than in areas of greater prosperity.[44] Access to and delivery of health services is closely linked to social disadvantage and people on low incomes have difficulty accessing primary and specialist healthcare services.[45]

Housing

Poorer families are more likely to be homeless or live in low-quality accommodation. While people who live in privately rented or social housing are more likely also to be poor, home ownership is no defence against poverty: homeowners account for half of all people in poverty.[46] Many of these poorer householders cannot claim benefits for housing costs and struggle to keep their home in adequate repair. Poor housing conditions, overcrowding and homelessness have implications for physical and mental health and have especially damaging effects on the well-being of children.[47] While some success has been claimed in tackling street homelessness, with a disputed claim of a 70 per cent reduction in rough sleeping since 1997, the number of homeless families placed in temporary accommodation, 101,020 households in September 2005, is high and has more than doubled in the same period.[48] Homelessness, though, is one area in which limited social rights have been recognised. Legislation introduced in April 2004 allows people in bed and breakfast accommodation the right to challenge councils if they are placed in such conditions for longer than six weeks. Clearly this is not a radical move but it is an alteration in the balance of power and one that acknowledges some basic right to decent housing.

Falling through the net
It was long recognised that the levels of income for families or individuals on benefit, especially those who were long-term beneficiaries, were inadequate to meet various contingencies, for example the need to purchase or replace kitchen equipment, bedding and so on. The social security scheme used to administer special grants to meet various types of contingency or even chronic short-falls, such as in children's clothing. However, these grants were replaced in 1988 by the much more limited discretionary Social Fund, which is designed to help the poorest and most vulnerable by providing financial assistance in times of need.[49] It offers community care grants (CCGs) for people leaving institutional care and repayable budgeting and crisis loans (in place of grants) for others. While potentially a lifeline for the poorest, the Social Fund has significant flaws:

- Many people applying for budgeting loans are refused because of outstanding debts – 65 per cent of pensioners, 72 per cent of lone parents and 80 per cent of disabled people refused a loan were turned down on these grounds;
- Rationing of resources means that CCGs just do not go round: just 45.8 per cent of applicants for CCGs were successful in 2004/5;[50]
- Unsuccessful applicants for CCGs often experience real hardship

as a result, managing for several months without essentials, such as beds or cookers.[51]

Four out of ten families in receipt of income support are repaying a loan to the Social Fund,[52] with an average deduction of £11.24 a week in 2005,[53] a substantial amount from a limited income. Consequently, repaying a social fund loan may result in increased hardship for many low-income families.

Exclusions from equal participation

Exclusion from services

As the National Consumer Council recognised in 2004, 'people who are poor often pay more or get less across a range of essential services'. The most extreme form of such exclusion which poor people experience is the withdrawal of basic essential services because of the inability to pay. Although water disconnections of domestic properties have been prohibited since 1999, power and communication supplies can still be cut off for monies owed. In 2003, 17,334 disconnections from gas and electricity supplies were made in Great Britain.[54] This dramatically decreased to 3,280 in 2004 after British Gas and other major suppliers temporarily halted disconnections for non-payment in response to the cold-related deaths of a pensioner couple after their gas supply had been disconnected. In addition:

- One third of gas and electricity disconnections are of people living in areas with the highest levels of multiple deprivation in Great Britain;[55]
- Energywatch figures for 2003 show a twenty-fold rise in disconnections for debt in Scotland since 2001;[56]
- In the year from July 2002 to July 2003, 1.1 million consumers were disconnected by BT for non-payment of bills.[57]

Because of irregular payments and debt, low-income households may be subject to compulsory installation of pre-payment meters by energy suppliers, even though these are the most expensive form of payment. Energywatch figures show that 50 per cent of all lone-parent families use pre-payment meters and 30 per cent of all pre-payment consumers have incomes of less than £6,500.[58] One disturbing aspect of pre-payment meter usage is that customers will self-disconnect, rather than incur debt – 27 per cent of low-income consumers themselves cut off their gas supplies, and 24 per cent their electricity, during 2003. Children lived in a third of these households.[59]

Financial exclusion

Market-based exclusion has been identified as a significant problem for poor and disadvantaged consumers.[60] At a time when the banks and other mainstream financial institutions swamp well-off households with glossy invitations to take up offers of credit, poor and disadvantaged people may be excluded from their financial services because their incomes are too low, or they lack 'creditworthiness', or because the institutions do not serve their needs.[61] Basic bank accounts are one government scheme to combat financial exclusion but such accounts do not offer the range of credit services taken for granted by better-off consumers. The inadequacy of a poverty-level income, though, often means that credit may be needed to meet daily requirements. 'Doorstep' lenders and mail-order catalogues fill this gap but are considerably more expensive than standard financial institutions and thus it is not surprising that debt is a significant problem for many people in poverty.[62] More than half of households with problem debt have incomes of less than £7,500 a year; families with children, especially lone-parent families, are most at risk of arrears with bills, housing costs and debt repayments.[63] Savings, as a buffer against unexpected events or for future plans, are not a possibility for many people in poverty. In 2003/4 more than half of individuals in low-income households had no savings.[64]

Geographical exclusion

The poorest are more likely to suffer from crime and the fear of crime; unemployed people are three times more likely than average to be the victims of violent crime; and deprived areas suffer the worst effects of environmental degradation.[65] In some of the most deprived areas in Great Britain:
- unemployment is three times the national average;
- income support claims are twice as high;

- health and educational attainment are well below average;
- housing is often sub-standard with poor local environments and high rates of crime and anti-social behaviour.[66]

The government's Neighbourhood Renewal Fund has targeted the eighty-eight most deprived local authority districts in England in order to tackle multiple deprivation and improve local core services, with the stated intention that no-one should be seriously disadvantaged by where they live in between ten and twenty years' time.[67] However, as noted in a document from the Centre for Analysis of Social Exclusion, 'the problems of poor neighbourhoods demand solutions that lie beyond the neighbourhood, in the tackling of inequalities between people as well as places'.[68] Thus, while neighbourhood renewal strategies may bring about beneficial changes, they may also have limited effect. An additional problem with area-based policies is that many people experiencing hardship do not live in areas classified as 'deprived': almost half of children in poverty do not live in the most disadvantaged areas.

Political exclusion

The ability to utilise political and civil rights is often compromised by poverty. A correlation exists between area deprivation and reduced civic engagement, and households with high levels of material and social deprivation have lower levels of political activity.[69] Research in Nottingham found that the wards with the highest levels of multiple deprivation had the lowest electoral turnout.[70] The negative consequences of poverty for equal citizenship and political participation are clear, especially when you consider that the policies and election campaigns of the political parties are driven by their competition for the votes of well-off 'swing voters' in a handful of marginal seats.

The government focus on work

Work-focused social security: aiding participation?

For New Labour, rights to social security go hand in hand with responsibilities, and the prime responsibility is to find paid work.

While some benefits in the UK, such as child benefit, are universal for British citizens, means testing has been gradually extended across the social security system. Entitlement to benefits is based on age, residency, illness and incapacity; and, in the case of jobseeker's allowance, on the recipient's obligation to be actively seeking paid work. Sanctions for failing to look for work can include the withdrawal of payments. The emphasis in social security overall is on getting people into paid work, a philosophy embodied in the introduction of in-work benefits, such as the working tax credit.[71] Compulsory work-focused interviews for some lone parents and those in receipt of incapacity benefit and their partners are a condition of receiving benefit. This 'work first' approach fails to address the problems of those whose labour market participation is limited because of caring responsibilities, or who are incapacitated for the purposes of most jobs that are available, or who do not have the appropriate skills. While one good that emerges from this focus on work is that many more people are now in employment, there is a lesser known advantage for the government. Expenditure on unemployment benefits in the United Kingdom is now one of the lowest in Europe, coming in at less than 3 per cent compared to the EU-15 average of 6.2 per cent. The UK social protection expenditure figure of 27.2 per cent of GDP is also slightly below the EU-15 average and now stands at a lower proportion of GDP than in the early 1990s.[72]

Paid work

The battle against 'worklessness' by successive New Labour governments has been closely bound to the ambition of tackling poverty and social exclusion. In part, this is in line with the European Employment Strategy, which incorporates the objectives of social inclusion and cohesion alongside full employment.[73] One government strategy to encourage entry into paid work has been the New Deal programmes.[74] Considerable success has been claimed for these schemes: for example, 42 per cent of all those who took part in the New Deal for lone parents (NDLP) in 2005 entered paid employment.[75] However, while paid work may help some people out of poverty, return-to-work jobs are often unstable and low paid, forcing many people to return to benefits within a short space of time. Thus one third of those entering paid work after leaving the NDLP lost their job within three months.[76] Although any paid work may appear better than none, research has found that switching between low-paid work and benefits may be more financially precarious, leading to an increased risk of poverty, than remaining on benefits alone.[77]

Another part of the drive against worklessness has been to 'make work pay' and the national minimum wage (NMW) has gone some way towards this ambition. In October 2006, increased minimum wage will be £5.35 an hour for adults, £4.25 for 18–22-year olds and £3.30 for 16–17-year-olds. The NMW has certainly increased the earnings of the poorest 10 per cent of workers, especially women and part-time workers,[78] and goes some way to ensuring a minimum in-work income. But the relatively low value of the minimum wage is no guarantee against poverty: in 2004/5, 42 per cent of all households in poverty had at least one member in paid work.[79] A recent study found that only 8 per cent of low-paid workers were able to keep their households out of poverty by means of their earnings alone, indicating the high risk of poverty for the low paid.[80]

Poverty trends and patterns

The government's current measure of poverty is households with an income below 60 per cent of national equivalised median income, after housing costs have been allowed for.[81] By this standard, overall poverty rose dramatically during the 1980s, continued to rise at a slower pace in the early 1990s and has fallen since the mid-1990s. Child poverty has also been on a downward trend since 1996/7, although it remains twice as high as in 1979.[82] In 2004/54, the overall proportion of people living in poverty was 20 per cent, or 11.4 million people. Of these, 3.4 million children – 27 per cent of all children – were living below the poverty line (see Table 7.2).[83]

Persistent poverty – defined as those living at least three years out of the last four in poverty – is high in Britain compared to the rest of Europe. Between 1998 and 2001, 11 per cent of UK citizens lived in persistent poverty, more than double the rate in the Netherlands

(5 per cent) and above the EU-15 average of 9 per cent.[84] Some groups, such as children, women (especially lone parents), workless households and particular ethnic minority groups, are more likely to have a low income and be vulnerable to poverty and persistent poverty.

Table 7.2: Proportion of children and total UK population living in poverty between 1996–97 and 2003–04 (living in households with below 60 per cent median income after housing costs)

Year	% children	% total population	Actual figure, total population (millions)
1996/7	34	25	13.9
1997/8	33	24	13.5
1998/9	33	24	13.4
1999/2000	32	23	13.3
2000/1	31	23	12.9
2001/2	30	22	12.5
2002/3	28	22	12.4
2003/4	28	21	12.0

Source: *Households below Average Income 1994/95–2001/02* (Department for Work and Pensions, 2003); *Households below Average Income 1994/95–2003/04* (Department for Work and Pensions, 2005). Number differences are due to rounding.

1. Child poverty

The UK government recognises the UN Convention on the Rights of the Child and argues that changes are being implemented in accordance with its principles.[85] The UK, however, is clearly failing to meet the standard of adequate living set out in the convention for a significant proportion of the child population. In 2004/5:

- 3.4 million children were in poverty;
- nearly half of all lone-parent families were at risk of poverty;
- the child poverty rate in inner London was 52 per cent.[86]

In 1998, the UK child poverty rate was the worst of the fifteen

European member states. By 2001, Britain had improved slightly to eleventh position, but still leaving a shockingly high proportion of children in the UK (23 per cent) living in poverty for such an affluent country. By comparison, Denmark's child poverty rate was just 5 per cent.[87] The consequences of poverty for children are substantial and enduring: they include increased health problems, low educational achievement, low self-esteem and a higher risk of early pregnancy and of accidental death.[88]

Despite a favourable economic climate, coupled with welfare reforms, the government's pledge to reduce child poverty to a quarter of the level of 1998/9 by 2005 was missed. Achieving the longer-term objective, of halving child poverty by 2010 and eradicating it by 2020, is consequently in doubt. In any case the semantic gymnastics of New Labour means that the 'abolition' of child poverty no longer means *no* child poverty but merely that 'child poverty might be judged as being among the best in Europe on relative low incomes'.

Children 'looked after' in local authority care have an increased risk of facing social exclusion and severe disadvantage in later life. One quarter of the prison population have been in care, as have between a quarter and a third of rough sleepers. Children in care are two and a half times more likely to become teenage parents, both a cause and a consequence of poverty. They are less likely to flourish in education: 40 per cent of 'looked after' children in England obtained no GCSE qualifications in 2005 and just 11 per cent obtained five GCSE passes, compared to a national average of 56 per cent of all children.[89]

Women

Women in the UK are at higher risk of poverty and have a higher risk of persistent low income than men.[90] Around 40 per cent of women had individual incomes of less than £100 a week in 2001/2 compared to less than one in five men.[91] Women employees are three times more likely to be low paid than men[92] and also more likely to receive means-tested rather than contributory benefits, often because time out of the labour market for the care of children or the elderly means that they do not have sufficient national insurance contributions. Thus in 2005 around two thirds of income support claimants were women. The UK has the highest rate of teenage pregnancies in western Europe and high number of lone-parent families (overwhelmingly female headed). These groups are especially vulnerable to poverty. Women are also more likely to face poverty in old age since they often retire earlier and live longer than men, but without adequate pension or social protection to prevent poverty.

Pensioners

Currently 1.8 million pensioners are in poverty, 17 per cent of all pensioners.[93] In past decades, pensioners were at high risk of poverty but since the late 1990s poverty for this group has steadily declined. The government has committed itself to tackling pensioner poverty, introducing the means-tested MIG as a preliminary to the pension credit scheme in late 2003, thus ensuring an income base that no pensioner should fall below. This of course relies upon full take-up. While the principle of this benefit goes some way towards a minimum adequacy standard, income inequality between the richest and poorest pensioners remains significant and is increasing.

Disabled people

Around a fifth of people living in poor households (approximately twelve million people) report a limiting long-standing illness, disability or infirmity.[94] Lack of paid work and higher expenses because of sickness or disability can lead to a particular risk of low income and poverty. Almost a third of working-age disabled adults live in poverty – higher than a decade ago.[95] The gap between the employment rate for those disabled and the overall employment rate is 28 per cent[96] and the unemployment rate for disabled people is almost double that of non-disabled people. Many black and minority ethnic disabled people have difficulty in obtaining information about services, including information about rights. This lack of information can lead to some individuals experiencing isolation and exclusion.[97]

Ethnic minorities

Some ethnic groups are significantly more at risk of being poor: 52 per cent of Pakistani and Bangladeshi and 34 per cent of black or black British people were at risk of poverty in 2004/5, compared with 18 per cent of white people.[98] Some ethnic minority groups also suffer low employment rates and high unemployment, illustrated by the 16-point employment rate gap between white and ethnic minority workers in 2005. Asylum seekers are also at significant risk of poverty and social exclusion. Indeed, government policy has increased exclusion for this group and resulted in a reduction of rights in the areas of income, employment and housing.[99] Since January 2003, asylum seekers who do not apply for asylum 'as soon as is reasonably practicable' (in practice, usually immediately) fail to qualify for support.[100] Asylum seekers who do qualify for the National Asylum Support Service receive an income well below basic income support rates and are not permitted to undertake paid work. If a single person's claim to asylum fails, all support is ended, leaving them to face destitution and homelessness (but see Chapter 4).

Inequality

Although poverty levels began to fall after 1997/8, inequality dramatically increased and by 2000/1 the highest income inequality levels since 1961 were being recorded.[101] While the years since 2000/1 have shown a decline, the end result is that income inequality in 2003/4 is more or less unchanged from the situation in 1996/7 and remains at historically high levels.[102] Arguably, income inequality would be even greater without a series of Budgets that have benefited the poor and the Chancellor's 'passive redistribution strategies.'[103] But such measures have halted a rise in inequality in incomes rather than directly reducing it. In 2003/4, the poorest fifth of the population received 5.9 per cent of total income while the richest fifth got 43.6 per cent, more than seven times as much.[104] There is no explicit government intention or target in place to tackle income inequality, and indeed the Prime Minister and his ministers publicly disavow any such idea.

Wealth inequality is even greater than income inequality:

- Between 1990 and 2002 the percentage of wealth held by the richest 10 per cent of the population increased from 47 per cent to 56 per cent;

- By 2002 the wealthiest 1 per cent of the UK population owned 23 per cent of the UK's marketable wealth and the wealthiest half owned almost all the wealth, 94 per cent.[105]

The latest Europe-wide figures confirm that the UK was the fourth most unequal society across the EU–15 in 2004 and more unequal than six of the ten new member states.[106] Only the poorer southern nations in the EU–15 – Portugal, Greece and Italy – showed greater inequality.[107]

Conclusion

This outline of poverty in the UK today reveals a mixed picture. Clearly, in some ways, things *have* got better – child and pensioner poverty are both on a downward trend and the incomes and living standards of many low-income groups have risen. Despite this, poverty, social exclusion and inequality remain significant problems, with many people socially and economically disenfranchised from full citizenship because of their poverty. Meanwhile, without social and economic rights in place, there is little opportunity for people in poverty to seek remedies in domestic law and the political arena. While a notion of a guaranteed minimum income underlies the new tax credits and the minimum wage, a tangible minimum income level does not exist. As such, there is no financial low point or living standard that is legally unacceptable. A joint team from the New Policy Institute and the Fabian Society has argued the case for a 'minimum income standard' to describe an expected level of adequacy 'for maintaining good health and essential needs and meaningful participation in the community'.[108] But the government has rejected this proposal on the grounds that it is unfeasible to define 'adequacy' in practice.[109] But it is certainly feasible, in fact all too easy, to define 'inadequacy'. The government routinely states the moral, social and economic need to end poverty and social exclusion, but is unwilling to commit the resources necessary or to empower people living in poverty through an effective legal framework of social and economic rights to ensure protection against falling below an adequate minimum standard of income, education, housing and health care. Accordingly, the most vulnerable citizens are left without protection in law and so without the means to campaign for justice. This is not an oversight, it is a failure of political will. The price paid is the daily human tragedy in the form of millions of people living and growing up in poverty within one of the richest economies in the world.

8

New life for health?

The right of everyone to the enjoyment of the highest attainable standard of physical and mental health ('right to health') under the International Covenant on Economic, Social and Cultural Rights (ICESCR) has a very broad scope. It gives rise to a variety of freedoms and entitlements, including health care and determinants of health, such as adequate nutrition and a healthy environment.

The population of the UK enjoys a high standard of health compared to the population of many other countries. But compared to other OECD counties the UK does not perform so well overall. For example, it has poorer (though improving) cancer survival rates than other European countries: the European average is 40.5 per cent, compared to 37.1 per cent in England, 35.6 per cent in Scotland and 34.7 per cent in Wales. For women the corresponding averages are 53.6 per cent, 50.8 per cent, 49.5 per cent and 47.3 per cent.[1] And within the UK, significant inequalities persist – for example, certain ethnic and racial minorities and unskilled labourers have far poorer health outcomes than the rest of the population. The United Nations treaty bodies and the European Committee on Social Rights (ECSR) have expressed their concerns about these inequalities, as well as obstacles to the right to health, including health-care waiting lists, hospital bed shortages, domestic violence and the persistence of female genital mutilation, despite its illegality.

This chapter is primarily limited to a survey of the right to health in England. Since health policies and programmes tend to differ between England, Wales, Scotland and Northern Ireland, there is not scope to review and audit the situation in each country. However, reference is made throughout to health issues in Scotland, Wales and Northern Ireland.[2]

International norms and obligations

The right to health was first articulated in the Constitution of the World Health Organization in 1946. Two years later, the Universal Declaration on Human Rights recognised the right of everyone to a standard of living adequate for health, and the right to security in the event of sickness. Since then, the right to health has been enshrined in international and regional human rights treaties ratified by the UK: the ICESCR, the Convention on the Elimination of All Forms of Racial Discrimination, the Convention on the Rights of the Child, the Convention on the Elimination of All Forms of Discrimination against Women (CEDAW), and the European Social Charter. The European Union's Charter of Fundamental Human Rights recognises a right of access to preventative health care and the right to benefit from medical treatment. These, and other, human rights treaties recognise other rights closely related to the right to health, which have been used indirectly to protect the right to health. For example, the provisions on the right to privacy and on the prohibition on torture contained in the European Convention on Human Rights (ECHR) have given rise to jurisprudence indirectly protecting the right to health.

Analysis of international, regional and UK law has given rise to a range of interpretations of the right to health over the years.[3] This chapter bases its analysis on the right to health norms and corresponding obligations under the ICESCR set out in the General Comment on the right to health adopted by the UN Committee on Economic, Social and Cultural Rights in 2000. [4] The authoritative General Comment confirms that the right to health:

- is not a right to be healthy. It should be understood as the right to the enjoyment of a variety of facilities, goods, services and conditions necessary for the highest attainable standard of health;
- contains freedoms and entitlements. Freedoms include the right to control one's health, including the right to be free from non-consensual medical treatment. Entitlements include available, accessible, acceptable and good quality goods, facilities and services connected with the right to health, including health care;
- contains specific entitlements, such as the rights to maternal,

child and reproductive health and access to essential medicines;
- is an inclusive right, extending beyond health care to the under-lying determinants of health, such as access to safe water and adequate sanitation, occupational and environmental health, and access to health-related education and information;
- is closely related to the enjoyment of other rights, including to education, housing, food, work, life, non-discrimination and participation, access to information, the prohibition of torture, and freedoms of association and movement.

The government has obligations to respect, protect and fulfil this right under the UN treaties that the UK has ratified. The obligation to respect includes refraining from denying or limiting equal access of all people to health services and refraining from enforcing dis-criminatory practices as a state policy. The obligation to protect requires the government to take measures that prevent third parties from interfering with right-to-health guarantees. This means that the government must ensure that privatising health-care services does not threaten the availability, accessibility, acceptability and quality of these services. The obligation to fulfil requires the government to give sufficient recognition to the right to health in the national political and legal systems, and to adopt other measures to give effect to the enjoyment of health.

Ideally, this audit would also be able to draw upon a full set of universally accepted right-to-health indicators. The UN Committee on Economic, Social and Cultural Rights, the monitoring body for the ICESCR, has suggested that the most appropriate device to monitor progressive realisation is the combined application of national right-to-health indicators and benchmarks.[5] The committee gives a degree of discretion, and responsibility, to individual states to select appropriate indicators to help monitor different dimensions of the right to health.[6] However, the UK government has not gone so far as to do this. This chapter therefore follows a framework of indicators to audit UK performance in relation to right-to-health norms based on the approach of the UN Special Rapporteur on the right to health. He has suggested that there be three different types of health indicator: structural indicators (key structures, systems and mechanisms conducive to the realisation of the right to health), process indicators (which provide information on the processes by which a health policy is implemented) and outcome indicators.[7] For reasons of space the author has chosen a series of indicators for this chapter out of a full list, which is set out in Appendix B.

The Committee on Economic, Social and Cultural Rights and the UN Special Rapporteur on the right to health both propose that the indicators should be 'appropriate national targets' and should 'provide useful background indications regarding the right to health in a particular national context'.[8] Some indicators used in this chapter are right-to-health indicators suggested by the Special Rapporteur;[9] others include those commonly employed to monitor health internationally or in the context of developed countries. Where possible, indicators are broken down according to the grounds of discrimination which are explicitly prohibited under international human rights law, such as gender and race. Given the broad scope of the right to health and the narrow remit of this chapter, it does not give a comprehensive audit of the enjoyment of the right to health in the UK, and other chapters address critical right-to-health issues, such as health and safety in the workplace (Chapter 11) and healthy living conditions (Chapter 9). This chapter covers protection of the right to health in domestic law; national human rights institutions and other accountability mechanisms; the national health strategy and budget; health status on the basis of equality and non-discrimination; child health; sexual and reproductive health; mental health; and the right to health care.

Is the right to health protected in domestic law in the UK?

Key indicators

Has the United Kingdom constitutionalised the right to health?

Has the UK passed other legislation that expressly recognises the right to health?

Have any judicial decisions expressly considered the right to health?

The Committee on Economic, Social and Cultural Rights has encouraged incorporation into the domestic legal order of international instruments recognising the right to health, since this can 'significantly enhance the scope and effectiveness of remedial measures'.[10] However, as with other economic and social rights, there is no free-standing recognition of the right to health in UK domestic law. So far as the author is aware, there are also no judicial decisions that expressly consider the UK's international right-to-health obligations, in contrast with other countries. The national constitutions of, among others, Belgium, Finland, the Netherlands, Portugal and Spain contain provisions on the right to health.[11] Where constitutions or other domestic legislative arrangements recognise the right to health, a body of jurisprudence has often developed: in Colombia alone, there are as many as 400 rulings from domestic courts on the right to health. Regional courts and commissions in Africa, Europe and the Americas have also passed down decisions on, or informed by, the right to health.

However, domestic human rights and health laws afford some protection for right-to-health norms. This chapter does not give an exhaustive examination of the legal provisions and jurisprudence on health issues, but provides illustrative points on two relevant Acts, the National Health Service Act 1977 and the Human Rights Act 1998.

The National Health Service Act 1977

The NHS Act contains provisions which correspond closely with the government's right-to-health obligations under the ICESCR to prevent, treat and control diseases, and to create conditions which would assure everyone of medical attention and medical services in the case of emergency (Article 12, ICESCR). Section 1 of the Act provides that the Secretary of State for Health is responsible for the promotion of a comprehensive health service in England and Wales, designed to secure improvement in the physical and mental health of the people in those countries; for the prevention, diagnosis and treatment of illness; and for that purpose, for providing or securing effective provision of services in accordance with the Act. Section 3(1) provides that the Secretary of State is obliged to provide, so far as he or she considers it reasonably necessary, hospital and other accommodation for providing services; medical, dental, nursing and ambulance services; such other facilities for the care of expectant mothers and young children as he or she considers are appropriate; facilities for the prevention of illness and after-care of persons who have suffered illness; such other services as are required for the diagnosis and treatment of illness.

This Act should therefore indirectly provide legal guarantees for the right to health, including through judicial review. However, the courts have often exhibited deference to the executive in judicial review decisions relating to health-care entitlements, especially where decisions on resources are involved.[12] *R v. Central Birmingham Health Authority ex parte Walker* involved a decision not to offer surgery to a 'hole in the heart' baby, which the applicants held contravened the provisions of the 1977 Act. Lord MacPherson held that the case did not involve 'an attack upon the actual decision made' but involved 'a general criticism of the decisions as to the staffing and financing of the health service'. These were questions of enormous interest and concern, but they were questions to be raised and dealt with outside the court. This approach contrasts to the approach of courts in some other countries, such as South Africa and Colombia, which have found violations of the right to health or other related human rights on account of public policy decisions.[13]

Nevertheless, at times, the UK courts have taken different approaches. The case of *R v. Cambridgeshire Health Authority ex parte B* (*Child B*) concerned a ten-year-old girl who was suffering from acute myeloid leukaemia (see also Chapter 4). She had previously undergone two courses of chemotherapy and had received a bone marrow transplant.[14] Her doctors considered that continued treatment only had a small chance of success and would be very expensive. The Court of Appeal held that it was not in a position to decide on the correctness of the difficult decision made by the health authority and how it decided to distribute its finite resources, and therefore could not hold that the decision made by the health authority violated the right to health.[15] However, Mr Justice Laws had previously argued in the divisional court:

Merely to point to the fact that resources are finite tells one nothing about the wisdom or what is relevant for my purposes, the legality of the decision to withhold funding in a particular case. But where the question is whether the life of a ten-year-old child might be saved, by however slim a chance, the responsible authority must in my judgment do more than toll the bell of tight resources. It must explain the priorities that have led it to decline to fund the treatment. It has not adequately done so here. I accept that at present no sufficient justification has been shown to refuse this chance to B.

The scope of the Human Rights Act 1998

The ECHR, and the Human Rights Act (HRA), which incorporated its provisions into domestic law, contains a number of rights which are closely related to the right to health, and which have been, or may potentially be, used to protect this right 'by the back door'. They include the right to life, to privacy and family life, the right of men and women of marriageable age to marry and found a family, and the prohibition of torture and other cruel, inhumane and degrading treatment.

The right to be free from torture and other cruel, inhumane and degrading treatment has given rise to cases on access to medical treatment. In *D v. UK* (1997), the European Court of Human Rights found that it would be a violation of this right to remove the applicant, an alien suffering from HIV/AIDS, to St Kitts since he would lose access to medical and other care, which would hasten his death and expose him to a real risk of dying in very distressing circumstances. According to the court, this amounted to inhumane treatment. However, in a recent decision, *N v. Secretary of State for the Home Department*, involving deportation of a failed asylum seeker living with HIV/AIDS, the Law Lords ruled that there was no obligation on the UK not to deport the applicant, even though returning the applicant to Uganda would reportedly result in 'ill-health, discomfort, pain and death within a year or two'.[16]

The right to respect for private and family life has been invoked in cases involving the confidentiality of medical records, including *Robin Ackroyd v. Mersey Care NHS Trust*[17] and *R (on the application of*

S) v. City of Plymouth,[18] as well as at the European Court of Human Rights, for example in *Z v. Finland* and *MS v. Sweden*.[19] The ICESCR requires respect for privacy and confidentiality in health-care settings.[20] Under the ECHR, the right to respect for private and family life may be invoked where environmental health problems cause an infringement of privacy and family life: in *Lopez Ostra v. Spain*, the European Court ruled that an infringement of the right to respect for private and family life occurred on account of, among other things, environmental pollution which affected the applicant's well being and denied her family the full enjoyment of their private and family life.[21] This judgment resonates with the right to a healthy environment, an underlying determinant of the right to health.[22]

The right to be free from torture and the right to respect for private and family life have been used in relation to accessing certain health-care procedures, including challenging resource allocation decisions of health authorities. However, as has been the case in judicial review cases involving the National Health Service Act 1977, the courts have tended to show deference to policy-making bodies on resource issues. In the case of *R (on the application of Yvonne Watts) v. (1) Bedford Primary Care Trust (2) Secretary of State for Health*, involving a patient awaiting a hip operation, the High Court held that neither the prohibition of torture or other cruel inhumane and degrading treatment, nor the right to privacy and family life, give rise to entitlements to free health care.[23] The judge held that 'the Convention does not give the applicants rights to free health care' and that, even if applicants were to have such a right under the right to family and private life, 'it would be qualified by the authority's right to determine health-care priorities in the light of its limited resources'.[24] In the case of *North West Lancashire Health Authority v. A, D & G*, which involved a refusal of gender re-assignment surgery, the Court of Appeal held that the prohibition of torture and other cruel, inhumane and degrading treatment was not designed to be used in cases involving allocation of resources among competing priorities.[25]

How effectively is health care made accountable to the public in the UK?

Key indicators
Are there effective, accessible and independent mechanisms of monitoring and accountability by which local communities may hold local and national public officials to account over the delivery of health policies and programmes that affect them?

The low level of accountability in the National Health Service has been illuminated by a series of recent scandals in the UK that have dominated politics and the press, such as Alder Hey, the Harold Shipman murders and the deaths of young children undergoing heart surgery at Bristol Royal Infirmary. Ministers have resorted in each case to special inquiries. A recent study of accountability in the NHS by the ad hoc Commission on the NHS concluded that the constitutional doctrine of ministerial responsibility to Parliament disguised 'a wider absence of accountability and transparency within NHS structures' and expressed concern that the government and NHS were not sufficiently accountable 'across the gamut of decision-making on health care – from the overall level of funding and planning of services, to the redress of individual patients' grievances and the say that they have in their medical treatment'.[26] The doctrine of ministerial responsibility itself (the convention that ministers are responsible for all that happens within the departments that they head) is widely criticised for being a diffuse and ineffective mechanism of accountability.

At the international and regional level, the government engages in a state party reporting process with relevant UN treaty bodies, including the ICESCR, and with the ECSR. The government's reports and the responses of the monitoring bodies provide a measure of independent international accountability, but these processes are poorly reported in the media and do not seem to be regarded as anything more than a formality within government. The failure of the UK to sign up to the individual complaints mechanism of the

CEDAW, or the European Social Charter, however, denies direct international avenues for complaints for individuals; but the European Court of Human Rights does provide more indirect avenues of complaint on some health issues (see above).

At the national level, new arrangements for complaints and accountability have been introduced in response to criticisms that the complaints procedure set up in 1996 was 'incompetent, opaque and ineffective in bringing about reforms in the system';[27] even the then health secretary admitted it was 'a bit of a shambles'. It is too soon to evaluate the new system, but it too places great emphasis on local resolution of complaints. In the first instance people must complain to the NHS trust, organisation or practitioner providing the service. If they are not satisfied with the response, they can then ask a new national body, the Healthcare Commission, for an 'independent review'; one of its strategic goals is to ensure an explicit focus on human rights, inequalities and diversity in assessments. Finally, they may take their case to the Health Service Ombudsman, who investigates complaints of unsatisfactory treatment or care by the NHS or NHS-funded private providers. Professional bodies for doctors and practitioners also organise their own procedures for hearing complaints and maintaining standards. The Healthcare Commission is also tasked to assess the management, provision and quality of NHS health care and public health services and to review the performance of NHS trusts; and there are other accountability mechanisms, such as the Commission for Healthcare Audit and Inspection, the National Audit Office, the Mental Health Commission, the Audit Commission and the Commission for Health Improvement (CHI).

There is only tentative democratic input into the NHS. Patients, carers and others may become members of foundation trusts and may vote or stand in elections to their boards of governors alongside staff representatives and a variety of official and appointed members.

Does the UK have a national strategy and plan of action for health?

Key indicator

Within the last five years, has the government adopted or updated a national strategy and plan of action on health? If so, does the strategy

a) expressly recognise international and domestic human rights law?

b) systematically take into account and integrate the provisions of international and domestic human rights law?

c) include measures that are specifically designed to reach and benefit vulnerable groups?

Since 2000, the government has adopted a wide range of strategies for health care, including the NHS Plans for England and Wales and for Scotland, as well as a range of strategies in the field of public health (see below). The plans are framed with clear objectives and include schedules and measures that are designed to reach vulnerable groups. These plans do not expressly recognise the right to health, or other internationally recognised human rights. However, the Department of Health must contribute to cross-cutting targets on gender, disability and race equality set out in its public service agreement, and ensure compliance in the health sector with the HRA and the Race Relations (Amendment) Act 2000. Even so, the culture of human rights does not strongly permeate the health sector. Under the HRA, public authorities have a statutory duty to carry out their duties in a manner compatible with the Act. The Audit Commission found in 2003 that 73 per cent of health trusts surveyed were not taking action to adopt a strategy for human rights, and that 'health bodies consistently lag behind other public services' in this respect.[28]

Expenditure on health care
The UK government is obliged under the ICESCR to devote maximum available resources to the right to health. General

Comment 14 also suggests that 'a State which is unwilling to use the maximum of its available resources for the realisation of the right to health is in violation of its obligations under article 12'.[29]

The ageing population and the costs of new treatments and drugs have greatly increased resource demands in health care. In 1998, health expenditure per capita in the UK was 6.8 per cent of GDP, lower than the average of 8.4 per cent among EU countries. The total health expenditure per capita was 25–30 per cent lower than in Australia, France and the Netherlands, and 35 per cent lower than in Germany and Canada.[30] The report *Securing Our Future Health: Taking a Long Term View* (2002) argued that years of under-investment in the health service had resulted in the UK falling behind comparable countries in terms of key indicators relating to the provision of health care services, such as waiting lists.[31] In the 2002 budget, Gordon Brown, the Chancellor of the Exchequer, announced a significant five-year increase in expenditure – £40 billion – for the NHS, to match average European health expenditure.[32]

How far does the population of the UK enjoy the highest attainable standard of physical and mental health, on the basis of equality and non-discrimination?

Key indicators (disaggregated)
Life expectancy at birth
Infant mortality rate
Mortality rate for major causes of mortality

While the population of the UK overall enjoys a high standard of health, the national average masks significant disparities in health status and access to care, according to gender, age, ethnicity, social class and other factors. In some cases, these inequalities are widening. Non–discrimination and equality are fundamental human rights principles, at the heart of the right to health. Examples of inequalities in health outcomes and access to care between groups include:

- *Racial and minority ethnic groups.* Many minority ethnic groups have poorer health outcomes. Black (Caribbean, African and other) groups and South Asian, and in particular Pakistani and Bangladeshi, populations have higher rates of long-standing illness. In 2000, infant mortality among babies of mothers born in Pakistan was 12.2 per 1,000 live births, more than double the overall infant mortality rate.[33] In 2003, the Committee on the Elimination of Racial Discrimination expressed its concern about discrimination faced by Roma, gypsies and travellers, reflected in, inter alia, their higher child mortality rate and shorter life expectancy than the population as a whole, and their limited access to health services, as well as about the discrimination that other minority groups experience in gaining access to health care;[34]

- *Social class and economic status.* In Britain, in the 1970s the mortality rate among working-age men was almost twice as high among class V (unskilled) as among class I (professional). By the 1990s it was nearly three times higher. Life expectancy has been increasing at a greater rate for men in classes I and II than for men in classes IV and V. Rates of obesity are higher among unskilled than among skilled groups, in particular for women.[35] People living in households with incomes of £350 or more per week have significantly lower rates of self-reported long-standing illness than those living in households with an income of £200 per week or less,[36] while the gap in survival chances between rich and poor widened between 1986–90 and 1996–9 for twelve of sixteen cancers in men and nine of seventeen in women.[37]

Tackling inequalities: government responses

The government is obliged to take measures to ensure de facto equality between different groups. This requires addressing underlying causes of inequality, including its political, social, economic and cultural roots. In 1980, the Black report identified social deprivation as a major determinant of ill health. However, it was only when a Labour government was elected in 1997 that these social links were significantly addressed by government policy. In an answer to a parliamentary question on low income, inequality and health in 1997, Tony Blair emphasised: 'These inequalities do matter and there is no doubt that the published statistics show a link between income, inequality and poor health. It is important to address that issue, and we are doing so.'[38]

The Labour government's 1999 White Paper, *Saving Lives: Our Healthier Nation*, set out a strategy to tackle poor health, particularly of those worse off in society; to narrow the health gap; and to reduce the number of preventable deaths. The government also established some key targets in relation to reducing inequalities, including, by 2010, to have reduced inequalities in health by 10 per cent, as measured by infant mortality rate and life expectancy at birth; and, in particular, to reduce the gap by 10 per cent between 'routine and manual groups' and the population as a whole, and between the fifth of areas with the lowest life expectancy and the population as a whole. Programmes established to reduce inequalities include the health action zones, which ran from 1999–2003, and Sure Start, which is designed to support pre-school children from poorer families.[39] The government's strategy, *Tackling Health Inequalities: A Programme for Action*, sets out detailed interventions from a range of government departments, as well as specific targets to be reached between 2003 and 2010.

However, a Department of Health report, *Tackling Health Inequalities: Status Report on the Programme for Action*, showed in 2005 that health inequalities are widening despite these pledges. The gap in life expectancy between the poorest quintile and the general population widened by 2 per cent for men and 5 per cent for women between 1997–9 and 2001–3. Infant mortality has also increased: in 2001–3 mortality rates were 19 per cent higher among routine and manual groups than for the general population, a rise of 6 per cent since 1997–9.

Determinants of the right to health

The right to health gives rise not only to an entitlement to health care, but also to underlying determinants of health, such as food and nutrition, housing, access to safe and drinkable water, adequate sanitation, safe and healthy working conditions and a healthy environment.[40] Inequalities in health status in the UK, between men and women, different racial and ethnic groups and different areas, are often derived from determinants such as the environment, income, educational attainment, quality of housing, quality of diet and poverty. Public health strategies in the UK tend to focus on health care and individual diseases, rather than on the social and environmental causes of ill health. A right-to-health approach would give greater focus to these social and environmental determinants. This chapter surveys just one determinant, nutrition. Other underlying determinants of the right to health are addressed in other chapters in this book, and should also be considered vital to a right-to-health approach to public health.

Do people in Britain eat well enough to protect their health?

Key indicators (disaggregated)
Proportion of the population who are (a) obese (b) overweight
Proportion of population who eat at least five portions of fruit and vegetables per day

Article 11(1) of the ICESCR recognises the 'right of everyone to an adequate standard of living for himself and his family, including adequate food'. General Comment 12 of the Committee on Economic, Social and Cultural Rights clarifies that, among other factors, food must be of an adequate quality sufficient to satisfy the dietary needs of individuals (that is, it must contain a mix of nutrients for physical and mental growth) and free from adverse substances (in other words, there must be adequate food safety and freedom from contamination). Adequate food and nutrition is an underlying determinant of the right to health.

A recent survey of thirty-five countries by the World Health Organization (WHO) found that Britain's children have among the worst dietary habits. Over two thirds of children aged eleven to fifteen said that they did not eat one portion of fruit or vegetable a day (compared to a recommended five portions), while almost half of Scottish, and one third of English, eleven- to fifteen-year-olds drank one sugary drink a day.[41] Only 30 per cent of men and 35 per cent of women living in affluent parts of the country eat the recommended amount, and in the most deprived areas these figures drop to 18 per cent and 20 per cent respectively.[42] Only 15 per cent or less of girls aged thirteen to fifteen eat the recommended amount of fruit and vegetables.

Unhealthy diet, combined with inactivity (in 1998, two thirds of men and three quarters of women were not exercising as much as recommended targets),[43] contributes to obesity, which gives rise to major health problems. In 2002, more than 20 per cent of women and men were obese, an increase from 8 per cent and 6 per cent for women and men respectively in 1980; over half of all women and men were overweight or obese.[44] Among children, obesity increased by more than 25 per cent between 1995 and 2002.[45] In the UK, there is a high incidence of chronic diseases such as heart disease, cancer and respiratory infections, and the incidence of diabetes is rising. These conditions are linked to lifestyle factors such as poor diet, smoking, alcohol consumption and a lack of exercise.

In 1998, the Acheson report made a number of recommendations regarding lifestyle factors, including policies and measures to improve nutrition provided at school, to reduce the sodium content of foods, to increase exercise, including more cycling and walking routes to school, and to reduce smoking, including among women before or during pregnancy. The government has adopted a 'five a day' programme that builds on WHO guidelines to encourage people to eat five portions of fruit and vegetables per day. As part of this scheme, a National School Fruit and Vegetable Scheme was introduced after the NHS Plan introduced a commitment to a national fruit scheme by 2000. All four- to six-year-old children in state infant, primary and special schools are entitled to a free piece of fruit every day. Despite the benefits of this programme and scheme, other efforts may be needed if children are to receive adequate nutrition. The 2004 Wanless report argued that people need to be supported more actively to make better decisions about their health and welfare 'because there are widespread, systematic failures that influence the decisions individuals currently make'.[46] It took the 'Feed Me Better' campaign, headed by the TV chef Jamie Oliver, to get the government to increase expenditure on school dinners in schools with a view to improving nutrition.[47]

The right to health of children and infants

Under Article 12(2)(a) of the ICESCR, the government is required to take steps towards 'the provision for the reduction of the still-birthrate and of infant mortality and for the healthy development of the child'. Infant mortality rates have steadily declined and stood at 5.7 deaths per 1,000 live births in 1998. The recent decline has been attributed to the decline in sudden cot death. However, the UN Committee on the Rights of the Child has expressed its concern 'at persisting inequalities in health and access to health services, including mental health services, across the [United Kingdom] linked to socio-economic status and ethnicity (like high rates of infant mortality among the Irish and Roma travellers)'.[48]

There are pressing concerns about obesity and poverty among British children, linked to falling rates of exercise and poor diet. The committee expressed its concern about the low rates of breast-feeding in the UK, and encouraged the government 'to promote breast-feeding and adopt the International Code for Marketing of Breast-milk Substitutes'.[49] Of all young people aged between two and fifteen years, 6.6 per cent of boys and 7 per cent of girls were obese,[50] while 20 per cent of young people aged thirteen to sixteen are over-weight.[51] Other concerns are related to lifestyle choices of adolescents: 25 per cent of fifteen- and sixteen-year-olds smoke, 10.5 units of alcohol are consumed each week by those aged eleven to fifteen who drink, and 11 per cent of those aged eleven to fifteen have used drugs at least once in the last year.[52]

According to the UNICEF Innocenti Centre, the UK has the

second highest child poverty rate in Europe. The government has announced plans to eradicate child poverty by 2020 and there has already been some progress towards this goal in recent years. A range of initiatives, such as the Children and Young People's Unit, the Social Exclusion Unit, health action zones, and the National Childcare Strategy are important, although Save the Children notes that 'they are often difficult to evaluate separately and there is a concern that they may be based on the displacement of funding for other initiatives rather than new funding'.[53] In reducing poverty, there is still progress to be made, in particular in addressing the needs of children in the most impoverished families and communities (between 2000 and 2002, children in the poorest 10 per cent of households actually became worse off).[54] Recent reports have also revealed that the worst-off households – those who need it most – do not take advantage of the Sure Start schemes that are designed to improve their children's life chances early.

Sexual and reproductive health

The right to health 'may be understood as requiring measures to improve child and maternal health, sexual and reproductive health services, including access to family planning, pre- and post-natal care, emergency obstetric services and access to information, as well as to resources necessary to act on that information'.[55] The rights to sexual and reproductive health are expanded in the CEDAW General Recommendation 24 on women and health, in the Declaration and Programme of Action of the International Conference on Population and Development, and in the 2004 annual report to the Commission on Human Rights of the UN Special Rapporteur on the right to health.

Are the government and society safeguarding the sexual health of the young?

Key indicators (disaggregated)
Incidence of sexually transmitted infections
Incidence of teenage pregnancies

In the UK a range of problems concerning sexual and reproductive health are to be found among vulnerable groups. Many of these problems reveal themselves in poor sexual and reproductive health outcomes among women, men who have sex with men, teenagers and young adults, and black and minority ethnic groups. Between 1995 and 1997, cases of chlamydia rose by more than half (53 per cent) among adolescents, cases of gonorrhoea by 45 per cent and cases of genital warts by 24 per cent.[56] In 1999, most people questioned in a survey did not know what chlamydia was, while over a quarter of fourteen- to fifteen-year-olds think that the contraceptive pill prevents infection.[57] In its Concluding Observations on the UK in 1999, the Committee on the Elimination of Discrimination against Women expressed concern at the high rates of sexually transmitted infections (STIs), especially among teenagers aged sixteen to nineteen, and recommended that the government should allocate resources targeted on adolescents to prevention and treatment programmes for sexually transmitted diseases, with a holistic focus on reproductive health, including violence.[58] In 2001, there were an estimated 41,868 teenage pregnancies in England and Wales, up from 40,966 in 2001 (teenage pregnancy rates are the highest in western Europe, and the rate is higher in Wales than in England).[59] Teenage pregnancies can result in health complications in both the mother and the infant. In 2002, the Committee on the Rights of the Child expressed its concern about the rates of teenage pregnancies, and recommended that the UK 'take further necessary measures to reduce the rate . . . through, *inter alia*, making health education, including sex education, part of the school curricula, making contraception available to all children, and improving access to confidential and adolescent–sensitive advice and information and other appropriate support'.[60] A further problem is the persistence of female genital mutilation in the UK, despite its illegality. The committee urged the UK to 'to enforce, through educational and other measures, the prohibition of female genital mutilation'.[61]

More people than ever – 50,000 – in the UK are living with HIV and the number of those with diagnosed HIV has been increasing by nearly 50 per cent in recent years.[62] In 2001, the All-Party Parliamentary Group on AIDS made a number of recommendations to the government on HIV and human rights, based on a hearing and evidence submitted by a range of domestic and international actors.[63] The group made recommendations based on the international guidelines on HIV/AIDS, including:

- increasing opportunities for people living with HIV/AIDS to participate in planning and implementation of policy;
- enhancing prevention among vulnerable groups;
- establishing a cross-departmental HIV/AIDS strategy to consider where further anti-discrimination legislation would help address the social exclusion of vulnerable groups and protect against HIV transmission.

Sexual and reproductive health care is relatively widely available in the UK, although the increase in STIs is placing new pressures on some services. Contraceptives are available free from the NHS, and emergency contraception is available in most pharmacies. Abortion, which is governed by the Abortion Act 1967, as amended by the Human Fertilisation and Embryology Act 1990, is available without cost on the NHS, subject to the consent of two doctors. The Act does not extend to Northern Ireland, and there are no other providers there, making abortion very hard to obtain (and thus constituting a threat to a woman's health).[64] There is increased demand for sexual and reproductive health-care services, in particular genito–urinary medicine, where there are now average waiting times of ten days for men and twelve for women, and six to eight weeks in some areas.[65]

In 2001 the government launched, among other initiatives, the National Strategy for Sexual Health and HIV in England, which set targets for reducing the transmission of STIs and HIV, increasing diagnosis, reducing unintended pregnancy rates, improving health and social care for people living with HIV and STIs and reducing stigma. The strategy included a national chlamydia screening programme, but currently it covers only one in four primary care trusts in England, is targeted only at 16–25-year-old women, and doesn't cover other UK countries. The Scottish Executive has also taken the initiative with a draft Sexual Health and Relationships Strategy, and in Wales there is the Strategic Framework for Promoting Sexual Health in Wales, which outlines a number of priorities for action and an action plan for improving access to good quality sexual health advice and services and reducing teenage pregnancy rates and the incidence and prevalence of STIs in Wales.[66]

Neglect of psycho-social care

The right to health must be guaranteed to all groups, including people with psycho-social disabilities. In 1998, the government announced its intention to review and update mental health law comprehensively for the first time since the 1950s, in part to comply with the HRA. However, the influence of public opinion about psycho-social disabilities has also significantly – and adversely – influenced the review process. Public opinion has been broadly geared towards protecting the public rather than the human rights of people with psycho-social disabilities. Three homicides committed by two men with severe psycho-social disabilities, of Jonathan Zeto and of a mother and daughter in the 1990s, both of which were widely reported in the press, have had a profound impact on popular opinion and thus on the government's proposals.

A draft Mental Health Bill was presented in September 2004 which aimed to balance internationally recognised human rights of persons with mental disorders (for example to autonomy, participation, the least restrictive options, non-discrimination) with public protection. However, the second objective dominates the Bill, which fails to enshrine fundamental human rights principles, relegating them to a code of practice. Among other criticisms, the Bill also contains a very broad definition of mental disorder which, among other faults, risks making far too many people subject to compulsory treatment. New guidelines, the Mental Health Draft Code of Practice, which may be included in the Mental Health Bill, increase the maximum period a person can be sectioned before they must appear before a tribunal to forty-two days. The new Mental Health (Care and Treatment) (Scotland) Act, which was introduced in 2003, provides a telling contrast and better safeguards the rights and needs of persons with mental disorders.

Violence against women and children

Violence, which disproportionately affects women and children, has a significant impact on the right to physical and mental health. The Convention on the Rights of the Child places an obligation on the government to take all appropriate measures to protect children from all forms of 'physical or mental violence, injury or abuse, neglect or negligent treatment, maltreatment or exploitation, including sexual abuse, while in the care of parent(s), legal guardian(s) or any other person who has the care of the child'.[67] General Comment 14 elaborates that the right to health gives signatory states the responsibility for reducing women's health risks, including 'protecting women from domestic violence'.

Key indicator (disaggregated)
Deaths from inter-personal violence

Violence against women takes many forms, including rape, domestic violence, sexual harassment, honour crimes, female genital mutilation, forced marriages and killing. Domestic violence affects one in four women over their lifetime, and claims the life of two women every week. A 1992 survey of female college students found that 12 per cent had been raped and a further 8 per cent had experienced attempted rape.[68] A shadow report on violence against women by non-governmental organisations to the Committee on the Elimination of Discrimination Against Women at the time of its review of the UK, drew attention to a range of problems regarding violence, including the lack of a coherent prevention strategy, the difficulties and dangers confronting immigrant, asylum seeking, or trafficked women who have been or may become victims of violence, and the absence of systematic, consistent or reliable data on violence against women.[69] The committee expressed concerns in relation to violence against women and the government's response:

> While noting the legislation and measures in place to address violence against women, the Committee is concerned at the absence of a national strategy on the prevention and elimination of violence against women. According to information available to the Committee, women in Northern Ireland are particularly affected by violence. The Committee recommends that a unified and multi-faceted national strategy to eliminate violence against women be implemented to include legal, educational, financial and social components, in particular support for victims.[70]

In February 2000, Victoria Climbié tragically died following starvation and torture by her great-aunt and the woman's boyfriend. There was a series of failures by child protection authorities that had been alerted to her vulnerability to protect her. Between one and two children die every week from physical assault or neglect in England and Wales, with many thousands more suffering repeated beatings that may amount to torture or inhumane or degrading treatment and punishment, and may have a significant impact on their health and development. Smacking is still permitted in some circumstances under domestic UK law, when it constitutes 'reasonable chastisement'. In 2003, a ban on child minders smacking children was introduced, although UK law still allows parents to exercise reasonable physical chastisement.

In 2002, the Committee on the Rights of the Child expressed deep concern at violence and neglect of children in the home, and violence, including sexual violence, directed at children in schools, institutions, the care system and detention. The committee noted its alarm at the lack of a co-ordinated strategy to limit the extent of these phenomena. It particularly notes the absence of adequate, systematic follow-up of child deaths and that crimes committed against children below the age of 16 are not recorded. In the care system, the Committee notes a lack of consistent safeguards for children who are privately fostered. The Committee welcomes the steps taken by the Government to support child witnesses in court, but notes the lack of public education on the role of the child protection system.

The committee made a number of linked recommendations, centring on the need to develop a co-ordinated strategy for the reduction of child deaths caused by violence and of all forms of violence against children; to carry out large-scale education and information campaigns; and to strengthen detection and reporting systems.[71] The committee also recommended that the UK 'with urgency' adopt legislation throughout the country to remove the defence of 'reasonable chastisement' and prohibit all corporal punishment.[72]

Right to health care

The right to health includes a right to health care. Under Article 12 of the ICESCR, the government has an obligation to prevent, treat and control epidemic, endemic, occupational and other diseases; to create conditions to provide everyone with medical services and attention in the event of sickness; to give them 'equal and timely access to basic preventive, curative, rehabilitative health services and health education; regular screening programmes; appropriate treatment of prevalent diseases, illnesses, injuries and disabilities, preferably at community level'; and to provide 'essential drugs' and 'appropriate mental health treatment and care'. General Comment 14 further expands on these basic obligations and explains that the right to treatment includes 'the creation of a system of urgent medical care in cases of accidents, epidemics and similar health hazards, and the provision of disaster relief and humanitarian assistance in emergency situations'.

The NHS came into being in 1948, with the mandate to provide a 'comprehensive health service designed to secure improvement in the physical and mental health of the people . . . and the treatment, prevention, diagnosis and treatment of illness'.[73] The founding Act introduced into practice the principle of state responsibility for a comprehensive health service, free at the point of delivery for all those in need, which to this day informs the popular understanding of its role.[74] Yet since 1948, the provision of health-care services has undergone significant transformation. The NHS was once an international flagship for health care around the world, but in a recent survey by the London School of Hygiene and Tropical Medicine, the UK's health system came eighteenth out of nineteen industrialised countries, looking at health outcomes, responsiveness and financing.[75]

The availability, accessibility and acceptability of health care

The ICESCR establishes a framework for health care goods, services and facilities, ruling that they must be available, accessible, acceptable and of adequate quality. This chapter uses the framework to assess whether health care in the UK complies with the UK's obligations arising from its ratification of the ICESCR and other international treaties recognising the right to health.

Availability
The basic rule is that 'functioning public health and health-care facilities, goods and services, as well as programmes' should be available in sufficient quantity within a country, though their precise nature will vary according to a variety of factors, including the country's level of development. They will include, however, the underlying determinants of health, such as safe drinking water, adequate sanitation facilities, hospitals, clinics and other health-related buildings, trained medical and professional personnel receiving domestically competitive salaries, and essential drugs (as defined by the WHO action programme). Within the UK, issues of availability

include the types of service available, waiting lists and the number of health professionals per capita.

The National Health Service Act 1977 imposes some obligations on the health secretary to make hospital and community services available, but does not specify a list of services and gives him or her a wide degree of discretion, requiring the provision of services 'to such an extent as he considers necessary to meet all reasonable requirements'. The NHS and Community Care Act 1991 gave health authorities greater responsibility as purchasers of health-care services within limited budgets, which obliges them to make choices about the services they provide, in what quantities and who benefits from them. Thus while many health-care services are, broadly speaking, available throughout the UK, there are some shortcomings in availability of some services, goods and facilities. One service that is insufficiently available is dentistry. In May 2004, researchers at the University of Bath estimated that an extra 5,200 dentists are needed to bring dentistry up to the standard of other countries, with rural and impoverished areas being particularly under-served at present.[76] Within hospitals, there have also increasingly been delays in access to dental treatment.

Another significant measure of availability relates to the number of trained medical and other staff. The number of practising doctors per head of population is relatively low in the UK compared to many other EU countries: in 2000, there were 1.8 practising doctors per capita, compared to the EU average of 3.1,[77] though there has been an increase in numbers since 1999.[78] This low level of staffing is compounded by the desire of some health professionals to leave the profession. In 2001, a poll conducted by the Royal College of Nursing found that 25 per cent of nurses aged between eighteen and forty-four intended to leave the profession in the next decade. Most blamed poor pay and problems combining home and family.[79] As well as shortages in some services, and of staff, there is also a shortage of certain types of facility. In the UK, the number of hospital beds declined during the 1990s by around 10,000 per year. Part of the decline is accounted for by the increasing movement towards care in the community for people with psycho-social disabilities. However, there are concerns that the reductions are too large: there are now significantly fewer beds per capita than in some other European countries. When there are great demands, such as during influenza outbreaks, capacity does not always match need. The NHS Plan in 2000 included a commitment to increase hospital beds by 7,000 by 2004 and adult critical care beds by 30 per cent by 2003.

In 1997, the UN Committee on Economic, Social and Cultural Rights noted with concern the length of waiting lists across the UK. In 2001, the ECSR concluded that waiting lists, coupled with the decrease of beds available (see below), meant that 'the organisation of health care in the United Kingdom is manifestly not adapted to ensure the right to health of everyone'.[80] The reduction of waiting times was a specific commitment of the Labour government elected in 1997, which pledged that no-one would have to wait for more than eighteen months for a hospital in-patient admission and a 100,000 reduction in the total numbers of people waiting by the time of the next election. Specific targets were also set for key sectors: for example, the NHS Cancer Plan in 2000 included the commitment of a maximum one-month wait from diagnosis to treatment for breast cancer by 2001 and for all cancers by 2005. By 2002 the government was able to report to the UN committee that progress had been made in some areas – for the first time in UK history, no patient had to wait more than eighteen months for admission, with very few cases waiting even this long. Between 2001 and January 2003, waiting lists fell by 20,000 and waiting times also fell. Even so, in 2002, more than a million people were waiting for treatment with particular dangers for some patients – one in four cardiac patients, and one in five lung cancer patients, die while waiting for treatment.[81]

The government is addressing the problems of shortages of beds and of staff. In recent years there has been an increase in NHS staffing – since 1997, staff numbers have increased by over 15 per cent for medical doctors, dentists, qualified nurses and midwives, and other therapeutic, support and infrastructure staff. The NHS Plan in 2000 aimed for 7,000 extra hospital beds, 7,500 more consultants, 2,000 new GPs, 20,000 more nurses, and better pay and training for health professionals.[82] Agreements concluded with NHS staff in 2003 will mean that their pay increases over the next three years will be ahead of projected increases in earnings in the private sector. For doctors working in hospitals, average earnings will increase by 25–35 per cent between 2003 and 2006. Other NHS staff will have a 10 per cent pay increase over the same period and may be upgraded to higher-paying jobs. The introduction of the European Working Hours Directive means that health professionals should no longer have to work their customary long hours.

One reason for the recent staff increases is that the UK health sector has been able to attract health professionals from other countries. One in four medical staff now comes from South Africa and India. In 2004 the Department of Health updated its code of conduct (first introduced in 2001), which prohibits NHS trusts from actively recruiting permanent staff from developing countries, in the absence of a government-to-government agreement: however, private sector recruitment agencies are not covered by this ban, and few are believed to ascribe to government guidelines.[83] And, despite the code of conduct, the number of health professionals being employed from developing countries has increased over the last five years.[84] The skills drain can have serious implications for source countries: South Africa's health system is reportedly short of 1,000 nurses and was losing 300 of them a month in the early 2000s.[85] While overseas recruitment may help the realisation of the right to health in the UK, it may also be incompatible with the UK's obligation to give international assistance and co-operation to enable the right to health in other countries.[86]

Accessibility

The accessibility of health-care services has four main components: physical accessibility, economic accessibility, accessibility on the basis of non-discrimination and accessibility of information. This chapter deals just with accessibility on the basis of non-discrimination and economic accessibility.

Non-discrimination: health facilities, goods and services must be accessible to all, especially the most vulnerable or marginalised sections of the population, in law and in fact, without discrimination on any of the prohibited grounds.[87] While the government is committed to access on the basis of non-discrimination, discrimination is a significant problem facing some groups, including the elderly, people with disabilities, people living with HIV/AIDS, people in detention, and failed asylum seekers and illegal immigrants.

More than one in six people aged over sixty-five report that they have experienced discrimination in access to health care on account of their age.[88] Three quarters of senior health managers surveyed believe that age discrimination existed in their local health service, and many thought this discrimination was endemic.[89] In 2001, the government launched a national service framework for older persons. This outlines national target standards in health care, and effectively bans the refusal of treatment to persons on grounds of age alone.[90] The national service framework admits that 'there have been reports of poor, unresponsive, insensitive, and in the worst cases, discriminatory, services' in the NHS.[91]

Aside from the discrimination faced by older people, some dentists have refused to treat people with HIV, others have requested that they treat them at the end of the day on the grounds that surgical instruments can be properly sterilised.[92] According to a study of infertility clinics and HIV, only 44 per cent of units agreed to treat a couple where the man alone was infected.[93] Similarly, People with intellectual disabilities are more likely to have long-term physical and psychiatric problems, but their health needs are not always adequately met. For example, there are very low cervical screening rates among women with intellectual disabilities.[94] Failed asylum seekers and undocumented migrants are not able to access health services equally and without discrimination. In 2004, the government made changes to the National Health Service (Charges to Overseas Visitors) Regulations 1989, obliging NHS hospitals to withdraw free secondary-level care to failed asylum seekers and undocumented migrants, except in cases deemed life-threatening or needing immediate attention (according to the regulations this does not include anti-retrovirals for HIV/AIDS). In 2004, the Department of Health published a consultation document proposing to exclude failed asylum seekers and undocumented migrants from free primary health-care services, unless their condition requires immediate treatment.[95] With only limited access to free primary or secondary care, there would appear to be a significant risk of deteriorating health for failed asylum seekers and undocumented migrants, especially those who are pregnant or who have chronic disorders, such as diabetes.

The prison population is at particular risk of certain health problems, including HIV and hepatitis B and C infection: infection rates among women in prisons are around thirteen times higher than among the general population. Drug misuse in prison is abundant. One in four prisoners report having injected drugs, and nearly a third of them continue to inject while in prisons. Condoms and clean needles are not made available in prisons, neither are hepatitis B vaccinations routinely given to those at risk.[96] The All-Party Parliamentary Group on HIV/AIDS has recommended that 'needle exchange schemes should operate inside prisons on the same basis as outside' and that 'Prison Service Instruction should be issued to ensure that all prison staff know that they have a duty to provide condoms in an effective and confidential way and not merely through medical officers'.[97]

Economic Accessibility: health facilities, goods and services must be affordable to all. Payment for health-care services has to be based on the principle of equity, ensuring that these services, whether privately or publicly provided, are available to all, including socially disadvantaged groups. According to the UN Committee of Economic, Social and Cultural Rights, equity demands that poorer households should not be disproportionately burdened with health expenses as compared to richer households.[98] The ethos underlying the NHS, of universal free health care on the basis of clinical need, means that health care is in general economically accessible in the UK, in particular in comparison to other countries. But there is an increasing tendency to offer patients in urgent need chargeable operations on the private sector far earlier than they are available free on the NHS by the same surgeon. There are charges for prescriptions and dental and optometric services, although a range of categories of people are eligible for free prescriptions, and 'passports' at lower rates are available for those who need a continuing supply of drugs.

Acceptability

'All health-care facilities, goods and services must be respectful of medical ethics and culturally appropriate, i.e. respectful of the culture of individuals, minorities, peoples and communities, sensitive to gender and life-cycle requirements, as well as being designed to respect confidentiality and improve the health status of those concerned.'[99]

Quality

The UN committee requires that health facilities, goods and services must 'be scientifically and medically appropriate and of good quality'.[100] Improving the quality of health services is at the heart of the government's commitment to health. In 1997/8, the government articulated a ten-year quality agenda, comprising a range of policy, legislative and regulative initiatives to improve access, effectiveness, equity, responsiveness and capacity.[101] Policy documents, including the White Papers *The New NHS: Modern, Dependable* and *NHS Wales: Putting Patients First*, signal the importance of quality. The consultation document *A First Class Service: Quality in the New NHS* opens with the statement 'High quality care should be a right for every patient in the NHS'.[102] The 15 per cent rise in qualified doctors, dentists, nurses and midwives and therapeutic and other staff since 1997 is vital to such a goal. A range of initiatives has been introduced to ensure quality in the NHS. The National Institute for Clinical Excellence (NICE), the CHI and the Healthcare Commission have been created to assess the contribution of drugs, provide guidance on best practice to patients, the health profession and the public, and to regulate NHS performance. Other newly created agencies include the National Patient Safety Agency and the National Clinical Assessment Authority. Even so, quality control has sometimes been criticised – there is, for example, concern over the length of time that it takes NICE to undertake appraisal processes for the licence of new drugs. There is also widespread alarm about the high incidence of MRSA, the multiple antibiotic resistant bacteria, in hospitals. Every year around 300,000 (nine in every 100) people in hospital contract an infection there, and 5,000 of them die.[103] The need to ensure greater hygiene in hospitals became an election campaign issue in 2005 and still haunts the government.

Another running problem is that the quality of health-care goods, services and facilities varies between regions and areas, giving rise to what is widely known as the 'postcode lottery'. In some respects, differences stem from variations in the policies of NHS trusts, which are an inevitable side effect of the desirable aim of decentralising decision-making in the NHS to render it more efficient and responsive. But the postcode lottery also reflects profound regional and local inequalities in the UK. For example, nearly a third of women (30 per cent is the estimate) in the north-west and north-east have a mastectomy following diagnosis of breast cancer, compared to about one in eight (12 per cent) of women in London and the south-east. Differences of this kind, and it would be possible to give multiple examples, derive in part from variations in resources; in this case, over-stretched radiography services and long waiting lists in some areas.[104] A guide compiled by the *Sunday Times* in 2001 found that for every ten patients who died at the University College hospitals in London, which have the lowest mortality rate in the country, seventeen patients died in Walsall NHS Trust, which has the highest rate.[105]

There are renewed fears about maintaining or achieving equality arising from the government's recent and proposed health-care reforms in its search to improve services. Critics argue that the creation of foundation hospitals will create a two-tier health system, in which well-performing hospitals will continue to do well, enjoying greater financial freedoms, while hospitals which perform less well may be driven into financial crises and may be left behind.[106] The government's reliance on private finance initiatives (PFIs) has also been criticised, not only over the long-term costs that are involved but also on grounds of the poor quality of some PFI hospitals and poor planning. For example, a number of PFI hospitals have planned extensions to support extra beds and facilities not properly integrated into the original building, while others have had poor ventilation and temperature control.[107] There are also documented complaints about the way PFI schemes in the NHS, as in other public services, have been driven through with 'a disturbing degree of manipulation, bullying and refusal of basic information'.[108] But underlying the debates over PFI schemes and the further involvement of the private sector in providing care is the fear that privatisation will exacerbate inequalities in standards of care.

Conclusion

While the right to health is not recognised in domestic law, many UK health policies are animated by the right to health norms and principles, such as equality and non-discrimination in access to health care, combating inequalities that give rise to poor health among some population groups, and ensuring that care is available, accessible, acceptable and of good quality. However, this is not always the case, and some policies, institutional structures and health outcomes are unacceptable. This includes inequalities in health outcomes, the denial of certain types of health care to particular groups, such as the denial of secondary health care to failed asylum seekers and illegal immigrants, and the lack of recognition of the right to health in UK law. Moreover, the changing structures of health care, with increasing emphasis on the market and moves towards privatisation, may well bring new right-to-health challenges – when reforms are pursued, a thorough human rights impact assessment should be undertaken.

9

Home truths

People in Britain do not have an overall constitutional right to housing, unlike citizens in other EU states, such as Belgium, the Netherlands, Portugal and Spain, nor is the right to housing inscribed as a 'fundamental aim' of the state, as in Sweden.[1] Such a right is not even conceivable in current circumstances, given that there is not sufficient housing to go round, especially for those who require rented accommodation because they cannot afford to buy their homes. Nor is there any realistic prospect of there being sufficient housing to meet the need in particular of those who cannot afford to buy, partly because the UK's house-building programmes are not large enough to meet acute demand, partly because resources are concentrated on homes for sale rather than renting. Thus the idea of a right to housing is utterly unrealistic, especially as there has been a pronounced shift towards owner occupation in government policies for the past quarter century. For some thirty years after the Second World War, government policies sought to hold a balance between social housing for rent and private ownership, which shifted over time from the public to private sector. The decisive shift came with the 'right to buy' under Margaret Thatcher's government in 1980, which hollowed out the public sector as tenants bought previously rented council houses and flats on advantageous terms. Since then too, both major parties have abandoned the shared goal of building sufficient housing to house the nation that animated policy until the mid-1970s.

Some housing rights are protected under the law: for example, the UK is the only EU member state that gives certain categories of homeless people an enforceable right of access to housing, though it is subject to stringent conditions that housing authorities can manipulate (see below). People who rent their homes either from private or public landlords are protected against arbitrary eviction and harassment by the Protection from Eviction Act 1977 and Housing Act 1985 (though most private tenants do not enjoy secure long-term rights to their home). In addition, people in housing need can claim the right to respect for their private and family life, as provided for by Article 8 of the European Convention on Human Rights (ECHR), which has been interpreted by the European Court of Human Rights to protect some housing rights (see Chapter 4). However, neither the convention nor (for that matter) the International Covenant on Economic, Social and Cultural Rights (ICESCR) guarantee accommodation for homeless people, and judicial deference tempers interpretation of the ECHR in the sphere of housing rights. Various Acts address the need for good repair and fitness and the Housing Act 1985 established fitness standards for publicly owned housing. But there remains no general obligation on landlords to make premises they let fit for habitation (except in Scotland). However, the Housing Act 2004 aims to raise housing standards through a new rating system operated by local authorities and introduced a new licensing regime for properties in multi-occupation (and also gave people in same-sex couples equal rights with those in heterosexual couples to inherit a partner's tenancy). Private tenants may appeal against excessive rents to a rent assessment committee, which sets 'market' rents. They are also protected against unreasonable service charges. Tenants in public and private housing sectors may apply for means-tested rent rebates to assist them in paying the rent.

In addition to specific legislation, the race relations and sex and disability discrimination Acts apply within the housing sphere. Limited rights to basic utilities are guaranteed under the Gas Act 1986, the Electricity Act 1989 and the Water Industry Act 1991 and regulated by Ofgem (for gas and electricity) and Ofwat or the Water Industry Commission (for water).[2] Other relevant legislation includes the Environmental Protection Act 1990, which enables people to take proceedings against premises prejudicial to health and to seek orders for remedial works.

Significant omissions remain. For example, some council tenants may lawfully be evicted from their homes in the first year of their tenancy; tenants of social landlords may automatically be evicted if they are more than eight weeks in arrears with their rent; most private tenants moving in since January 1997 hold shorthold tenancies, which give protection for only limited periods. In the first two cases, landlords are not obliged to give reasons for seeking possession. Furthermore, it is estimated that each year landlords unfairly withhold part or all of the deposits of more than 100,000 private tenants. But the major deficiency remains the absence of sufficient affordable housing for rent and the weakness of safeguards for vulnerable households. This failure of state policy is significant because a decent and secure home underpins the well-being and performance of all citizens and especially children.

Aside from the serious gaps of coverage in housing entitlements, government housing policy has often actively contravened inter-national human rights obligations. For instance, the Homelessness Act 2002, various aspects of which are discussed below, was a cause of concern for the parliamentary Joint Committee on Human Rights. The committee expressed doubts about the part of the Act that prevented local housing authorities from allocating accom-modation to certain categories of people. It argued that there would be possible breaches of Articles 3, 8 and 14 of the ECHR, Article 5 of the International Convention on the Elimination of All Forms of Racial Discrimination and Article 11 of the ICESCR.[3]

However, access to decent housing is the crucial issue for a wide range of British citizens. For many citizens the failure to provide fully for a right to housing is acute: in 2000 alone, Shelter, the housing charity, had to assist over 176,000 homeless or badly housed people. Recent information shows that the number of families waiting for a council house has risen by more than half since 1997, now standing at 1.5 million.[4]

The housing divide

Britain faces a housing crisis that has been neglected since at least 1979 and is only now being acknowledged. It is driven by a high and growing single population, continued immigration and the abandonment and demolition of existing housing. Lack of access to decent, affordable housing is a major problem in the UK. British society is polarised between the two-thirds of the population who are generally well housed in owner occupation and those who live in rented accommodation, very often in the rump of the public sector and in privately owned slums in the inner city – that is, in areas of acute social exclusion with a multitude of communal deprivations. Their housing conditions are often poor: in 1996, 40 per cent of public housing and 29 per cent of the private sector failed to meet official standards of decency.

But homeless people are clearly worst off – those who live rough, families in emergency accommodation, couples who cannot live together, households without self-contained homes. They are the obvious casualties of the acute housing shortage that governments have neglected.

The vast majority of people – nearly 90 per cent – would prefer to buy rather than rent their homes, if cost were not an issue.[5] House building has fallen to historically low levels. Only 175,104 new dwellings were completed in the UK in 2001/2 – the lowest level since the Second World War. Since then there has been a slight increase, to 205,961 for 2004/5, although this is still only just past the figure of 198,074 for 1990/1. Partly as a consequence, the entry point for owner occupation is now higher than it has ever been. House prices have risen by 2.4 per cent a year in real terms during the past thirty years, compared with an EU average of 1.1 per cent. As a result, in 2002, only 37 per cent of new households in England could afford to buy, compared with 46 per cent in the 1980s.[6] The rise in house prices has now generally slackened off, but without bringing relief to those in need. The number of first-time buyers in 2004 was 361,000 – the lowest annual total since 1981. While on the one hand the shortage of homes for sale has led to property becoming increasingly unaffordable, on the other there is a desperate shortage of affordable homes for the less well off, which we consider in detail here.

Affordable housing

The severe lack of affordable housing has been created by the failure to build sufficient quantities for rent or sale – and by the cumulative loss of better-quality social housing over twenty years, as a result of the introduction of the right to buy by Margaret Thatcher in 1980. Since 1980, 1.7 million homes in all have been lost from social housing, and the annual loss of re-lets now stands at 22,000 homes.[7] The amount of new-build social housing for rent fell by half from 1994 to 2003. Of the 176,451 new dwellings completed in 2000/1, only 18,000 were affordable homes. In the same year, 53,000 social homes were sold off.

Urban areas suffer particularly from the need for affordable housing. A survey by the Halifax bank published in January 2005 indicated that first-time buyers, usually young people, could not afford to buy a home in 92 per cent of English towns and cities. For many people across London and southern England, particularly those working in the public sector, the cost of property is simply out of reach. During the past thirty years wages have risen by 60 per cent compared to 135 per cent in property prices.[8] Research carried out in 2000 showed that there were nineteen local authority districts in south-east England where fewer than one in five younger working households living locally could afford to get on the bottom rung of the housing ladder.

But the housing shortage is affecting rural as well as urban Britain. In the five years to 1995, 80,000 affordable homes were needed in rural England, but only 17,000 were actually built between 1990 and 1997. Wealthy home owners, many of them buying second homes, are forcing out local families: a study from Aberdeen University found that four out of ten new households in rural areas are unable to buy a home, disrupting local communities and their way of life. Young people are particularly badly hit. They cannot afford to live independently of their parents into their twenties and must choose between living with their parents or moving to urban areas. Meanwhile, once established in an area, richer home owners seek to protect their 'rural idyll' by opposing new developments that could benefit the wider community and provide some social housing. The trend towards larger detached houses for ownership in suburban and rural Britain is also denying most of those in need the kind of housing they require.

In 2005, for example, south-west England was facing an unprecedented housing crisis. The number of people living in temporary accommodation had risen by 70 per cent over the previous five years – and far more in some parts of the region.[9] The familiar malign combination of high-priced private housing and neglect of social housing had created the crisis. In half of local authority areas average house prices were more than ten times local income. The cheapest homes averaged 6.3 times income. Average house prices were 6 per cent above the national average, while average incomes were nearly 14 per cent below the national average. Some 134,000 homes had been lost to the public sector since the 1980s under the right to buy, but in 2004, for example, only 1,300 affordable homes were built. Council house waiting lists had nearly doubled; the number of homeless households rose by 26 per cent over five years; households in temporary accommodation had more than doubled since 1997. These problems were compounded by low incomes, holiday and second homes, and retirement accommodation.

Affordable tenancies

The rental market in the UK is not as large as other European countries at about 30 per cent of all housing. Currently in England some 3.7 million households rent from the social sector and 2.2 million rent privately, out of a total of 20.5 million households.[10] During the 1990s those having to rent were hit with huge rent increases across both sectors, and the upward trend has continued. By May 2003 the average monthly rent amounted to £1,619 in London and £714 in the rest of the country. For most tenants there is little protection against excessive rents, although they can be adjudicated by an independent rent assessment committee if considered beyond the market rate – but this may be meaningless if the market itself is skewed so much in favour of the landlord; and those who have only limited protection in the private sphere would risk losing their home if they took a case forward. Moreover, for those at the poorest end of the scale, benefit levels have not kept pace with rent increases, especially in London. For them, social housing offers the security of affordable rents with benefits if required, but public housing policies are less targeted to meeting such needs. For example, Shelter noted that of the affordable homes built in London in 2003, only 54 per cent were for rent, compared to 72 per cent in 2002.[11]

Young people are particularly subject to prejudice. A survey of single people under twenty-five on housing benefit found that the combination of landlords' negative attitudes towards the young and those on benefits, combined with their low incomes and limited savings, conspired to make it difficult for them to rent accommodation. Even if they do manage to find somewhere and can afford the deposit and advance rent, their benefit may well prove insufficient to meet the regular payments.[12]

Despite the perceived unpopularity of rented council housing and the actual problems that many tenants suffer in relation to fitness and disrepair (see below), it remains significantly more acceptable than other forms of tenancy. The British Social Attitudes survey found that more than three-quarters of council house tenants would prefer to rent from their local authority than another landlord and that more than a quarter of housing association tenants would rather live in council property. Furthermore, more than half of the general public believe that councils provide better value for money than private landlords. These results arguably reflect the lack of alternative affordable good-quality rented accommodation as well as the greater security of tenure that council tenants generally have. However, the same survey found that only 32 per cent of the public and 52 per cent of council tenants regard council estates as 'generally pleasant places to live'.

The Barker review and building plans

Action on house-building – particularly of affordable homes – is clearly needed to tackle the problems described above. It has been estimated that there is a house-building shortfall in England of at least 39,000 each year, of which 31,000 should be affordable. The position is worst in London (already the second most densely populated city in Europe) and south-east England, where demand and house prices are soaring and social housing provision is at an all-time low. Shelter has estimated that 25,700 new affordable homes are needed in London every year and yet in 2002 only 4,300 were built.[13] It has further been estimated that England alone will need four million new homes during the next twenty years – 25 per cent of the existing stock – but is nowhere near achieving such targets.

Labour's 2001 manifesto made commitments to improving sub-standard housing,[14] but was silent on new house building. Since early 2003, the Deputy Prime Minister, John Prescott, has been issuing plans to increase the stock of affordable housing in south-east England and to refurbish derelict stock in northern England. In April 2003, he and Gordon Brown, the Chancellor of the Exchequer, commissioned the economist Kate Barker to 'conduct a review of issues underlying the lack of supply and responsiveness of housing in the UK'. When she reported in March 2004, her review illustrated the continuing failure to bridge the huge gap between rampant and over-priced owner occupation and the inadequate and under-funded affordable sector. There is an urgent need for a vast house-building drive to close it.

The report estimated that 179,000 new households would form annually in England from 2002 to 2011, of which 28,000 will need affordable housing. But losses of re-lets through the right to buy (22,000 homes each year), losses of privately rented homes for sale and other changes in the housing market bring the total number of new households requiring housing in England to 206,000 every year to 2011, of which 67,000 will require affordable homes. Aside from this annual flow of new households which need subsidised housing, there is a substantial backlog of households which are likely to need help to access housing. Barker used figures from the Office of the Deputy Prime Minister (ODPM) to revise previous estimates of need published by the National Housing Federation. She calculated that there is a backlog of some 948,000 households in need of affordable or social housing. They encompass homeless households in emergency accommodation, families not in self-contained accommodation, owner-occupiers and private tenants needing social housing, and other tenants in overcrowded or otherwise unsuitable housing (see Table 9.1).

Table 9.1: Backlog of households in need of sub-market housing, England

Households without self-contained accommodation

Households in temporary accommodation	94,000	
Concealed families	154,000	
Households in shared dwellings	53,000	
Would-be couples living apart	74,000	
Single homeless people: hostel residents etc.	110,000	
Adjustment for those saving to buy	−23,000	
Sub-total		462,000

Owner-occupiers and private sector tenants needing social rented sector homes

Households applying for age or medical reasons	70,000	
Households who cannot afford mortgage payments	20,000	
Expiry of lease or inability to afford or rent	30,000	
Over-crowding	20,000	
Sub-total		140,000

Local Social and Registered Social Landlord tenants in unsuitable housing

Overcrowding	206,000	
Households with children living above the ground floor	150,000	
Overlap in categories	−10,000	
Sub-total		346,000
TOTAL		948,000

Source: Barker, K., Review of Housing Supply: Delivering Stability: Securing Our Future Housing Needs, Final Report – Recommendations (HM Treasury, 2004), Table 5.2.

The Barker review also addressed the problem of high house prices. It was calculated that, in all, 120,000 private sector houses would have to be built annually to reduce the rise in house prices to the EU average of 1.1 per cent. However, the review accepts that even if more private homes are built, the government will have to double the rate at which social homes, provided either by local councils or social landlords, are built to meet the needs of the less well off. Barker calculated that an extra 17,000 homes will be required annually to meet 'newly arising need' on top of another 23,000 to make inroads into the backlog 'of the most needy' described above. She threw down the gauntlet to the government by calculating that these targets would require an extra investment of £1.2 and £1.6 billion respectively each year (although not all of this need come from the Exchequer).

Barker made it clear that the current rate of house building is not a realistic option, 'unless we are prepared to accept increasing problems of homelessness, declining affordability and social division, decline in standards of public service delivery and increasing costs of doing business in the UK'.

Measuring up to the Barker review

Addressing some of the concerns raised by Barker, the ODPM published its five-year plan, *Sustainable Communities: Homes for All*, in January 2005. It set out plans to build an extra 200,000 homes in London and south-east England, over and above the 2001 plans, by 2016. To that end £1.1 billion was promised over three years. The ODPM also promised £2 billion for social housing in 2007/8. Local authorities wishing to be involved in building new social housing were given three options: a private finance initiative, funding housing associations and bidding in partnership with private developers. In other words, the more traditional statist model was ruled out. Then in its 2005 general election manifesto, Labour proposed to 'increase the annual supply of new social homes by 50 per cent by 2008, an extra 10,000 homes a year' – a pledge that was first made in the government's spending review in 2004 in response to Barker.

Organisations such as Shelter and the Chartered Institute of Housing continue to question whether sufficient resources are being committed to deliver required levels of affordable housing. The use of resources for other purposes, such as expanding low-cost home ownership schemes, is often viewed as a questionable approach. For instance, the five-year plan promised schemes to assist first-time buyers. It was also stated that right to buy in public housing would be continued, including for tenants of social landlords if they agree, with a few limitations. For example, since March 2003 discounts on purchase have been reduced in forty-two areas of high housing demand and the Housing Act 2004 also introduced restrictions to prevent abuses. Nevertheless, the general drive of policy remains the same – valuing the extension of ownership above the need for affordable social housing and seeking in particular to assist middle-income households to get into owner occupation through shared ownership and other intermediate schemes. In its 2005 manifesto, Labour boasted:

> Home ownership has increased by over one million with Labour and by the end of our third term we aim for it to have risen by another million to two million . . . We want to widen the opportunity to own or part-own, especially for more young people and those tenants who rent in the private or public sector.

After Labour's third election victory, the government continued in a similar vein. On 25 May 2005 John Prescott and Gordon Brown launched a pamphlet entitled *Extending Home Ownership*. It described a scheme whereby equity loans would be jointly funded from public and private sources. It is intended to introduce the loans from April 2006. The plan has been criticised on the grounds that if it is not accompanied by an increase in housing supply, it will mean further increases in house prices.

Adequacy and quality of housing

Another manifestation of the housing divide is in the variable condition of housing. Living in poor housing is not only degrading and a source of discomfort; it has health consequences. Poor health is the third most common problem after homelessness and eviction that Shelter's helpline has to deal with. A study conducted for the Joseph

Rowntree Foundation in 2002[15] found a strong correlation between poor housing conditions and excessive winter deaths, of which there are on average 40,000 per annum – greater than in most other European continental countries and Scandinavia. The percentage rise in deaths in winter was greater in those dwellings with low energy efficiency ratings and those predicted to have low indoor temperatures during cold periods. In particular the absence of central heating was a major contributory factor along with fuel poverty. The report concluded that substantial public health benefits could be expected from measures that improve the thermal efficiency of dwellings (see further under 'Older people' below).

As far back as 1980, after years of under-investment, Britain was faced with a massive legacy of unfit and poor living conditions, especially for the disadvantaged. But the massive right-to-buy sale and the withdrawal from investment in council housing made overall conditions far worse; and Labour ministers were confronted in 1997 with a £1.9 billion backlog of investment in a housing stock much of which was way below average EU standards. Part of the problem is that the UK has the oldest housing stock in Europe: 39 per cent of the housing stock (8.1 million houses) was built before 1945 and 21 per cent (4.4 million) built before 1919. Half of all pre-1919 stock is non-decent compared to just over a third of stock dating from between 1919 and 1980. Virtually all post-1980 stock is decent. The extent of unfit housing in Britain bears testimony to the decline in slum clearance from its height in the 1970s, when 80,000 properties per year were being demolished (although much of this demolition was in fact unnecessary), to less than 1,000 per year in 1997 – an annual replacement rate of less than one in every 23,000 dwellings.[16]

Just before Labour came to office, in 1996, some 1.45 million homes (one in every sixteen dwellings in the UK) were classified as 'unfit for human habitation'.[17] In that year the European Community Household Panel comparative survey of specific housing problems showed the UK in a poor light compared with other European countries. The survey found that for three out of four categories the UK had a worse record than the EU average. It had the fifth highest level of complaints regarding lack of space; the fifth highest level concerning leaking roofs and damp; the sixth highest level about excessive noise and the highest level regarding vandalism or crime in neighbourhoods. Altogether the survey found that approximately 9.5 million people in Britain (nearly one in five households) could not afford to keep their home adequately heated, free from damp or in a decent state of decoration.[18]

Table 9.2: Percentage of households declaring that they experience specific problems with accommodation

UK	19	21	27	27
EU	15	17	30	18

Source: Eurostat – European Community Household Panel 1996 and national data 1995

When it came to basic amenities – bath/shower, indoor flushing toilet and hot running water – the UK performed better, with only 1 per cent of older people living alone lacking at least one of these. This compared with 11 per cent in Germany, 13 per cent in Italy and Spain and 17 per cent in France.[19]

With Labour in office, the number of people living in poor housing has remained unacceptably high. Every five years the Housing Condition Survey assesses the state of the housing stock. The survey defines a 'decent home' as (a) meeting the statutory minimum standard for housing to be fit; (b) in a reasonable state of repair; (c) with reasonably modern facilities; and (d) providing a reasonable degree of thermal comfort. Fitness is further defined under Section 604 of the Local Government and Housing Act 1989 as satisfying criteria relating to disrepair, structural stability, dampness, lighting, heating and ventilation, water supply, drainage, facilities for food preparation and presence, and location and functioning of bath and toilet facilities.

The latest survey carried out on behalf of the ODPM in 2001 found that seven million dwellings failed to provide a decent home. (It pointed out that many homes continue to fall into unfitness, but their numbers are beginning to be exceeded by those being made fit.) Although this is a fall of 2.4 million since the last survey in 1996 it still amounts to a third of all dwellings. Social sector non-decent homes account for 1.6 million (38 per cent) of non-decent dwellings (an improvement of 700,000 since 1996) compared to 5.5 million in the private sector (down from 7.1 million). Significant improvements include higher levels of amenities, central heating and double glazing. The number of unfit homes stands at 900,000 (or 4.2 per cent of the total stock), an improvement of 600,000. However, a higher proportion of unfit homes fail on more than one item than in 1996, suggesting a hard core in the very worst condition. The most common reason for unfitness is disrepair (46 per cent) followed by inadequate cooking facilities and dampness.

Nearly half a million households continue to live in overcrowded homes,[20] and householders in the UK in general live in more crowded conditions than in other EU countries when the number of persons per room is considered: 2.2 against an EU average of 1.8.[21] The 2003 Poverty and Social Exclusion Survey concluded that while the proportion of people living in overcrowded conditions fell by more than a third between 1990 and 1998, there had been no fall since that date.

Disrepair remains a widespread problem. Almost a third of all English, and a quarter of Welsh, homes require £1,000 worth of urgent repairs. It is much worse in Scotland, where nearly a third of dwellings need repairs costing over £3,000.[22] At the same time the number of renovation grants has fallen by one third to the level of the early 1980s – a trend which is unlikely to be reversed given the continued constraints on local government spending. Perhaps not surprisingly the problem of disrepair is particularly acute in the private rented sector, where about one in five dwellings are unfit. Many council housing estates are also notorious for their poor state of repair. A British Social Attitudes survey found that 56 per cent of their tenants thought the standard to be poor.[23]

The proportion of 'vulnerable' households – those who receive income- and disability-related benefits – in the private sector living in non-decent homes is 43 per cent, amounting to some 1.2 million people (a fall of 300,000 since 1996). While all social groups have benefited similarly from the overall improvement of the stock, the poorest fifth of households remain twice as likely to be living in non-decent homes as the wealthiest fifth. One in ten low-income people live in unfit homes. More than three quarters of those living in housing which was unfit or in serious disrepair in Scotland and Wales had incomes of less than £12,000 in 1996.[24] In the most deprived 10 per cent of wards, two fifths of homes are non-decent, compared to a quarter in the least deprived wards. Overall over 10 per cent of those on the lowest incomes (below £4,000 per annum) live in unfit housing compared to only 4 per cent of those on the highest incomes (above £24,000). At least three quarters of those living in housing which is unfit or in serious disrepair had incomes of less than £12,000 in 1996.[25]

Regional variations have long been pronounced when it comes to housing conditions. A survey in 2000[26] drawing on a range of unpublished data concluded that a line could be drawn from the Wash to the Bristol Channel. Above the line, conditions are generally worse, with south Wales, rural Wales and Scotland, the industrial areas of north England, especially north-west England, and some parts of the Midlands standing out for poor quality. The only real exception to the higher standards found in southern England is in some London boroughs. In northern England there is now little or no housing demand in many areas and housing conditions are generally poor. A study by Sheffield Hallam University of eighteen housing associations and councils in the cities of Newcastle, Salford, Manchester, Sheffield, Liverpool and Leeds paints a picture of sink housing estates where poor conditions are made worse by social disadvantage.[27] Another study, focusing on Manchester and Newcastle, found that poverty and joblessness were more significant causes of low demand than the quality of the housing itself, with the decline of large-scale manufacturing during the 1980s and 1990s having had a major impact.[28] Whatever the causes, it is clear that the situation has got worse during Labour's tenure, with up to 60 per cent of English councils reporting that an increasing number of homes are difficult to let, the majority being in northern England.

In Scotland, a comprehensive survey by Scottish Homes published in October 1997 painted a grim picture of the condition of the country's housing.[29] One in four houses (representing 534,000 properties) suffered from dampness or condensation, based on surveyors' assessments.[30] New data produced for a successor survey in 2002 suggested no significant improvement in housing conditions.

Scottish housing is plagued by poor energy efficiency, forcing people on low incomes to spend a much greater share of their income on energy than the wealthy. One third of low-income households have to spend more than 20 per cent of their income on energy. In May 2003, the leading environmental health body, the Royal Environmental Health Institute of Scotland, found that as many as 88,000 properties failed to meet the basic habitation standards laid down in the Housing (Scotland) Act 1987 and some of these lacked basic amenities – 3,500 lacked a bath or fixed shower, and half of those had to share whatever washing facilities existed with other households.

Poor housing in Britain is often located in poor areas – over half of all dwellings in poor neighbourhoods were classified as non-decent by the 2001 House Condition Survey. Whether or not a house is adequate, the surrounding area is important to residents. The UN Committee on Economic, Social and Cultural Rights has emphasised that the right to adequate housing includes the right to enjoy a safe and clean local environment with decent amenities for all. The House Condition Survey found 2.5 million dwellings affected by substantial problems connected to heavy traffic and parking; one million by poorly maintained or neglected buildings, private gardens and public spaces; and 500,000 by vandalism, graffiti and boarded-up buildings – some were affected by more than one of these problems. A comprehensive survey of English housing carried out for the ODPM during 2003/4 found that around half of households perceived crime, litter, traffic and/or vandalism and hooliganism as problems in their area. According to the ODPM, with the exception of litter and traffic, these figures reflect a marked improvement on recent years.

It is a terrible indictment of the world's fifth largest economy that a third of its homes are not considered to be of a decent habitable standard and nearly a million are unfit to live in. In its 2002 report on the UK, the UN Committee on Economic Social and Cultural Rights expressed concern about the poor quality of housing and the fuel poverty experienced by many families and individuals and recommended that immediate remedial measures be taken. The scale of the task of achieving fitness should not be under-estimated – the average cost of making a home decent is £7,200, representing a total cost of £50 billion; 40 per cent require expenditure of up to £1,000 per dwelling, while 10 per cent need £20,000 or more.

It was only in its second term that the government seemed ready to try and get to grips with the problem of poor housing. The investment of nearly £5 billion in housing during the first parliament was quite insufficient to fulfil a grand policy objective of 'offer[ing] everyone the opportunity of a decent home and so promot[ing] social cohesion, well-being and self-dependence'.[31] Labour's 2001 manifesto made a commitment to 'reducing by a third the backlog of substandard housing by 2004', and the party has set itself a target to 'eliminate fuel poverty in vulnerable households in England by 2010' (fuel poverty is a responsibility of the devolved administrations).[32] There is also an ambitious strategy for improving existing council stock. Outlined in the 2003 paper *Sustainable Communities*[33] the strategy mostly consists of a target of bringing all stock up to a decent standard by 2010. The public service agreement (PSA) enforcing this objective (which now covers all social housing stock and some private sector housing) states that the intention is 'by 2010, [to] bring all social housing into a decent condition with most of this improvement taking place in deprived areas, and for vulnerable households in the private sector, including families with children, [to] increase the proportion who live in homes that are in decent condition'.

Homelessness

Homelessness is the most acute form of housing distress. People living and sleeping on the streets are a minority of the homeless; there are also families and individuals living in temporary accommodation (such as hostels, bed and breakfast accommodation, night shelters, squats, living with relatives and friends). Half a million more live in overcrowded conditions. The rate of homelessness in the UK is incompatible with international human rights obligations. The Commons Select Committee on Housing, Planning, Local

Government and the Regions noted in January 2005 that 'every person has the right to a secure home . . . The Government should aim not to reduce homelessness but to eradicate it.'[34] Unfortunately such an objective seems far off. The UN Committee on Economic, Social and Cultural Rights drew attention to the failure of successive governments to remedy homelessness in its 1997 report, just as Labour was coming into office, and deplored the continued failure to protect vulnerable groups such as travellers and ethnic minorities.[35]

But Labour failed to respond. Homelessness worsened considerably in its first term, rising by a third in two successive years and reaching 166,760 households, or 400,000 people, by 2000. Some 104,770 people were officially recognised by local authorities as being in priority need for accommodation.[36] London had by far the worst problem, with 48,000 families officially recognised as being homeless – the highest level for twenty years. Moreover, official statistics do not tell the whole story and can be manipulated to the disadvantage of the homeless. They excluded most of the 41,000 people living in hostels and squats and 78,000 couples or lone parents sharing accommodation because they could not set up their own home.[37] Further, it is known that between 1996 and 1998 substantial numbers of households, perhaps 200,000, were probably kept off the local authority registers that grade people in housing need.[38] The charity Crisis recently estimated that there were 380,000 'hidden homeless' people – including those who do not approach a local authority, or do not meet the necessary statutory criteria.[39] Moreover, Shelter revealed early in 2005 that some two thirds of council housing staff they interviewed said that they felt under pressure to reduce the number of people they accepted as homeless.[40]

Such figures are alarming. The insecurities of homelessness impact on the other economic and social rights, such as health, education and social security, of these usually vulnerable people. The effects on the health of people sleeping rough and families living in bed and breakfast accommodation are well documented.[41] Crisis's December 2002 report found that homeless people were forty times more likely than other citizens not to have access to a family doctor, instead having to rely on hospital casualty units once a medical problem became serious. Nearly two in five of those surveyed were not registered with a GP – the figure for the population as a whole is 1 per cent – and more than half of them had had no contact with a doctor during the previous year. Moreover, homeless people often do not receive the social support they need. In January 2003 the Audit Commission criticised the extensive use of bed and breakfast and other forms of temporary accommodation and the weak priority given to preventing homelessness.[42]

The government's real achievement has been the 'rough sleepers' initiative. The figure for rough sleepers has now bottomed out at around 500 (504 for 2003, 508 for 2004). Over half of rough sleepers are in Greater London – with 175 of a national total of 508 in the City of Westminster alone. (Though, as homeless charities argue, putting a roof temporarily over people's heads is only a start; to meet its international obligations, the government must give rough sleepers the social support required to reintegrate them in society.) In its 2002 report, the UN Committee on Economic, Social and Cultural Rights praised the new measures taken to reduce homelessness and rough sleeping, but expressed concern about the persistent homelessness among ethnic minorities, those with alcohol and mental health problems and other vulnerable groups.[43]

Labour has been committed since its 1997 manifesto to legislate for a preventative strategy in place of simply responding piecemeal to crises and setting one-off targets. A Homes Bill was held up in the Lords in 2001 and fell at the general election. The Homelessness Act 2002 required local authorities to put in place five-yearly action plans to tackle homelessness, to conduct annual censuses of rough sleeping, and to give temporary accommodation to unintentionally homeless people in priority need until they can be provided with more permanent housing. The Act also insisted on new safeguards to prevent homeless families with children and vulnerable homeless people being housed in inappropriate private rented accommodation.

More importantly, the government added new vulnerable groups to those already recognised as being 'in priority need'.[44] This is the passport to re-housing under the Housing Act 1996, which entitles homeless people in priority groups to social housing – broadly, families with dependent children, those living in unsanitary or overcrowded conditions, those vulnerable due to older age and others with certain welfare and medical needs. New regulations added vulnerable sixteen- and seventeen-year-olds, young people leaving care, people in danger of violence or harassment, and ex-service people, offenders and others from an institutionalised background to those being recognised as being in need; and the government allocated nearly £200 million over two years to meet the costs. But despite an earlier amendment tabled by the Liberal Democrats, the protection of these groups was not included in the primary legis-lation, arguably making their entitlement less secure. The Act still leaves local authorities with discretionary powers to refuse accom-modation, for example, on the grounds that a family or someone in priority need have intentionally made themselves homeless, and to exclude or suspend people from tenancies for arbitrary reasons; and the courts refuse to intervene even on behalf of families in desperate need that is officially recognised (see Chapter 4, page 61).

The need for such an Act was made evident by the continuing toll of homelessness: the official figures for 2003, just a year later, reached their highest level since records began in 1976 – a staggering 135,590 households. Even today, the official figures show 127,760 households accepted as homeless and in priority need for 2004, although it should be added that these figures increased partly because more groups of people were considered to be in priority need. Never-theless, temporary housing for homeless people, and especially the continuing high, though falling, use of bed and breakfast accommodation, remains a scar on the government's record. The government does recognise the scale of this problem and one aim of the ODPM five-year plan, published in January 2005, is to cut the use of temporary housing for homeless people by half by 2010. Since April 2004, local authorities have not been permitted to place homeless families with children in bed and breakfast accommodation for longer than six weeks.

Scotland

One part of the UK that does seem to have adopted the human rights principle of the progressive realisation of rights to housing, at least in legislative terms, is Scotland. In 2003 the Scottish Executive was awarded the Housing Rights Protector Award by the Centre on Housing Rights and Evictions, a leading international housing non-governmental organisation, for its Homelessness Act 2003. The centre described the Act as the most progressive in Europe. The legislation, largely developed from the work of a task force, effectively guarantees the right of access to adequate housing for everybody within ten years. It seeks to achieve this by gradually expanding the categories of people defined as being in 'priority housing need' and giving households classified as intentionally home-less accommodation with greater social support. The Act adopts a multi-agency approach, demonstrating the indivisibility and inter-dependence of different economic and social rights. It gives ministers the power to make regulations banning the use of unsuitable accom-modation, such as bed and breakfast, and requires local councils to accommodate homeless people who apply for re-housing in their area rather than shuffling them off, as many councils do, to other areas where they have a local connection.

But progressive legislation is only half the story – local authorities must have sufficient resources to implement the Act. A study for Shelter Scotland in May 2003, noting that the number of households living in temporary accommodation had risen by 147 per cent since the Labour–Liberal Democrat coalition assumed power, found that 85 per cent of Scottish councils considered they had insufficient temporary housing to cope with demand already created by the previous Housing (Scotland) Act 2001.

Exclusions and suspensions

Anti-social behaviour, sometimes racially inspired, is an increasingly severe problem around Britain. Too often violence, vandalism, disturbances and noise cause great distress to people in many localities. But the growing use of anti-social behaviour orders, often against children, raises general civil liberties concerns. In housing, Shelter has expressed concern that local authorities and social landlords exclude or suspend people from tenancies for unproven anti-social behaviour. Shelter also argues that some local authorities operate punitive and wide-ranging exclusion policies for rent arrears caused solely by delays in payments of housing and other benefits.

Before Labour took office, local authorities already had discretion under the Housing Act 1996 to run introductory tenancy schemes of a year, during which time it is easier for them to evict tenants for anti-social behaviour. This policy has been upheld in the face of challenges under the Human Rights Act. Like other policies directed towards anti-social behaviour, it falls unfairly upon those in social housing, as opposed to private tenants or owner-occupiers, who are also capable of anti-social behaviour.

The Homelessness Act 2002 removed the power of local authorities to operate blanket exclusions of categories of people from social housing, but people may be treated as ineligible for housing because of their behaviour. If a person or household becomes home-less as a result of their anti-social behaviour they may be deemed 'intentionally homeless' – meaning the local authority is under no obligation to secure them permanent accommodation. There is evidence that the government would like to go further still but is constrained by human rights safeguards. In 2002 a private member's Bill was introduced that was designed to deny housing benefit to households guilty of persistent anti-social behaviour. The government sympathised with the Bill's objective but it fell. Now, however, similar proposals are emerging in the government's 'respect' agenda.

A study by Shelter in Scotland of approximately 36,000 cases found a distinct lack of due process and consistency in the processes that councils and social landlords adopt towards evictions for anti-social behaviour.[45] Very few operated clear written procedures, appeals systems were seriously under-used and monitoring was poor. Some social landlords operated blanket policies that did not allow individual circumstances to be taken into account; others employed discretionary policies that were open to abuse. Two in five landlords excluded at least some people merely on suspicion of anti-social behaviour as opposed to concrete evidence.

There is a clear need for common standards and regulation. The government's housing Green Paper in 2000 said that people should be suspended from allocation processes only in exceptional circumstances, but the subsequent Homelessness Act did not contain any safeguards or rights of appeal against arbitrary action. And in April 2002 Stephen Byers, then the local government minister, announced sweeping new powers to enable landlords to evict anti-social tenants. 'We are not on an eviction crusade,' he said, but the homeless charities, Crisis and Shelter, feared that the measures were badly timed at a period when the rate of home possession orders taken out against council and housing association tenants had doubled within the space of eight years. These measures would make anti-social behaviour a mandatory ground for possession, thus opening up the prospect of automatic eviction and removing the discretion the courts now have to respond leniently according to the individual circumstances.

Vulnerable groups

Widening categories of people are given priority status for housing because of their vulnerability, as we report above.[46] However, certain groups, most notably asylum seekers, continue to be excluded; and certain groups experience disadvantage and discrimination in housing.

Ethnic minorities

People from the ethnic minorities are vulnerable to homelessness and poor housing conditions. Official figures state that in 2004 73 per cent of homelessness acceptances in priority need were white people, 10 per cent were African/Caribbean (clearly a high figure), 5 per cent were Indians, Pakistanis and Bangladeshis, and 6 per cent were of other ethnic origin, with 5 per cent not known. In 1996, half of all residents of emergency homeless hostels in London were from ethnic minorities, and of them 12 per cent were refugees or asylum seekers.[47] Other surveys and advice agencies have found that younger people from ethnic minorities are very vulnerable to homelessness, especially among those who are not employed. Their homelessness is often 'hidden' as they tend to stay with friends or relatives rather than sleep rough.[48]

Minority communities in inner city areas suffer from over-crowding and poor housing conditions. The English Housing Survey found that 46 per cent of Asian and 36 per cent of black households lived in non-decent homes (the figure for white households is 32.5 per cent). Asian and black households were also more overcrowded in their homes, and were nearly three times as likely to live in poor neighbourhoods as white households.[49] Bangladeshi and Pakistani families experienced the worst and most isolated conditions and often had insufficient bedrooms to meet their needs while black Caribbeans are better housed, primarily as a result of moving into public housing in the 1970s. But generally local authorities tend to discriminate against the ethnic minorities in the allocation of housing; officials restrict their access to waiting lists and offer them poorer quality housing. The failure of local housing departments to keep desegregated data on their ethnic minority clients and hence to monitor their work and promote equal opportunities only exacerbates the problem.[50]

Asylum seekers and refugees

The position of refugees and asylum seekers is especially insecure under continuing legislation, which removes benefit and housing entitlements from those who fail to register immediately on entry while prohibiting access to work. Under the Asylum and Immigration Act 2004, failed refugee families who have not left the UK are also refused benefits and welfare services and may have their children taken into care. Local authorities tend to deny asylum seekers access to social housing. In April 2000 nearly 32,000 destitute asylum seekers (including families with children) were living in temporary accommodation in London.[51] Those in private rented accommodation scarcely fared better. A Shelter report in January 2001 took data from five environmental health departments on 154 dwellings housing 309 refugees, including 48 children. One in five were unfit through disrepair or lack of cooking facilities; one in five were infested. Houses were often damp with mouldy walls and little or no heating.[52] Nearly all the properties in multiple occupation were unfit, with unacceptably high fire risks in 83 per cent of them. One in three did not have enough beds for the occupants. The report revealed that the authorities did not inspect such properties to ensure that they met statutory minimum standards before they moved asylum seekers in, and they encouraged overcrowding by paying landlords per person rather than per unit of accommodation.

Some asylum seekers may be able to obtain accommodation under the 'Hard Cases' scheme, administered by the National Asylum Support Service (NASS), part of the Immigration and Nationality Directorate, though the availability of Hard Cases support was restricted by the Nationality, Immigration and Asylum Act 2002. And it seems NASS is not culturally disposed towards promoting economic and social rights. It did its best to keep potential claimants in the dark as to the existence of Hard Cases support. In October 2003 the High Court ruled that NASS had been unlawfully withholding information on the scheme in order to avoid more applications being made. Up to that point, its only published guidance on Hard Cases had been in a letter to the Refugee Council in November 2001. Placing asylum support within the Home Office may have been administratively neat, but has possibly meant that the dispersal of necessary benefits and assistance has become increasingly subordinate to the desire to discourage asylum seekers from coming to the country and to encourage those who are here to leave, even at the expense of their housing and other rights.

The impact of government policy upon the lives of asylum seekers continues to be devastating. The Refugee Council announced the findings of a survey in February 2004 that showed that 61 per cent of asylum seekers seen by refugee organisations were sleeping rough. In April 2004, the council issued a report, *Hungry and Homeless*, based on a broader survey showing that three quarters of clients of refugee organisations were sleeping rough. Many clients were refused support, despite applying for asylum within a few days of arrival. Clients had physical and mental health problems, lacked essential items such as clothes and toiletries, experienced hunger and were denied emergency shelter. A report by the Refugee Council and

Refugee Action, based on their work in Leeds, London and Manchester with 116 failed asylum-seeking families targeted by the government in a pilot scheme designed to encourage them to go home, found that over half the families had all their state housing and welfare support withdrawn and a quarter of them had gone underground to avoid having their children taken into care, losing all contact with services and leaving themselves and their children acutely vulnerable. Some housing authorities refused to evict some of the families.

Roma

The housing needs of the Roma, travellers and gypsies, can differ significantly from those of the settled community. But attempts to provide for them can be discouraged by negative popular and media portrayals. The government often accedes to the negative image of travellers, even when purporting to assist them. The ODPM's five-year plan of January 2005 referred to the need for provision for gypsies and travellers, 'while taking action to tackle unauthorised development'. Given this environment, it is not surprising that the UN Committee on the Elimination of Racial Discrimination (in August 2003) expressed concerns about the continued discrimination against Roma in housing as in other areas of life, their experience of poor housing conditions and lack of available campsites.[53]

A particular issue for these groups is the need for camping sites, though this need varies between full-time or seasonal travellers and settled travellers (who suffer discrimination and racism in social housing). The Caravan Sites Act 1968 placed a duty on local authorities to provide accommodation for gypsies. But this obligation was repealed by the Criminal Justice and Public Order Act 1994. Local authorities have proved reluctant to provide sites for fear of offending local populations and attracting more travellers. Between 1994 and 2000, forty-nine caravan sites were closed down.[54] Officially travellers fall within the statutory definition of homelessness if they are without an authorised place to stop. By this token, 18 per cent of travellers are homeless, compared with 0.6 per cent of the settled population.[55] As a result, there are an estimated 3,000 unauthorised sites. The result is a cycle of trespass and eviction for many travellers. Those without permanent sites also find it hard to access health and education services – not to mention basic amenities such as running water, electricity and sanitation – and tend to be over-represented on nearly all indices of deprivation. Where sites are provided, they are rarely suitable for other residential use, are usually remote from services and amenities, and are more likely to suffer from heavy traffic, intrusive industry, dereliction, vandalism, and so on.[56]

The government provided £16 million over three years from 2001 to refurbish authorised sites. But far more needs to be done. Housing laws rarely cover caravan sites and gypsies on these sites have less security of tenure than any other residents: they can be evicted within twenty-eight days from a site they have occupied for years. Permanent and transit sites should be brought within the broader housing and planning laws to allow for more security and better-planned facilities.[57]

The Housing Act 2004 requires local housing authorities to assess the needs of and produce strategies for gypsies and travellers in their area. These are fine words, but local authorities are reluctant voluntarily to provide sites for them and succumb to pressures to try and prevent them making their own arrangements. There is a clear case for the government to restore the duty on local authorities to provide sites, as recommended by the Commons Housing Select Committee in 2003 and 2004.

Women, young people and children

Home ownership among women has risen over the last twenty years, though they still lag behind men, be they married or unmarried. Some categories of women are also more vulnerable to housing problems than men. Young and older women, single mothers on low incomes, those trying to escape abusive and violent relationships and ethnic minority women are all more likely to be homeless or live in poor housing. Single mothers are significantly at risk of homelessness and life in temporary accommodation or bed and breakfast.[58] Such insecurity harms not only the physical health of the mothers and their children, but also their mental health. Ethnic minority women tend to be more vulnerable to homelessness and poor housing conditions than white women and are liable to suffer racial abuse or damage to their homes.[59]

Financial hardship often puts young people, especially those leaving care and other sixteen-year-olds, at risk of homelessness. Although they may now be classified as in 'priority need' under the Homelessness Act 2002, a restriction to housing benefit for single people under twenty-five living in private rented homes often means that the benefit for a significant minority of young people does not match the rent and the shortfall can be so large as to be unmanageable.[60] The average shortfall is around £35 a week. Few of them know of the hardship fund that is available, though only in 'exceptional circumstances'.

Children are notable casualties of the housing crisis. More than 900,000 families with children live in poor housing conditions; more than 300,000 families with children live in overcrowded conditions; and in excess of 100,000 children become homeless each year.[61] They are not always properly supported by official authorities. An extreme example of systemic failure is that of the Victoria Climbié case. She was murdered through systematic abuse, dying in February 2000. In January 2003 the Laming inquiry into her death found significant errors in the way that the housing services in three London boroughs dealt with her case and a failure to coordinate with social services which could have prevented her death.[62] In the same month the Audit Commission found that fewer than a quarter of local authorities offered satisfactory help and advice to homeless families and recommended improved joint working with social services.[63]

The Chancellor of the Exchequer's Child Poverty Review was announced as part of the 2003 Budget. Included in its terms of reference was the devising of policies to 'improve the effectiveness of public services that tackle material deprivation, for instance housing and homelessness'. It was published with the July 2004 Spending Review[64] and noted that in 2002/3 2.6 million children lived in low-income households in Britain. It found that the number of families placed in temporary accommodation had risen from around 11,000 to nearly 100,000 over twenty years. Nearly two thirds of those families included dependent children or a pregnant woman. Only 29 per cent of homeless children attended mainstream schools. Loss of access to other services, as well as to networks of family and friends, was likely. Some 400,000 vulnerable families with children lived in non-decent homes in the private sector, 380,000 in the public sector. The review found that children living in bed and breakfast accommodation were twice as likely to be admitted to hospital and two fifths of children in temporary accommodation for a year developed mental health problems.

Older and disabled people

People over the age of fifty, and especially those aged over eighty, tend to have low incomes and to live in some of the oldest – and worst – housing stock.[65] Nine out of ten older people continue to live in their own homes, either owned or rented. Only 5 per cent live in sheltered housing and another 5 per cent in institutional care.[66] Many of them live in unfit properties built before 1914. Their homes are often cold and damp and they cannot afford to heat them. The link between low income and poor housing among older people is strong. The English Housing Condition Survey found that although older people were only a little more likely than other age groups to be living in a non-decent home, they were much more likely to do so when their incomes were low.

A small but significant minority of older people is homeless – that is, living in temporary accommodation or actually sleeping rough. In 2004, of the 127,760 households accepted in priority need, 3,740 were deemed vulnerable due to a member's older age. The UK Coalition on Older Homelessness (composed of Age Concern, Help the Aged and the National Homeless Alliance) has estimated that as many as 7,840 older people live in unsuitable hostel accommodation in London and a further 13,200 outside the capital. Moreover, nearly 27,000 older people also referred themselves to bed and breakfast hotels and thereby failed to access statutory or voluntary support. Surveys have shown that between about 10 and 35 per cent of street and hostel dwellers are aged sixty or over. Taking into account these trends, the Commons select committee responsible for scrutinising housing policy argued in January 2005 that all older people should be treated as in priority need for housing, whether or not they were vulnerable. The government did not agree to this proposal.[67]

One in four households in non-decent homes include somebody who is long-term ill or disabled.[68] In 2002, the first national survey of the housing needs of disabled children and their families[69] found that they experience considerably more problems with unsuitable housing than other families. Nine out of ten families with a severely disabled child report at least one significant difficulty, while one in four identify six or more problems. But few families with disabled children receive help with housing needs from statutory agencies, and no single agency takes lead responsibility.[70]

Conclusion

Housing stands at the crossroads of deprivation in British society. A decent home provides the soundest foundation for good health, a good education and taking work and other opportunities. The absence of a decent home contributes to deprivations across the board. After 1945, governments stood or fell upon their ability to build homes, but from the 1970s onwards governments gave housing supply an increasingly low priority and switched their attention to the growth of owner occupation. The most urgent need now is building social housing for rent to satisfy desperate shortages in urban and rural areas. But still the government gives priority to expanding owner occupation for those on intermediate incomes. This is a policy that makes electoral sense, but at the expense of those on lower incomes.

10

Education, education, education

The oft-repeated mantra by Tony Blair, Prime Minister since 1997, that his top three priorities in government are 'education, education, education' has led to record levels of investment in all stages of education and a drive to raise the educational achievement of the whole population. Although this record investment has not yet reached the levels of many of the UK's major European partners, an incidental by-product is that government policy has improved access to, but not guaranteed, the education rights enshrined in the International Covenant on Economic, Social and Cultural Rights (ICESCR). However, those rights are not enshrined in UK domestic law. This approach was summed up by the report of the UN special rapporteur on the right to education in the United Kingdom in 1999 when she said: 'Silence prevails with regard to the right to education and even more with regard to rights in education.'[1]

The UK government, and the separate administrations for Northern Ireland, Scotland and Wales, are, however, making progress in establishing rights for children through putting duties on public bodies. England is the last of the four UK countries to establish a children's commissioner under the Children Act 2004. The England commissioner, who also has a UK-wide remit for promoting the interests of children in areas not devolved to the separate administrations, must have regard to relevant provisions of the UN Convention on the Rights of the Child. A key task of the commissioner is to be concerned with the views and interests of children and in particular their well-being with regard to various issues, including their education, as part of the Every Child Matters programme. Local authorities are in turn charged with making arrangements to promote the well-being and education of children.

This development is at an early stage and will almost certainly lead to demands for more rights for children, but these changes are not, on the whole, being led by the UK's international treaty obligations.

The Human Rights Act 1998

The one explicit reference to the UK's treaty obligations in domestic law is the Human Rights Act 1998. The Human Rights Act 1998 gives a qualified right to education, which is enforceable in the UK courts by way of Article 2 of the first protocol to the European Convention on Human Rights. The right, though, is expressed negatively: 'No person shall be denied the right to education.'[2] It then goes on to require the state to enable education to be available in conformity with the religious and philosophical convictions of parents. There is a UK reservation that parental convictions have to be met only if they are 'compatible with the provision of efficient education and training and the avoidance of unreasonable expenditure' for the state.[3]

Looking back in 2006 on the Human Rights Act eight years after enactment, it is possible to conclude that the effect has not been significant. There has been a trickle of cases testing Article 2 in the UK courts but, as Simon Whitbourn, consultant to EMIE at the National Foundation for Educational Research, argues, areas where UK law was not compliant with the European Convention had already been tested in the European Court of Human Rights and reformed as a consequence.[4]

International conventions

A right to education in one form or another appears in many of the treaties and conventions to which the UK is a signatory. For example, Article 26 of the UN Universal Declaration of Human Rights begins: 'Everyone has the right to education.' The UN Convention on the Rights of the Child proclaims that state signatories must 'recognise the right of the child to education and with a view to achieving this right progressively and on the basis of equal opportunity' (Article 28).

This chapter is about the right to education contained in Article 13 of the ICESCR. The historical and legal context is explained, and

UK government policy examined in the light of each paragraph of Article 13. Mention is made of under-performing groups in the light of Articles 2(2) and 3 on non-discrimination. For reasons of space, this chapter is mainly concerned with the legislation as it applies in England.

In its General Comments on the covenant, the UN Committee on Economic, Social and Cultural Rights has described Article 13 as 'the most wide ranging and comprehensive article on the right to education in international human rights law'.[5]

Article 13 states why education is important and what it should enable people to do. The article goes on to specify, for each phase of education, what a developing education system should achieve for learners. The conditions of teaching staff should be improved. Parents must be allowed to choose a school which conforms to their own convictions although education does not necessarily have to be provided at the state's expense. Anybody can establish an educational institution as long as its objectives are consistent with the covenant and it conforms to minimum standards of provision.

The UK context

There are common aspects to educational provision throughout the United Kingdom. For example, compulsory schooling begins at the age of five years, and overall expenditure is controlled by the Treasury. However, responsibility for institutional resourcing, the curriculum, improvement of provision, equality compliance and staff employment is widely dispersed because of the different governance arrangements in the four United Kingdom countries and the move to greater devolution of decision-making and institutional autonomy in the latter part of the twentieth century.

The four UK countries each have their own national education system. Historically, the Scottish system was the first to develop and has many unique features: for example, there is no prescribed school curriculum, although there has been a long-standing advisory curriculum; local authorities have greater responsibility and school autonomy is less developed; the curriculum beyond the minimum school-leaving age and the Scottish Higher School Certificate support a broader range of subjects than the A-level-dominated curriculum elsewhere in the UK. The England and Wales systems are similar and have the same statutory basis. However, since devolution of responsibility to the National Assembly for Wales in 1999, the systems have begun to diverge although the Westminster Parliament still has responsibility to make primary legislation. As for Northern Ireland, thirty years of direct rule from Westminster has resulted in convergence between the education systems of England and the province, especially during the period from 1988 to 1996 as the Conservative government introduced the curriculum and assessment changes to Northern Ireland that had previously been introduced to England and Wales.

The school-leaving examination is an example of the relationship between the four systems. Introduced in the 1980s, the General Certificate of Secondary Education is used in England, Wales and Northern Ireland. The examination is set by five independent bodies, three based in England, one in Wales and one in Northern Ireland. The England qualifications body, the Qualifications and Curriculum Authority (QCA), leads on standards which are implemented by sister bodies in Wales and Northern Ireland. Scotland has a completely separate qualifications system.

In England, the Secretary of State for Education and Skills is the competent authority. The office holder sits in the UK Cabinet and is accountable to the Westminster Parliament. The national education department is the Department for Education and Skills (DfES). Responsibility for publicly provided school education is shared with an independent inspectorate, Ofsted (the Office for Standards in Education), the QCA, 150 elected local education authorities (LEAs) and the governing bodies of 23,300 schools. The Learning and Skills Council provides a strategic organisational overview of further education and training and funds the 400 further education and sixth form colleges, training provided by employers and in the private sector, publicly maintained school sixth forms and local authority adult education. Higher education is funded through the Higher Education Funding Council for England.

In Northern Ireland, because of the suspension of the Northern Ireland Executive, responsibility lies with the Secretary of State for Northern Ireland, who sits in the UK Cabinet and is accountable to the Westminster Parliament. Administrative responsibility is divided between the Department of Education Northern Ireland and the Department of Employment and Learning. The latter department funds the sixteen further education colleges and the four higher education institutions. There are five non-elected Education and Libraries Boards, which maintain or grant-aid 1,300 schools.

In Scotland, responsibility has been devolved to the Scottish Parliament. There are separate Ministers for Education and Young People (covering schools) and Enterprise and Lifelong Learning (covering post-schools learning). These ministers are members of the Scottish Executive, which is collectively accountable to the Parliament. There are thirty-two elected local authorities, responsible for 5,500 schools. There is direct funding of further and higher education.

In Wales, the competent authority is the National Assembly of Wales, although the Government of Wales Bill before the UK Parliament in the 2005/6 session separates the executive from the assembly, and the assembly gains additional legislation-making powers. There are twenty-two elected LEAs maintaining 2,000 schools. A few responsibilities remain with the Westminster-based Secretary of State for Education and Skills, such as teachers' pay.

Purpose and quality of education

Article 13(1) of the ICESCR sets out the objectives for the education system of each state:

> [Each state recognises] the right of everyone to education [that is] directed to the full development of the human personality and the sense of its dignity [and] strengthens respect for human rights and freedoms. They further agree that education shall enable all persons to participate effectively in a free society, promote understanding, tolerance and friendship among all nations and all racial, ethnic or religious groups, and further the activities of the United Nations for the maintenance of peace.

Assessing whether the UK, or any country, has met this standard is difficult. The General Comment on Article 13 states that since the covenant was adopted in 1966, other international instruments have further elaborated the objectives to which education should be directed and that education should conform to these instruments, including specific references to gender equality and respect for the environment.[6]

The Education Reform Act 1988 gave the first statutory aim for the school curriculum in England and Wales. Each school is required to have a balanced and broadly based curriculum which:

a) promotes the spiritual, moral, cultural, mental and physical development of pupils at the school and of society; and

b) prepares such pupils for opportunities, responsibilities and experiences of adult life.

The 1988 Act also introduced a national curriculum, which enabled the state to specify in great detail what should be taught. The 1999 revision of the curriculum established values, aims and purposes of the curriculum which are consistent with the covenant.

As mentioned above, assessing how well the education system in England achieves the 'full development of the human personality' and so on for each young person who participates in it is difficult. The main quality assessment tool, school inspection by Ofsted, essentially assesses education at system and school level, not at pupil level. Her Majesty's Chief Inspector of Schools summed up the 2004/5 school year thus: 'We have an improving education system and one that has the capacity for further improvement.' He judged that the majority of schools are effective and improving. The great majority of children are satisfied with their education.[7] However, no assessment is given as to whether the demanding objectives of the ICESCR are being achieved.

Of particular importance was the introduction of a citizenship curriculum, mandatory since 2000, for secondary school pupils, which actively supports the aims of the United Nations. Pupils have to be taught 'the legal and human rights and responsibilities under-pinning society', including the role of the United Nations. A non-statutory curriculum has been introduced for primary pupils.

The Chief Inspector of Schools' annual report for 2004/5 found that the performance of secondary schools at teaching citizenship was improving and that substantial developments have been made since its introduction. However, citizenship is marginalised in the curriculum in one fifth of schools. If schools are using the 'scheme of work' on human rights, available from the DfES website, to teach citizenship to fourteen- to sixteen-year-olds, then the young people will learn little of the covenant's economic, social and cultural rights. Examples of the rights described are civil and political rights: freedom from discrimination, fair trial, freedom from cruel and degrading punishment, the right to vote and so on, but there is no mention of the right to work, family protection, right to an adequate standard of living, and other socio-economic rights. As the UN special rapporteur noted,

> human rights are perceived as different from and alien to the rights and freedoms that learners will recognise in their everyday lives – their rights as subjects of the right to education, as future employees, as future parents or voters. 'Human rights' seems identified with international issues and foreign countries and dissociated even from concepts such as equal opportunities and gender equality.[8]

Right to education: UK government policy and law

Article 13(2) of the ICESCR sets out the right to education for each phase. Before a detailed look, some general comments are necessary. Children and young people in the UK have no right in domestic law to school, further education or higher education, except that in Scotland the Standards in Scotland's Schools etc. Act 2000 gives a right to school education for children.[9] Education is provided free to children and young people between the ages of three and nineteen years. There are very high participation rates in education from five to sixteen because parents and guardians are under a duty to ensure their children receive 'efficient full-time education suitable to the child's age, ability and aptitude' and any special educational need either through regular attendance at school or otherwise.[10] Vocational and further education (for those aged nineteen and over) and higher education are not free; see the description of higher education below for a discussion of recent changes on student contributions to higher education.

Children's rights and parental duties

The current UK arrangement, dating back to the nineteenth century, of placing a duty on the parent while not at the same time giving any rights to the child does produce anomalies. For example, the parents of a sixteen-year-old transferring to a new school for post-compulsory studies have to make the application. However, for the 21st-century education maintenance allowance, a means-tested allowance to support him/her in continuing to study, the young person has to make the application and receives the allowance.

When a pupil is excluded from school for alleged misbehaviour in England, it is possible to appeal to an independent panel, but if the child is under eighteen, it is the parent who has to decide whether to do so. In Wales, this anomaly has been recognised and, using the freedoms now acquired by the National Assembly of Wales, pupils over the age of eleven can appeal in their own right.[11] This is not to say that the child's voice is not listened to in England at critical episodes of his or her school career, it's just that it is only in Wales that the child has a right to be heard. There is also the possibility that appeals in England are not heard because the parent, for language reasons or otherwise, does not wish to appeal even though the pupil has a genuine issue which should be appealed.

As has been mentioned previously, the Every Child Matters programme may lead to a demand for specific education rights for children and young people. The government has recently recognised in law that children have views which relevant authorities must take into account. For example, Section 176 of the Education Act 2002 requires governing bodies to consult pupils and consider their views. Section 7 of the Education Act 2005 requires school inspectors when inspecting a school to take account of the views expressed by children attending the school. In Wales, under the School Councils (Wales) Regulations 2005, every school has to establish a school council in order to enable children to express a collective view on the operation of their school, and consideration is being given to requiring every school to establish a children's complaints procedure.

Availability of education

The ICESCR's General Comment on Article 13 indicates that certain conditions, related to the arrangements and resources prevailing in each state, must be met if the right to education is to be achieved. These are that educational institutions and programmes have to be available in sufficient quantity, the provision must be accessible to everyone without discrimination, the provision must be acceptable (relevant, culturally appropriate and of good quality) to students and the provision must be adaptable to the changing needs of society. The level of resourcing of education will have a bearing on these four criteria, although see below for a further discussion on accessibility and non-discrimination.

The late nineteenth-century debates on education in the UK established a consensus that compulsory education should be free and that the state should subsidise other educational provision. Support for free school education, though, has arguably been led by the need to have an educated and well-qualified workforce to support economic growth rather than a commitment to providing a right to education for all.

The UK government's record on investment in education is variable, especially when measured against the standard of the proportion of gross domestic product. Of the twenty-eight countries covered in the 2005 edition of the Organisation for Economic Co-operation and Development (OECD) publication *Education at a Glance*,[12] the UK came fifteenth for investment of GDP in education, using 2002 data. The performance was summed up in September 2005 by Andreas Schleicher, head of the OECD's indicator and analysis division, as showing that UK performance was 'a picture of stagnation' (as quoted in *the Times*).[13] Additional investment in education was minimal in the early 1990s and stood at 4.7 per cent of GDP in 1996/7. The Labour administration intends to increase investment to 5.6 per cent by 2007/8. The effect in cash terms looks more dramatic: DfES figures show that total expenditure in England in 1999/2000 was £33 billion, which is expected to rise to £64 billion by 2007/8.

An example of the under-investment in education in England is the ratio of qualified teachers to pupils. In the twenty-year period from 1984 to 2004, the ratio in maintained schools worsened from one teacher to 16.2 pupils to one to 17.0. In the same period, the ratio in independent schools improved from 1 to 11.6 to 1 to 9.4.[14] An international comparison of OECD countries using 2003 data places the UK twenty-fifth out of twenty-eight when ranked by favourable ratio of students to teaching staff for primary education. Only Turkey, Mexico and Korea had a worse pupil-to-teacher ratio.[15]

There are concerns about the cost of 'free' education. DfES research publicised by nine national organisations in August 2005 estimates that the parents of secondary school pupils spend on average £948.11 per year on their child's 'free' education, including uniform, PE kit, day trips, residential trips, classroom materials, music lessons and charity events. The DfES survey found that 55 per cent of respondents in the two lowest income groups found these costs difficult to meet. A report by Citizens Advice found that children whose parents cannot afford these costs may 'find themselves isolated, stigmatised and more likely to be bullied' and may also 'suffer academically if they cannot go on school trips, or cannot afford textbooks or lesson materials'.[16]

Primary education

Article 13(2)(a) of the ICESCR requires that 'primary education shall be compulsory and available free to all'. Parents in England and Wales had a duty placed on them by the Education Act 1876 to ensure that their children received efficient elementary instruction in reading, writing and arithmetic. In practice, it took until the mid-1890s for legislation and government policy to achieve sufficient free elementary-school places for all parents to discharge this duty, if they so wished, through the public education system, when compulsory education ran between the ages of five and twelve years. The elementary-school system was created by the state through locally elected school boards, which established new schools to complement the historic provision made by religious bodies. Gradually, the state took on the funding of education at the religious schools while leaving significant responsibilities with the religious bodies which founded the schools.

Although some children are educated at home and in the private sector, the great majority are registered at primary school, and those who are not are pursued by local authorities with an increasing array of legal devices, such as school attendance orders, education supervision orders and parenting orders. Attendance remains a problem: the proportion of half-days missed in primary schools was 5.43 per cent in 2004/5 (down from 6.06 per cent in 1996/7).[17] There are no reliable figures on the number of primary-age children not in education of any sort. However, it remains a matter of concern for the state that there are children missing from education. The DfES White Paper *Higher Standards, Better Schools for All* in 2005 stated that the government intends to place a duty on local authorities to identify such children. This task will be assisted by the new information databases under the Children Act 2004 being developed to assist professionals to share information about children in need.

In England, government policy since the mid-1990s has achieved a significant expansion of education and child-care provision for under-fives. Local authorities have to secure free part-time early-years education places for a minimum of five 2½-hour sessions per week, thirty-three weeks per year, for all parents who want the provision. The DfES provisional estimate for January 2005 is that 98 per cent of three- and four-year-olds have educational provision, although there is no duty on parents to ensure their children are educated.[18] The government consulted in 2005 on implementing one of the manifesto commitments from that year's general election, of halving child poverty by 2010/11, to ensure every child gets the best start in life as part of the objective of abolishing child poverty.[19] Specific proposals include developing early-years provision further and abolishing the legal distinction between education and child care for under-fives, requiring local authorities to secure sufficient child-care from birth and rationalising the charging regime. Education is currently free although parents are expected to pay for child care. The intention is to make child care affordable for all through remission of fees for parents who are unemployed or on low wages.

Secondary, further and vocational education
Article 13(2)(b) of the ICESCR states that 'secondary education in its

different forms, including technical and vocational secondary education, shall be made generally available and accessible to all by every appropriate means, and in particular by the progressive introduction of free education'. Free secondary and vocational education was achieved from the mid-1940s in the United Kingdom for those under the age of nineteen, although the parental duty to ensure their children are efficiently educated was last extended in 1972, when the age for compulsory attendance was raised to sixteen. Virtually all children are enrolled at an educational establishment up to that age, although the variable quality of educational provision is the subject of the October 2005 government White Paper *Higher Standards, Better Schools for All*. This is discussed further below. As with primary education, attendance remains a problem: the proportion of half-days missed in secondary schools was 9.07 per cent in 2004/5, up from 7.82 per cent in 1996/7.[20] Education and training between the ages of sixteen and nineteen years is not compulsory.

The expansion of secondary education occurred during the middle decades of the twentieth century, with new secondary schools being established while leaving the existing selective grammar schools untouched. During the 1960s and early 1970s many state-maintained secondary schools were reorganised to ensure an intake of pupils with a comprehensive range of abilities. Disquiet about comprehensive schools in the 1980s led the Conservative administration to enable some secondary schools to become 'grant-maintained schools', and a limited number of independent but state-funded city technology colleges were created. These new types of school were allowed to select a proportion of pupils by aptitude or ability.

On the whole, the current Labour government has not promoted comprehensive education enthusiastically and has left the previous administration's selection policies in place. Selective secondary education still affects the parental choice of secondary school for approximately a quarter of all children in 2005. The Labour administration since 1997 has added to the different types of school with foundation schools and academies while preserving the historic religious schools and promoting new ones, particularly for the new faith communities in the UK. In addition, schools have received various designations for subject specialisms, teacher-training expertise and 'leading edge' and 'beacon' status. A major theme has been to encourage diversity to improve the parental choice of school, leading to a concern that there has been a reduction in social mobility and a widening of the achievement gap between the best- and worst-performing schools. This is discussed further below.

There is a significant independent sector in England. Although only about 7 per cent of pupils attend independent schools, the places are not evenly spread throughout the country. Roughly half of the places are in London and the south-east.

Britain has one of Europe's lowest post-16 participation rates. In 2002, for example, three quarters of seventeen-year-olds were in education and training, while participation rates in OECD countries varied from 100 per cent in Belgium to about a third in Mexico. Britain was twenty-fourth out of the twenty-eight countries ranked. In a 2005 White Paper,[21] the government launched various initiatives to improve the 14–19 education phase and reform the qualifications system to improve the staying-on rate.

Higher education

Article 13(2)(c) of the ICESCR states that 'higher education shall be made equally accessible to all, on the basis of capacity, by every appropriate means, and in particular by the progressive introduction of free education'. Government policy on higher education since the 1960s is that it should be increased and access widened. Access to higher education was an issue of controversy during the 1990s as the then Conservative government introduced student loans to replace means-tested student maintenance grants. There was further controversy in the late 1990s when the Labour government introduced a requirement that undergraduates contribute to their course fees and at the same time set a target of achieving a 50 per cent participation rate in higher education for under-thirties by 2010. Variable tuition fees will be introduced in 2006 under the Higher Education Act 2004 in England; this is likely to result in a significant increase in course fees. A new means-tested maintenance system is being introduced to encourage students from low-income families to participate in higher education, and the requirement that course fees must be paid up front will be abolished and replaced by loans, to be repaid on a sliding scale in line with income, with any outstanding debt written off after twenty-five years. The 2004 Act also introduced a 'fair access' to higher education, which gives higher education institutions targets to broaden their intake and ensure that all social groups can gain fair access. At this stage it is too early to say what the effect will be on the take-up of student places in 2006. However, fears over the increase in fees have led to an 8 per cent increase in the number of students who started courses in 2005. Scotland continues not to charge fees and it is also proposed that the Welsh universities should drop fees.

The UN special rapporteur on the right to education reported in 1999 that the introduction of fees violated the UK's obligation under the ICESCR that access to higher education should be on an individual's capacity, and in any event equal access should be secured through 'progressive introduction of free education' and not the ability to pay. The rapporteur recommended that the government should 'prioritise its commitment to utilise funds generated within education to improve accessibility for disadvantaged categories'. The government would no doubt claim that the student support reforms introduced by the Higher Education Act 2004 meet this point, although the objective of free higher education has receded.

According to 2003 OECD data, the United Kingdom, at 48 per cent, is below the OECD average of 53 per cent for entry to 'tertiary type A' courses, to which degree-level courses are roughly equivalent.[22]

Adult and continuing education

Article 13(2)(d) of the ICESCR requires that 'Fundamental education shall be encouraged or intensified as far as possible for those persons who have not received or completed the whole period of their primary education'. The UK government has prioritised the improvement of adult basic skills. The national adult basic skills strategy, Skills for Life, aims to improve literacy, numeracy and English for those who struggle because it is not their first language. It is aimed at people over the age of sixteen who have not achieved basic school qualifications. A 1999 report[23] estimated that seven million people, or one in five adults in England, have poor literacy and numeracy skills. People with poor basic skills tend to be on lower incomes or unemployed and are more prone to ill health and social exclusion. The cost of poor basic skills among the workforce has been estimated at £10 billion annually and people with poor basic skills earn significantly below the average of those with sufficient basic skills. Skills for Life aims to help 1.5 million adults achieve a qualification recognising basic skills proficiency by 2007 and is being supported to the tune of £1.5 billion.

School development and teachers

Article 13(2)(e) of the ICESCR states: 'The development of a system of schools at all levels shall be actively pursued, an adequate fellowship system shall be established, and the material conditions of teaching staff shall be continuously improved.' The school system in England has been actively developed by the government since the early 1980s, with major statements on policy development and legislation being made almost annually. The system has been driven by curriculum reform to improve standards, for example the primary literacy and numeracy strategies coupled with an enhanced account-ability system which publishes inspection reports on every school and league tables of school performance. These performance tables are based on the assessment of children and young people carried out at the ages of eleven and fourteen along with GCSE and A-level results and their vocational equivalents. This system has highlighted inequalities between schools, which, coupled with greater parental awareness about the educational attainment of their own children, has arguably led to increasing covert selection of pupils by social class. The special rapporteur noted that 'inequalities between learners and schools tend to become accentuated and exacerbated, not perceived as a human rights issue that ought to be addressed so as to familiarise children to accepting and assisting their peers, but rather as a legitimate differentiation enhancing individualism and competitive-ness.'[24] One of the major themes tackled in *Higher Standards, Better Schools For All* is the inequality of school performance, and that social class remains a major determinant of educational success: 'Our goal is no less than to transform our school system by turning it from one focused on the success of institutions into one which is shaped and driven by the success, needs and aspirations of parents and pupils.'[25]

This chapter is not the place to comment on whether the UK government's latest prescription for the English school system will work. However, the government has placed at the centre of public debate the need to ensure that the system helps all children to develop their knowledge and skills and that a good education is available to every child in every community. The pity is that the government has reached this conclusion based on ideas of education producing 'human capital' and the need to ensure the UK economy is competitive, and not because education is a basic human right for all people.

The UK government's support for improving the material conditions of teachers has improved significantly since 1997. Pay has increased by approximately 20 per cent in real terms and school support staff have doubled in number to over 260,000, with more trained and qualified support staff playing leading roles in the classroom. These changes have not been without controversy. The Education Act 2002 introduced a new definition of a teacher, which enables support staff to take over certain teaching duties under the direction of a qualified teacher. The improved pay and promotion prospects have increasingly been linked to results and pupils' progress. As reflects the education funding relative to other OECD countries, teachers in England are paid around the average of the twenty-eight countries.

Parental choice and education in non-maintained schools
Article 13(3) of the ICESCR requires each state

> to have respect for the liberty of parents and, when applicable, legal guardians, to choose for their children schools, other than those established by the public authorities, which conform to minimum state educational standards, to ensure the religious and moral education of their children in conformity with their own convictions.

There is a fundamental duty on parents in the UK, as has been referred to above, to ensure that their children receive efficient full-time education suitable to their age, ability and aptitude and special educational needs by regular attendance at school or otherwise.

There is no requirement that a child attend a school provided by the state. The law on independent schools was recently reviewed and new provision made in the Education Act 2002. The state registers independent schools and inspects, or ensures that they are inspected by approved inspectors, against minimum standards for registration. Reports are published and schools can be, and are, closed down which do not meet these standards. Inspection reports are published. It is a criminal offence to run an unregistered independent school. There is an expectation that the curriculum of independent schools is suitable for the children in attendance and is appropriately broad. There is no requirement that children are educated in citizenship although no doubt most provide some education in human rights issues.

The standards, in terms of examination achievement, in many private schools are significantly higher than state schools, reflecting both the favourable class-based intake and the pupil-to-teacher ratio. The provisional 2005 GCSE results for England give the proportion of pupils in maintained schools who achieved five or more GCSE results at grades A★ to C as 53.8 per cent, while in the private sector the equivalent statistic is 92.6 per cent.[26] However, the quality of some independent schools has been criticised. Just before the introduction of the new standards, the chief inspector of schools commented that many private schools are worse run than their state counterparts.[27]

Schools with fewer than five pupils of compulsory school age, as long as they do not contain a child looked after by a local authority or a child with special educational needs, do not have to be registered. However, parents are advised to let their local authority know so that it can be assured that the education is appropriate and legal school attendance order proceedings are not commenced.

Freedom to establish private educational institutions
Article 13(4) of the ICESCR states: 'No part of this article shall be construed so as to interfere with the liberty of individuals and bodies to establish and direct educational institutions, subject [to] the principles set forth [above and] minimum standards as may be laid down by the State.' Individuals in the UK have absolute freedom to

establish educational institutions within minimum standards specified by the state (see above on parents' right to choose a non-maintained institution), and individuals and bodies can establish educational institutions at any level. There are a number of accepted safeguards in law: for example, individuals who have a criminal conviction for child abuse are not able to establish and manage a school even if they are not involved in direct work with children. The state also safeguards the power of bodies working in the higher education sector to award degrees. It is illegal for a body to award degrees without the permission of the state.

Conclusions

If the UK government's education performance is judged solely on Article 13 then on the whole it is satisfactory, not as the result of any specific plan to meet the standards contained in the article but through the business of government to extend and improve public services. The policies are in place and there is reasonable public funding to support their implementation, although the funding is not particularly generous when compared with other OECD countries. But there are problems. In particular, the commitment to introduce progressively expanded higher education is in conflict with the ICESCR's insistence on free education at this level and may well be undermined by the policy of charging students fees, albeit with generous relief for young people from low-income families. Another is the secondary school system, which ensures that parents with sufficient resources are able to obtain a form of education for their children which leads to higher examination outcomes and improved prospects for effective participation in society. This can be seen as a denial of the human rights of people who are not able to obtain such an education. However, to deny parents the right to secure education for their children at institutions not maintained by the state would also be a denial of a human right. The UK government would no doubt argue that it is attempting to secure the very best education for all children and would cite the White Paper *Higher Standards, Better Schools for All*.

The government's policies are based on the reasonable objectives of equipping the nation's workforce to compete in the international economy and improving parental satisfaction. There is beginning to be an objective 'to tailor education around the needs of each individual child', which would support a human rights perspective. There is, though, no commitment to develop policy from a human rights perspective, a point made strongly by the Joint Committee on Human Rights in its report on the covenant: 'Insufficient attention is currently given within government to the ways in which these rights [in the covenant] can be used to provide a point of reference in the development of policy and legislation.'[28]

The main characteristics of the right to education are that everyone has an equal access to educational provision and that school education should be free and compulsory. The right is nothing if the educational provision through one reason or another is conducive to racial or gender discrimination or religious intolerance and if children do not benefit as much as others solely because of their family background or other circumstances.

The non-discrimination provisions of the covenant
The literature on discrimination and under-achievement in the UK education systems is extensive and comes from the UK government, non-governmental organisations, academic bodies and the United Nations.[29] Discrimination is found on grounds of class, poverty and family background including refugees, gender, ethnicity including travellers, disability, and religious affiliation. Discrimination and under-achievement also occur with groups for which special provision is made: for example, those children who are excluded from school for misconduct and those who are detained by the criminal justice system. Children who are in public care also under-achieve in the education system.

Article 2 of the ICESCR makes clear, as has been explained elsewhere in this book, that governments must frame their policies with a view to achieving progressively the rights set out in the covenant and those rights must be exercised 'without discrimination of any kind as to race, colour, sex, language, religion, political or other opinion, national or social origin, property, birth or other status'. Article 3 requires that men and women should enjoy equally all economic, social and cultural rights.

The UK government has tackled, and continues to tackle, areas of under-achievement. Examples of this include the Aim Higher programme, which intends to encourage young people to think about the benefits and opportunities of higher education; especially young people from families with no tradition of higher education. The Aiming High programme to raise the achievement of ethnic minority pupils supports the raising of standards for all young people whatever their ethnic or cultural background so that 'all education policies truly address the needs of every pupil in every school'. Again, the government would argue, at least as far as its responsibility for England is concerned, and as shown in *Higher Standards, Better Schools for All*, that the whole thrust of its education policies is to provide the best education for each individual person, and that no person is held back from achieving his or her potential.

The English (and to some extent the whole UK) education system remains fundamentally class based. David Miliband MP, when Minister of State for School Standards at the DfES, frequently quoted evidence from the Programme for Internal Student Assessment study in 2000 to show the high level of average attainment of English school students compared to the other twenty-six countries in the study but also to show that the 'education system confirms socio-economic inequality, rather than challenging it'. England was sixth from the bottom on equality of achievement, nine countries below the average. DfES evidence shows that:

- poor children are still one third as likely to get five good GCSEs as their wealthier classmates;
- young people from unskilled backgrounds are more than five times less likely to enter higher education than those from professional backgrounds;
- the link between socio-economic status and educational achievement cuts in at a very early age, before primary school as well as within it.[30]

An example of the class-based nature of secondary schools is seen in the Sutton Trust report published in January 2006, which showed the social exclusiveness of 'high-achieving' comprehensive schools in terms of examination performance at sixteen. The overall proportion of pupils eligible for free school meals at the 200 highest-performing comprehensive schools is 5.6 per cent, compared to 11.5 per cent of children in the areas in which these schools are situated, and 14.3 per cent in secondary schools nationally. The study found that schools which control their own admissions are much more likely to be in the top 200 and are unlikely to be representative of the social mix of the area in which they are situated.[31]

It is therefore no surprise that the debate within the Labour Party during winter 2005–6 has been about who gets into which school and changing the law to place duties on local authorities and schools to ensure a fair and equitable distribution of pupils between schools. What has been missing from the debate has been the vision, supported by the UK's international treaty obligations, that education is a human right which the state must accord to all citizens. Schools are there not just to help the children of the middle classes to secure professional advancement, but are the means by which the children of economically, socially, and culturally marginalised persons can be equipped to play a full part in society and break the cycle of poverty and exclusion.

Justiciability

As has been shown above, the likelihood is that in the current UK legislative framework, based on the duties of public authorities to provide education rather than on an explicit right to education for children, young people and adults, the only claims which are likely to achieve judicial success are where negligence can be proved. There is no separate accountability for education policies except through parliamentary democracy with all its strengths and weaknesses. A strong argument for the justiciability of the rights in the ICESCR is that it will bring accountability to extensive policies now in place to improve the quality of education for all, although it is probably without question that the courts are not the best place to decide such questions, given their lack of competence and experience to assess detailed government policy. A quasi-judicial or expert tribunal system is perhaps a suitable place to determine the efficacy of complex educational policies.

11

Inequalities at work

Employment is central to the current government's economic and social policies and, by extension, to socio-economic rights in the UK. The UK, as we have seen, has made a range of commitments to employment rights through the major UN economic and social rights treaties, the European Social Charter (ESC) (but not in its more extensive 1996 version) and the International Labour Organization (ILO). Moreover, it is bound under European Union law to protect core employment rights, including equality, health and safety and pension rights; and in 1997 the Labour government signed up to the Community Charter of the Fundamental Social Rights of Workers, enshrining rights to four weeks' paid holiday, workplace consultation, pension rights for part-time workers, protection for workers in take-overs and anti-discrimination measures (protecting the rights of gay and lesbian workers for the first time). But as the government's position on the proposed EU Charter of Fundamental Rights (see Chapter 3) showed, it is far from whole hearted in its commitment to workers' rights.

Access to employment

Access to work is the key employment right under the International Covenant on Economic, Social and Cultural Rights (ICESCR, Article 6) and the ESC (Articles 1, 9, 10 and 18). The government's drive to reduce unemployment has thus in itself been a contribution to employment rights, especially in its New Deal programmes to improve access to work for young people and other unemployed groups and the introduction of new benefits for workers with dependent children.

The labour market, employment and unemployment

The shift from a largely manufacturing base to service industries among developed countries has been particularly marked in the UK, where a higher proportion of workers is employed in services than in the rest of the EU: 72.4 per cent compared to an EU–15 average of 66.2 per cent,[1] leaving this once heavily industrialised nation only tenth in the EU–15 table of the proportion of workers employed in industry. One aspect of this still continuing trend is the rise in call centre workers and teleworkers (i.e. people working from home or other bases outside the office). Between 1995 and 2001 the number of contact centres multiplied from 2,515 to 4,825 and agent positions from 143,900 to 538,700; the totals projected for 2007 are 5,980 and 647,600 respectively. Call workers made up more than 2 per cent of Britain's workforce in 2001 while the number of teleworkers more than doubled between 1998 and 2005 and now stands at 8 per cent of the workforce – that is 2.5 million workers.[2] Call centres have been singled out for their poor pay and work practices. But the government is reluctant to deal with the consequences of this revolution and to intervene to protect worker rights in the increasingly service-centred economy. The government is committed to a flexible labour market. Though business complains about government 'red tape', the UK has one of the least regulated labour markets in the world, coming tenth out of 130 countries according to the World Bank, and is ranked above the EU and the US as the most 'entrepreneur-friendly' environment by the international business consultants Arthur Andersen.[3] Moreover, the government's spending on positive labour market policies is low compared to that of its EU partners – 0.6 per cent of GDP compared to an EU–15 average of 2 per cent, with Denmark spending 4 per cent. The UK's record is even worse when expenditure on training, job rotation, integration of the disabled, direct job creation and start-up incentives is taken into account – at just over 0.1 per cent of GDP, the UK is next to bottom after Luxembourg in the EU, which has an average spend of 0.75 per cent (with Sweden top in this case at 2.5 per cent).[4]

On unemployment, the Labour government stumbled at first, since (contrary to what is generally believed) unemployment inactivity in its first three years was worse than the previous three years under the Conservatives, on the ILO's measure of labour market inactivity. But the government then relied on the traditional, but less accurate, measure of people drawing benefit and so was able to claim, in March 2001, that the psychological barrier of less than one million out of work had been reached. However, after adverse publicity and pressure from a number of organisations working with the unemployed, the government adopted the more realistic ILO benchmark. On this measure, the quarterly figures for three months up to April 2004 saw unemployment falling to 1.43 million, or 4.8 per cent, its lowest level in thirty years (compared to an average for the euro zone of 9 per cent, and 5.6 per cent for the US). At the same time, the number of people in employment rose to a record 28.3 million (a rise of 750,000 on the previous year), largely due to a growth in the public payroll of half a million over the previous two years.

However, this success brings problems with it. Many of the new jobs being created are low paid and part time, usually undertaken by women in service industries with high staff turnover. During 2003/4 part-time employment grew more than one and a half times faster than full-time work. Moreover, the rise in employment has failed to provide sufficient work in neglected workless communities stretching across northern England and into the former coalfields of south Wales, Scotland and Kent.[5] It is here that you will also find the 'hidden workless' – those on sickness benefit, who make up, for example, as many as one in four men of working age in south Wales. Under the Conservatives in the early 1990s, people were signed on for sickness rather than unemployment benefit to conceal the scale of unemployment. The number of people claiming sickness rather than unemployment benefit doubled between 1992 and 1997, and continued to rise to more than 750,000. The figure has fallen by 100,000 during the last two years, but only down to the level it was at when Labour took office in 1997. If everybody on long-term benefits is taken into account (2.1 million), there were actually 2.5 million people out of work in Britain in 2004, more than double the official government figure. Some academics estimate that nearly half these people would be at work if the industrial economy were stronger.[6]

The result is that the UK probably has more hidden jobless than any other country in Europe, particularly if you count the hundreds of thousands of women who have partners required to assume responsibility for them after six months of unemployment. Indeed, if the economically inactive – such as students, the long-term sick or 'discouraged workers' (those who believe there are no jobs for them out there) – are all taken into account, the unemployment rate actually rises to about 11 per cent of all possible workers. This is a long way from full employment. Such labour market exclusion is a significant aspect of social exclusion, particularly where all members of a household are jobless. It leads not just to poverty but a lack of the interaction that work brings. A comprehensive survey of poverty and social exclusion found that 43 per cent of socially excluded adults had no paid work.[7] Another recent study found that one-sixth of all British adults aged seventeen to fifty-nine have neither a job nor a working partner. It identified six characteristics associated with a high risk of unemployment – not having a partner (especially being a lone parent), being disabled, lacking qualifications or skills, being in one's fifties, living in areas of weak labour demand and belonging to certain ethnic minority groups. While only 4 per cent of individuals with none of these disadvantages are not in work, nine out of ten people with all six are.[8] We go on below (see pages 253–264) to consider groups who are disadvantaged in the labour market – women, members of ethnic minorities and others. Here we briefly draw attention to the marked regional inequalities in employment. The prospects for work have improved in some parts of the UK since the late 1990s (for example, in south-west and north-east England), but have worsened elsewhere, most notably in London. In January 2001 Gordon Brown committed the Labour government to creating full employment across the regions by 2006.[9]

A New Deal for the unemployed?
The main plank of Labour's efforts to tackle unemployment has been the New Deal. Successive UK governments have placed little

emphasis on staff investment and training and the UK continues to suffer a large skills shortage with investment in its workforce at only two-thirds the rate of its international counterparts such as the US, Japan, France and Germany. It is therefore not surprising to find that nearly 20 per cent of job vacancies remain unfilled because of a shortage of skilled workers.[10] Early in 2001 a third of employers surveyed admitted that it was largely due to their own failure to train staff. Business spends £4.5 billion on training staff each year, but only half their employees benefit. Four years into the new Labour government (and three years into the New Deal), ministers were forced to admit that Britain had a skills and recruitment crisis due in part to lack of training.

Welfare to Work, the forerunner to the New Deal, was launched in April 1998 to tackle unemployment among 18–24-year-olds by giving positive support to employment through Training and Enterprise Councils (later Learning and Skills Councils and the Small Business Service), providing job subsidies to the private sector, seeking to expand employment opportunities, providing special assistance to ethnic minorities, and withdrawing benefits from those who refused to participate. Within the space of three years 500,000 individuals had entered the programme and around half had found work at an estimated cost of £1.48 billion. More than 80,000 employers signed up to the scheme. Unemployment among young people fell by 70 per cent within four years (while 32,000 young people lost their benefits). By May 2005, 1.32 million 18–24-year-olds had joined the New Deal for young people. Of the 1.24 million young people who had left the scheme, 519,000 (41.9 per cent) went into employment.[11]

However, some have questioned the sustainability of the jobs created and whether natural growth would have accounted for many of them anyway. Some evidence has emerged to support such views. As the economy weakened slightly in the middle of the present decade, the small rise in unemployment appeared to impact disproportionately upon the young. Office of National Statistics (ONS) figures showed that in the twelve months to the end of June 2005, the number of 18–24-year-olds claiming jobseeker's allowance rose by 9.4 per cent, as compared to an overall rise of 1.6 per cent.[12] By then the New Deal had been extended to single parents and the partners of jobless people, to people aged 25-plus and 50-plus, and to the disabled, with varying rates of success. The New Deal for single parents has been the most prominent of these schemes, with the ambitious aims of raising the proportion of single parents in work from 50 per cent to 70 per cent by 2010, placing 375,000 more people in employment and lifting 600,000 children out of poverty. Under the new scheme single parents would not lose benefits if they refused to take up work or training. But the penalty would apply to 55,000 women under forty-five whose partners were jobless and who did not have children. However, the New Deal for lone parents has only marginally raised the number in work, a major obstacle being the lack of good child-care (see page 244). The success rate for those who took part in the scheme is mixed. Some 410,050 of the 771,550 people coming out of the scheme in May 2005 had found work. However, the TUC noted that 'only 269,040 [65.5 per cent] of them are listed as having achieved sustained jobs . . . We should be worried that a third of the lone parents who get jobs through the programme are unable to keep them for at least 13 weeks, and this figure needs further investigation.'

The government's employment drive took on an increasingly compulsory shift, with a tougher imposition of skills testing – including basic numeracy and literacy – on 'hardcore' benefit claimants and plans for a US-style 'workfare' system, with benefits being denied to adult workers and their partners who refused to opt for one of four New Deal choices: subsidised work, training, voluntary work or a place on an environmental taskforce. Compulsory interviews would be held for all lone parents, although they remained free to opt out of the New Deal without penalty. The then education and employment secretary, David Blunkett, justified the new approach on the basis that the unemployed had to 'accept the responsibilities they have towards society . . . those who are taking taxpayers for a ride will soon find that there is no hiding place'. And since 2005 the government has turned increasing emphasis on encouraging recipients of incapacity benefit to find work, finally publishing a Green Paper in January 2006 revealing an 'aspiration' to reduce the number claiming the benefit by a million over ten years, through improvements to workplace health, reform of the 'gateway' to claiming benefits and the removal of 'perverse incentives in the system'.[13]

Working rights and conditions

'The right to a fair remuneration' is established as a fundamental right under Article 4 of the ESC, while Article 23 of the UN Universal Declaration of Human rights states that 'everyone who works has the right to just and favourable remuneration ensuring . . . an existence worthy of human dignity'. Britain has professed its adherence to these principles for half a century, but has had a historically poor record on low pay. In 1993, the Conservatives abolished the wages councils that gave some protection to wage rates in a handful of industries, most notably agriculture. The UN Human Rights Committee of independent experts found the UK to be in breach of the right to fair remuneration under Article 4 of the ESC on a number of occasions. Thus the Labour government's decision to introduce the national minimum wage (NMW) in 1999 represented a significant, if modest, landmark for socio-economic rights in the UK. The NMW has been a central plank of its economic and social policies.

The National Minimum Wage (NMW)
The Council of Europe has defined a 'decency threshold' – the level of income that is deemed necessary to provide for a household's basic needs – as the equivalent of 68 per cent of the average (mean) earnings of all full-time workers. This threshold was put at £7.97 per hour in 2001, though the method of calculation has now changed, making a uniform figure difficult to arrive at. On this measure, the government's national minimum wage has had a significant impact in moving towards a decent living wage and is arguably one of the government's most significant economic and social reforms. The government also set up the Low Pay Commission to advise on the rates set and to monitor its effects. The government can ignore its recommendations, but has yet to do so in relation to the main rate. The commission estimates that the upratings of the minimum wage

have provided hundreds of thousands of workers with higher wages (see Table 11.1). In its most recent report in 2005, the commission reported that the October 2003 uprating benefited 900,000 workers and the October 2004 uprating to £4.85 per hour helped one million workers, or 4.4 per cent of the workforce. However, it conceded that 'throughout the life of this commission, the number of beneficiaries has turned out to be smaller than originally forecast'. The uprating in October 2004 (a second successive increase of more than 7 per cent) also meant that, for the first time, the wage was worth more in real terms than when it was introduced in 1999.

Table 11.1: National minimum wage rates, 2000–6

	Adult rate (22+)	Development rate (18–21)	Development rate (16–17)
1 April 2000	£3.60	£3.00	
1 October 2000	£3.70	£3.20	
1 October 2001	£4.10	£3.50	
1 October 2002	£4.20	£3.60	
1 October 2003	£4.50	£3.80	
1 October 2004	£4.85	£4.10	£3.00
1 October 2005	£5.05	£4.25	£3.00
1 October 2006	£5.35	£4.45	£3.30

Source: Low Pay Commission

However, the government has only just passed the £5.00 per hour rate that the trade unions and the former Low Pay Unit had been demanding since 1999 to bring the UK rate into line with its EU-15 counterparts. One break on the government's willingness to raise the rate in the first years was, as it explained in its response to the UN Committee on Economic, Social and Cultural Rights in 2001, that it was not a question of whether the NMW provided a reasonable standard of living, but rather whether it was affordable for employers in order not to put jobs at risk. Fears of the effect on employment also explain the lower rate for 18–21-year-old workers and the initial exclusion of sixteen- and seventeen-year-olds from the scheme. The UN committee has noted its 'concern' about the discrimination against younger workers. The Low Pay Commission and trade unions have also expressed concern about the treatment of younger workers. Despite the commission's recommendations, 18–21-year-olds continue to receive 80p less than older workers, a disparity that will increase to 90p in October 2006. Further, despite continued evidence from the commission and lobbying by the TUC and others that young workers were receiving little or no training and 'exploitative' rates of pay, it took until March 2004 for the government finally to announce that sixteen- and seventeen-year-olds would be included, though at far lower rates of pay (see Table 11.1). However, on the commission's own recommendation, apprentices were not covered. There remains a strong case for a flat rate covering all workers rather than a structure that encourages employers to implement age differentials, thereby allowing them to drive down rates for all employees.[14]

But the greatest defect of the NMW is that it is government ministers who determine its level, albeit with recommendations from the commission, instead of it being indexed against a suitable benchmark (such as median wages). It is not therefore a reliable feature of socio-economic rights in the UK because this or future governments could neglect to raise it for a variety of reasons. The principle of automatic uprating was established as long ago as 1914, when it was first introduced in Australia and New Zealand and was Labour party policy for thirteen years until the 1997 general election. The UK is out of step with most other European countries, where the minimum wage is uprated annually, and closer to the more erratic American model. However, despite this caveat, the NMW has made pay at the bottom end of the labour market more competitive, with some companies choosing to pay above the NMW rate in order to attract workers in a low-unemployment market. Non-compliance has not been as great an issue as initially envisaged, but even so, more than four years after its introduction, 170,000 workers were still being paid below the NMW level. At the same time, workers had recovered £13 million from law-breaking employers;[15] and from July 2003, workers could claim back pay not only from current employers (as had always been the case) but also from previous employers where they had been paid less than the NMW since it came into force.

Nevertheless low pay remains a reality for millions of workers. More than one in four workers across all sectors earn less than £6 per hour, but the position tends to be worse in particular regions and occupations and among certain groups of vulnerable workers – ethnic minority workers, young workers and older workers, those with low qualifications, part-time workers and home workers (see below). Non-unionised workers, encompassing many of these groups, are at particular risk.

In-work benefits

The government's strategy for reducing poverty has focused on 'making work pay', primarily by raising the incomes of low-paid workers through tax credits, underpinned by the NMW. Analysis has shown that, despite its symbolic significance, the NMW has delivered less new money to the poorest-paid workers than other government measures such as the working families tax credit and child tax credit, although these too are not without their difficulties.[16] Despite these measures in-work poverty has not been eradicated – partly because of the persistence of low wages and partly because of the complex interaction between benefits and household income. Of those living in poverty, 30 per cent – 3.5 million people – live in households with at least one wage earner. The working poor represent a larger group than the unemployed or pensioner poor. Nearly 2.5 million workers earn below the lower limit for national insurance contributions (currently £97 a week for 2006/7) and are therefore not entitled to basic benefits such as statutory sick pay and the basic state retirement pension. In this context, there is clear evidence that the NMW was introduced at a rate too low to have a major impact on lifting working households out of poverty.[17]

Moreover, it is difficult to break this cycle of poverty. Being low paid once makes it more likely that an individual will be low paid again. Low-paid workers are also more likely to experience periods of unemployment. The probability of escaping from low-wage employment decreases the longer an individual has been in that low-paid job and the longer the period spent in low-paid work over the course of his or her life.

Working hours and shifting work patterns

British full-time employees work significantly longer hours than their EU counterparts. Recent figures show 43.9 hours for a UK worker, compared to 41 for the EUR-12 (the Eurozone) and 41.4 for the EU-15. A government survey found that one in nine full-time employees work more than 60 hours per week and 80 per cent of workplaces have people working more than their standard hours (with 39 per cent for no extra pay).[18] The ESC's committee of independent experts has found that high levels of overtime are a persistent feature of British employment. Surveys have shown the detrimental impact on health of working long hours.[19] The EU working time directive provides for a maximum 48-hour average working week, but uniquely among member states, the UK exercised the right to allow individual workers to opt out of the 48-hour limit and it has had little initial or longer-term impact.[20] One in six male employees were working more than sixty hours a week in 2003, compared with one in eight in 2001 and twice as many women – up from one in sixteen to one in eight – were working long hours. Much of this overtime is unpaid – the UK continues to lack any legislation specifying when and how it must be paid. Moreover, not only do UK employees work the longest hours, academic research shows they also work more intensely than their counterparts in Europe.[21] The 400,000 employees in call centres, for example, work intensely hard on what is described as the 'assembly-line of the modern era',[22] offering in some cases 'sweatshop conditions'.[23] Unsocial hours are another UK employment problem. Some 12.5 per cent of the workforce usually work nights (the Eurozone average is 5.4 per cent; the EU-15 average 7 per cent) and shift working is also higher in the UK – the respective figures for shift workers are 19.2 per cent, 14 per cent and 15.7 per cent.

Parenting rights

Nearly half of all working women have children under five, but until recently the needs of working mothers were shamefully neglected by governments and employers alike. Nursery care was in short supply and maternity pay was less than half the EU-15 average. The Labour government has had a real impact in this area, introducing new parenting rights to bring the UK into line with the rest of the EU, including the right since April 2003 to request flexible working and the adoption of the directive giving fathers, as well as mothers, thirteen weeks' unpaid parental leave over the first five years of a child's life. At the same time, maternity leave and pay have been extended so that mothers can take up to twenty-six weeks' leave, receiving 90 per cent of earnings up to a maximum of £100 a week (although the UK still lags behind some other European countries, especially Norway and Sweden). For the first time, adoptive parents and same-sex parents are also eligible for the same rights.

The right to request flexible working represents a major advance. Not only blood parents but also guardians, adoptive and foster parents, with children under the age of six or a disabled child under the age of eighteen, may request flexible working arrangements from their employer and that request has to be taken seriously. This is not a right per se, but a right to have requests taken seriously with a strict written procedure to be adhered to and refusal on only one of eight grounds. Within a year of this measure being introduced a million working women requested flexible working, 80 per cent of them successfully.

The Labour government has also tackled the lack of affordable child-care after identifying it as a major constraint on working women entering or re-entering the labour market. Labour launched its National Childcare Strategy as early as 1998, which has begun to close the child-care gap.[24] By 2002 the government claimed to have created more than 553,000 new child-care places, benefiting more than 1,007,000 children. The lottery-funded Out of School Hours Programme had in addition created 288,000 new child-care places. The December 2003 Budget gave employees using registered child-care up to £50 per week in subsidised child-care services, child-care allowances or vouchers tax free (though this figure remains well below the £128 per week average cost of child-care). But those who rely on friends and relatives to look after their children while they are at work do not benefit. For all this progress, the need for a fully integrated child-care system and equal parental rights remains acute. Women continue to be the primary parent on every indicator despite being also the main earner in 40 per cent of households. And they still experience shocking discrimination from the moment they become pregnant. Active discrimination against pregnant employees amounts to about 27,000 cases handled by the Citizens Advice Bureau every year out of a total of 40,000 on parental rights.

Health and safety
The Health and Safety at Work Act 1974 established a regulatory framework overlooked and enforced by the monitoring and enforcement bodies, the Health and Safety Executive (HSE) and the Health and Safety Commission (HSC). This framework has been reinforced by subsequent EU directives, resulting in more than thirty sets of regulations (though the UK still lacks a single set of codified regulations covering health and safety in the workplace). Under the current government, the rate of non-fatal accidents at work has risen from 1,550 per 100,000 workers in 1996 to 1,607 per 100,000 in 2000, but this figure is well below the EU average of 4,088 per 100,000. As for fatal accidents, Britain is second lowest after Sweden among EU member states, with 1.7 fatalities per 100,000 workers compared with an EU figure of 2.8 per 100,000.[25]

On coming to power Labour signalled its intent to take health and safety more seriously. It provided substantial new resources for the HSC in order to implement a strategy of reducing work-related deaths, injuries and illness by up to 30 per cent by 2010. In addition, the government announced in 2003 that it would finally introduce an offence of corporate manslaughter in the wake of the Hatfield rail crash, something which trade unions and other organisations had been lobbying for since the *Herald of Free Enterprise* disaster in 1987.[26] A draft Bill was published in March 2005 and the Queen's Speech in May referred to the government's intention to take forward its proposals. The draft law states that an organisation will be guilty of corporate manslaughter if its senior managers organise or manage its activities in such a way that causes a person's death and amounts to a gross breach of its duty of care owed to the individual. The proposed law differs from existing legislation in that it provides a range of statutory criteria based on health and safety guidance and law by which culpability can be assessed. It also makes it possible to prosecute larger companies by removing the need to identify the 'directing mind' of the corporation. There will be no Crown immunity – though Crown immunity will still apply to breaches of health and safety legislation. It will not be possible to charge individuals, who can already be prosecuted under existing manslaughter laws – to date twenty directors have been prosecuted, of whom seven have been imprisoned. It is estimated that the new law will lead to an extra five prosecutions a year. While the TUC welcomed the draft Bill, some unions and the Centre for Corporate Accountability (CCA) have expressed regret that it is not sufficiently stringent. Suggestions for improving the Bill include allowing for the punishment of individual directors.

Whatever impact the new law may have, there is disturbing evidence that the HSE is giving insufficient attention to its enforcement role, due, in part, to a lack of resources. It took until July 2003 for the HSE to issue guidance to its inspectors on the prosecution of individuals for health and safety offences (and also on the investigation of directors and managers). In May 2004 the CCA uncovered an internal HSE memo that appeared to suggest that since November 2003 the agency had dropped routine investigations into deaths and injuries caused by the unsafe working practices of local authorities, hospitals, prisons and the police. As a result the HSE may be in breach of its statutory duties under the Human Rights Act by failing to protect life and guard against serious injury. In response the HSE stated that it needed to prioritise resources and would only look into cases where health legislation was breached. It is important for the HSE to maintain a high level of activity, for employers can be laggardly in responding to new standards and there are occasional worrying lapses, such as the deaths of nine apprentices on work placements funded by the government's Learning and Skills Councils, revealed in 2004 by the CCA.

There is also the need to adapt to the changing nature of work in the UK. There has for example been a large rise in stress levels, particularly among the more than two million teleworkers, often women in low-paid work with a high turnover who have no access to sick pay or trade union support. The government actively promotes teleworking in the interests of labour market flexibility; but in September 2003 it finally appeared to recognise that teleworkers needed greater protection when it introduced a new health and safety code for working at home to ensure that the latest EU employment regulations give protection to those out of the office.

Dismissal and redundancy

Private sector redundancies, sometimes on a large scale, like the 6,000 jobs lost at MG Rover in 2005, are a fact of life in the international economy. And they can also occur in the public sector. With the Gershon report on civil service efficiency, published in 2004, the government has committed itself to a reduction of 84,150 civil service posts by 2007/8. The poor state of worker protection was starkly revealed in October 2003 when government job centres sacked more than 400 of their own staff one week before they were due to qualify for job security, thereby ensuring they lacked any employment rights. According to the chief executive, this act was intended to 'support flexibility and responsiveness'. Not surprisingly, a survey of UK workers in May 2005 found that one in four believed they could lose their jobs in the next year (compared with 4 per cent of Norwegian workers, 19 per cent of US workers and 27 per cent of Germans).

What rights do employees have with respect to redundancy? The Employment Protection (Consolidation) Act 1978 consolidated rules on unfair-dismissal claims and redundancy pay, with some restrictions favouring employers being applied by the Employment Act 1989. Under the Trade Union and Labour Relations (Consolidation) Act 1992, which, as amended, implements the EU Collective Redundancies Directive (98/59/EC), employers must follow certain procedures for notification and consultation over redundancies of twenty or more. Failure to comply can lead to compensation payments on top of any redundancy payments. Currently workers receive full protection against unfair dismissal only after twelve months of employment. But while European directives govern the framework of redundancy law, the detail of implementation varies across countries – and it appears that the UK is among the least strict in its requirements. For instance, in the Netherlands and Spain redundancies have to be authorised by regional employment offices; and social plans to alleviate the adverse consequences of redundancy must be drawn up in Germany, France, Austria and Luxembourg. When Marks and Spencer announced its intention to close its continental branches in 2001, it became clear that although UK and French laws came from the same European sources, Britain required less consultation and imposed less severe penalties on companies transgressing the regulations.[27] In the same year the Commons Trade and Industry Select Committee stated that 'the suggestion that it is easier and cheaper to dispose of employees in the UK than elsewhere seems to us to have been shown to be factually correct'.[28] In response to such concerns the government introduced a limited reform with the Information and Consultation of Employees Regulations 2004, which require all companies with fifty or more employees to establish formal information and consultation procedures if 10 per cent of the workforce requests them – by April 2008.

Though imperfect, protection for full-time employees is favourable when compared to the plight of the increasing numbers of temporary and home workers,[29] of whom there are far more in the UK than in any other comparable economy. Labour did introduce new regulatory protection in 2002, but in so doing manufactured a new divide between workers on fixed-term contracts and those employed through an agency. At the same time, it has consistently opposed attempts at the European level to introduce better protection for agency workers. The result leaves agency workers in a legal limbo with only very limited rights under anti-discrimination legislation, the minimum wage and rules on working time, no protection from unfair dismissal and no access to the benefits of family-friendly legislation. Home-workers are another large group of workers who are readily exploited. Research for the TUC, Oxfam and the National Group on Homeworking published in May 2004[30] found that many lacked basic employment rights since they were not classed as employees. The government is currently considering a review of their employment status.

Trade union rights

Trade unions make an important contribution both to economic and social rights and also to democracy through their role as representatives of workers. However, in pursuit of the idea that they had grown too powerful, a series of major restrictive Conservative reforms during the 1980s and early 1990s – the Employment Act 1980, the Employment Act 1982, the Trade Union Act 1984, the Public Order Act 1986, the Employment Act 1988, the Employment Act 1990, the Trade Union and Labour Relations (Consolidation) Act 1992 and the Trade Union Reform and Employment Rights Act 1993 – had a devastating effect on Britain's unions, made worse by the decline in manufacturing. Employers were encouraged to end long-standing collective bargaining arrangements and unilaterally to derecognise unions. The right to strike was seriously restricted. While many in the labour movement recognised that some of the reforms were necessary, they undoubtedly went too far, attracting expert criticism from the ILO, the Council of Europe (and the ESC's committee of independent experts) and the UN Committee on Economic, Social and Cultural Rights. The International Confederation of Free Trade Unions concluded that by the end of the 1990s the UK had the worst record on organised labour of any EU country.

The Labour government was expected to redress the balance, but while the Employment Relations Act 1999 did restore some legal rights, the government did not repeal all the anti-trade union legislation, particularly in regard to industrial action, secondary picketing and balloting. There remains extensive interference in trade unions' internal affairs – for instance, they are prevented from disciplining members who refuse to participate in lawful industrial action voted for by members. The Institute of Employment Rights summarised the concerns expressed by international rights bodies in a paper in 2004 (see Table 11.2). As the institute pointed out in the paper, the ILO's committee of experts has repeatedly criticised intervention in the internal organisation of unions, as has the Council of Europe Social Rights Committee.[31] Furthermore, there are continuing statutory difficulties imposed upon unions seeking to organise or support industrial action by their members, which are discussed below.

Table 11.2: International concerns over trade union rights in the UK

Treaty	Monitoring body	Areas of concern
International Covenant on Economic, Social and Cultural Rights	Committee on Economic, Social and Cultural Rights	Article 8 – right to strike – violated and should be incorporated into UK law (1997, 2002 reports).
International Labour Organization Convention 87 – protection of trade unions from state interference	International Labour Organization Committee of Experts and Committee on Freedom of Association	Concerns regularly expressed over restricted right to strike, erosion of freedom of association, narrow definition of trade dispute, virtual impossibilty of secondary action; insufficient protection for dismissal in connection with a trade dispute; unions prevented from disciplining members.
European Social Charter (1961 version)	European Committee of Social Rights	Article 6(2) – the right to bargain collectively – violated. Article 6(4) – the right to strike or take other industrial action – 'subject to serious limitation'.

Source: Institute of Employment Rights

The right to strike is the backbone of collective action in pursuit of workers' interests and commands widespread public support: 86 per cent of respondents in a 2000 opinion poll for the Joseph Rowntree Reform Trust's State of the Nation series agreed that the 'right to join a legal strike without losing your job' should form part of a British Bill of Rights. The right to strike is protected under the ICESCR: Article 8(1)(d) provides for 'the right to strike, provided that it is exercised in conformity with the laws of the particular country'. Similar guarantees are included in the conventions of the ILO and the ESC, to which the UK is party. Yet the ILO, UN Committee on Economic, Social and Cultural Rights and the Council of Europe Social Rights Committee have all found major flaws with the protection of this right in the UK. The UN committee has criticised the omission of a specifically enshrined right to strike in its last two reports on UK compliance with the covenant. In evidence to the parliamentary Joint Committee on Human Rights (JCHR), the government insisted that it fulfils its international human rights obligations with respect to the right to strike and rejected the committee's proposal that it make this explicit in law. Its argument was that because under existing legislation striking workers could not be compelled to return to work and unions were free to organise industrial action (provided proper procedures were followed), 'a right to strike . . . is already enshrined in UK domestic law'.[32]

But despite the government's claims, existing legislation provides neither trade unions nor individual workers with sufficient protections. The legal definition of a 'trade dispute' – which lies at the heart of strike action – is narrowly drawn and hideously complex. The difficulties involved in the conduct of industrial action ballots and the rigours of the obligations to serve notices make trade union action very vulnerable to legal injunctions.[33] In short, the law is loaded against trade unions contemplating industrial action. Strikes are limited to disputes with immediate employers – it remains virtually impossible to engage in lawful secondary action, and the government has said that it has no plans to legalise such action. Unions cannot strike in situations where the employer with whom they are in dispute hides behind a layer of subsidiary companies, even when they have done so in order to render primary action secondary. The ILO

Committee of Experts has repeatedly criticised the present legal position, stating in 2002:

> Workers should be able to take industrial action in relation to matters which affect them even though, in certain cases, the direct employer may not be party to the dispute, and . . . they should be able to participate in sympathy strikes provided the initial strike they are supporting is itself lawful.[34]

A memorandum to the JCHR from the Communication Workers Union (CWU) in 2004 described how difficult it can be for unions to represent their members when in dispute with employers. The CWU noted that existing legislation makes it possible for employers to prevent action on unreasonable technical grounds. Furthermore, injunctions are granted to employers 'on the lowest conceivable legal threshold' – that of an 'arguable case'. The CWU has felt obliged to desist from industrial action it felt would otherwise be correct and to go as far as to repudiate members already engaged in action it nevertheless judged to be justifiable in principle. In the latter circumstances, the members concerned were thereby denied any protection they might have had from unfair dismissal for engaging in the action.[35] Other unions – the GMB and the National Union of Rail, Maritime and Transport Workers (RMT) – similarly complained to the JCHR that they were inhibited in supporting their members. Unions such as the CWU have proceeded with action which they have then been forced to abandon because of legal injunctions. To ignore an injunction is to risk, in the words of the CWU, 'fines, sequestration and imprisonment – even if the injunction at full trial is shown to have been unwarranted as a matter of law'.[36]

As well as there being no specific right to strike, there is a lack of the proper protection from dismissal that would necessarily accompany it. The RMT informed the JCHR that 'whilst the protection of the right of trade unions to call and support industrial action is very limited, for workers it is practically non-existent'. In the UK 'all forms of industrial action constitute a breach of an individual worker's contract of employment allowing the employer to dismiss them'. This applies to both unofficial and official, lawful and unlawful actions; and both all-out strikes and other forms of industrial action, even works to rule.[37] But the government also rejected the UN committee's suggestion in 2002 that there was a need for statutory protection against loss of employment for strike action, drawing attention to the limited measures it had introduced with the Employment Relations Act 1999. (These made dismissal unfair if the employee was on strike for less than eight weeks or if the employer had not taken reasonable steps to resolve the dispute from which the action arose.)[38]

The Employment Relations Act 1999 also left employers free to agree individual contracts with employees, even in a workplace where the union was recognised for collective bargaining. However, a landmark case decided by the European Court of Human Rights in 2002 forced the government to act.[39] The court agreed that UK legislation breached workers' right to free association under Article 11 of the European Convention on Human Rights (ECHR) because it allowed employers to treat employees who were not prepared to give up their collective bargaining rights less favourably than those who accepted personal contracts. The Labour government was forced to introduce the Employment Relations Act 2004, which tidied up and clarified some existing provisions on statutory recognition and requirements for strike ballots and outlawed some of the discriminatory practices identified by the European Court. Yet the JCHR argued that

> the Act leaves some incompatibilities [with international human rights obligations] unremedied. In particular . . . the failure to provide trades unions (rather than only employees) with an avenue of redress of their rights under Article 11 of ECHR, where inducements were offered to employees not to join the trade union, could result in a violation of both the Article 11 right and the right to a remedy.[40]

Equality at work

The UK's anti-discrimination legislation is long established, dating back to the mid-1970s in terms of equal pay, sex and race discrimination and augmented by the Disability Discrimination Act 1995 (see Chapter 6). However, as Chapter 6 makes clear, its protections are increasingly antiquated and fail to provide a coherent defence against discrimination in the workplace (as elsewhere). Moreover, gaps remain and in October 2000 the government responded to the new EU directive on discrimination in the workplace by pledging to introduce a package of new anti-discrimination legislation covering religion and sexual orientation by 2003 and age and disability by 2006. But the government also secured opt-outs from the directive, allowing the Army to continue to reject or dismiss people who are too old or disabled to serve and permitting religious schools to continue with the option of rejecting staff of other faiths.

Enforcement remains a key issue, with many companies failing to police themselves. A Department for Trade and Industry (DTI) taskforce on workplace equality recommended in May 2003 that businesses should be forced to disclose in their annual reports whether they pay their female staff fairly. It also suggested that firms publish a breakdown of their staff by age, gender and ethnicity and describe their training policies.

Disabled and mentally ill people

Disabled people account for nearly a fifth of the working-age population in Britain, but for only an estimated 12 to 16 per cent of those actually in employment. Only about 40 per cent of disabled people of working age are economically active compared with 85 per cent of the non-disabled population. In addition, they are more likely to be long-term unemployed, even though one million of the 2.6 million unemployed disabled people want to work.[41] One third of disabled people who do find work are out of a job again within a year (compared to one fifth for the non-disabled). Of those who become disabled while in work, one in six will lose their employment during the year after becoming disabled. Overall, those with a long-standing illness or disability are about half as likely to be in paid work than the rest of the population.[42] Those who do find work are more likely to be in low-paid occupations because of their relative lack of educational qualifications (even after taking account of differences in age, occupation and education) and the gap appears to have grown significantly since 1985.[43] Despite these constraints they do not receive any additional training over and above the norm.[44]

The Labour government created the Disability Rights Commission (DRC) in 2000, with the remit to enforce the Disability Discrimination Act 1995 and bring about 'the equalisation of opportunities for disabled persons'. The Act makes it illegal for employers to limit access on grounds of disability, but exempts companies with fewer than fifteen employees, even though such companies employ 90 per cent of the workforce. However, the government announced in March that it would strengthen the protection that the Act gives to 600,000 employees already covered and add some seven million additional workers who were previously excluded, such as firefighters and prison officers – but not members of the armed forces. The government also pledged to extend protection to people suffering from serious diseases, such as cancer and HIV/AIDS, from victimisation (including measures to this effect in the Disability Discrimination Act 2005). By 2004 small businesses would be required to make 'reasonable adjustments' to their premises for the benefit of disabled employees and job applicants. In addition all firms would have to remove unreasonable obstacles for disabled customers. Public bodies would be under a legal duty to provide equal opportunities for disabled people. Further, the New Deal for disabled people (see above) aims to find 'relevant and appropriate' employment opportunities for people with disabilities, and the disabled person's tax credit was raised in the 2000 budget. But in practice, as the DRC reported in 2003, it remains powerless to help thousands of disabled people sacked or refused access to services because the law does not protect them. The DRC asked the government to impose a duty on all public bodies to promote disability equality.

A year-long inquiry into social exclusion and the mentally ill found that as many as 80 per cent of people with a mental illness have given up looking for work, making them one of the most socially excluded groups.[45] Another study found that less than one in six mentally ill people were in work, more than half lived on a low income and virtually all of them said their diagnosis had affected their work prospects, with some stating that it made securing work virtually impossible.[46]

Women

During the last decade, the number of women in the labour market has increased dramatically, with more than twelve million working women representing nearly half the workforce compared to only a third in 1970. Women graduates are now more likely to be employed than men (95.3 per cent compared with 92.6 per cent).[47] Yet for all this apparent progress in accessing work, inequality remains in the type of jobs that women do, their work patterns and their pay. Women have benefited from a series of progressive legislative measures dating back to the early 1970s – the Equal Pay Act 1970 (EPA), the Sex Discrimination Act 1975 and a number of European directives. The Employment Act 1989 lifted certain restrictions on women's work and the Part Time Workers Regulations, which came into force in July 2000, gave part-timers rights equal to their full-time equivalents. There was no specific prohibition on sexual harassment at work until the Employment Equality (Sex Discrimination) Regulations 2005 came into force in October 2005.

Mirroring these initiatives, demographic changes have resulted in increasingly well-qualified women (better qualified than men for younger age groups) entering the labour market, more of whom become managers (the number has more than doubled within a decade). They are able to return to work straight after maternity leave, thereby avoiding the significant loss of pay from moving to a new, often part-time job after a gap of several years. Yet at the same time many women (particularly those at the bottom end of the labour market) remain subject to social constraints: for example, being a carer means exclusion from the labour market for six times as many women as men.[48]

The goal of equal pay remains out of reach, with wide disparities across employment from part-time workers to highly skilled professionals. The pay gap has closed in some areas. Between 1970 – when the EPA came into force – and 2000, the gender pay gap halved from 37 per cent to 18 per cent.[49] However, this still represents an estimated lifetime earnings gap of £241,000 for a 'middle-skilled' childless woman and £140,000 for a woman with two children. The gap for female part-time workers (the vast majority of part-time workers are women) stands at a vast 39 per cent, leaving the UK with one of the worst records in the EU-15. By October 2003, women's average hourly pay was 82 per cent of men's, but their annual earnings – a better indicator, according to the Fawcett Society, since they reflect the seasonal work of many women – stood at just 72 per cent of men's (£20,314 compared with £28,065).[50] At such a rate of progress since 1970, even if it is maintained, it would take eighty-five years for men and women to achieve parity. Inequalities extend into other work-related areas, such as bonuses and performance-related pay. Women are frequently illegally excluded (including more than 10 per cent of part-time employees) from pension schemes. The CBI has maintained that the pay gap can be explained by women's career and educational choices, but the Equal Opportunities Commission (EOC) disagrees, stating that it is more due to discrimination. It is usually the case that as more women enter an employment sector, the relative pay falls.

The government's Women's Unit has had little impact in redressing the balance. Instead it has had to respond to the EOC's own Equal Pay Task Force on making the EPA more effective by setting up the Kingsmill review in autumn 2001. The review emphasised the importance of voluntary pay reviews by private companies, recognised the adverse effect on women's pay due to the contracting out of public services and called for greater disclosure of pay information by companies. In December 2000 Labour pledged to strengthen the enforcement of equal pay laws by placing the burden of proof on employers in sex discrimination cases and widening their scope to include indirect discrimination (in line with EU directives). At the same time, the government has argued that the national minimum wage (introduced in 1999) has done more for women's pay than the thirty-plus years of the EPA. The NMW has certainly made a difference, since about two thirds of the millions who have benefited from it have been women; as a result, the pay gap narrowed by almost 2 per cent between April 1998 and 2000.[51] However, substantial proportions of full-time adult women workers, younger full-time women workers and part-time women workers still earned less than £5 an hour;[52] and women continued to make up nearly 80 per cent of all employees in the bottom ten paying manual and non-manual occupations.[53] In the lowest income decile the gap between the average male and female pay has narrowed by only 1 per cent over twenty-five years.[54] At the same time, while pay improves across the board, there is a downward pressure on wages in many female-dominated occupations, such as catering and cleaning, as public services are contracted out and firms compete to win contracts by cutting staffing costs. But women suffer by comparison at all levels of the job market. Female graduates anticipate earning less than their male counterparts and they do. The government is often the worst offender, with a 28 per cent pay gap within the civil service; and many women workers in local government, such as care workers and nursery nurses, have been earning less than £6 an hour.

What more could be done? The EOC highlights the failure of businesses to conduct equal pay audits. Only a third do so voluntarily and the government has continually refused to legislate to compel employers to conduct the audits. This laissez-faire attitude on behalf of business and government is mirrored in the general lack of awareness amongst employees. The Equality Bill, introduced in 2005, should improve matters in the public sector by creating a 'gender duty' on public authorities, requiring them to promote equality of opportunity between women and men (see Chapter 6).

Young people
Three issues affect the employment and social rights of young people – low pay, illegal child labour and the more insidious effect of living in or heading a workless family. One in eight young people aged sixteen to thirty-four live in households with no paid work, particularly those headed by single parents, usually a mother. A report by the Social Exclusion Unit in June 1999 found that teenage mothers were less likely to find a decent job and consequently more likely to bring their children up in poverty. Even where they do find work, their earnings are often insufficient to lift their families out of poverty.[55] The unit set out a ten-year national strategy for England. One of the objectives was to 'increase the participation of teenage parents in education and work to reduce their risk of long-term social exclusion'. Government figures suggested initial success, showing that from 1997 to 2001 the proportion of teenage mothers aged sixteen to nineteen in education, training or work increased from 17

per cent to 29 per cent, going on to reach 30 per cent over the period 2002–4.

In March 2000 the UK ratified ILO Convention 182 on the worst forms of child labour and Convention 138 on the minimum age of employment. Yet child labour continues to be a major problem. This is due largely, according to UNICEF, to the growth of the service sector and the demand for a flexible workforce, with the income from child work making an important contribution to the household budget of poor families.[56] It is illegal for under-thirteens to do any paid work and the employment of older children is supposed to be subject to strict regulation of hours in conformity with both ILO and EU guidelines. Yet a Council of Europe report in 1997 estimated that about half the children aged between thirteen and fifteen in the UK were engaged in some kind of part-time employment, most of them working illegally without formal registration, and thus without an assessment of whether their employment is exploitative. Another study, jointly compiled by the TUC and MORI in March 2001, suggested that 485,000 under-thirteens were working illegally, including 289,000 who are doing paid work either during term time or in the summer holidays (the rest were babysitting, doing paper rounds or other casual jobs that are strictly speaking illegal). Over 100,000 of these play truant from school to do paid work – with children as young as ten being employed as cleaners. The government's own figures show that one million eleven- to sixteen-year-old pupils (about one third of the total) do paid work of some kind.

Child prostitution is a common source of income for many homeless children. There are also a large number of street children in major UK cities who live and work under extremely hazardous conditions at high risk of abuse and criminal activities, though exact figures are hard to establish.

Ethnic minorities

Racial discrimination affects the employment rights of workers from ethnic minorities in three significant ways: they are disproportionately liable to be unemployed, they are less likely than their white counterparts to be promoted and they may suffer from racial harassment in the workplace. The UN Committee on Economic

Social and Cultural Rights has expressed concern that ethnic minorities continue to suffer higher levels of unemployment and occupy a disproportionate number of lesser-paid jobs. Employers say that tackling racism and sexism is a priority, but research has shown that in reality firms continue to pay lip service to equal opportunities and diversity issues and fewer than half have an equality strategy.[57]

Labour's Race Relations (Amendment) Act 2000 increased the reach of race relations legislation, obliging public authorities to eliminate race discrimination from their functions and to promote good race relations. New codes of practice encourage the authorities to monitor their employees by ethnic origin and to conduct pay audits similar to those being conducted for women. However, the Act does not cover the private and voluntary sectors.

Unemployment rates for ethnic minority groups are consistently higher than for whites, with some groups being up to five times more likely not to have a job. But it is important to disaggregate the data to obtain a true picture of how different communities fare. Black men from countries other than Africa or the Caribbean have the highest unemployment rate, at 26.6 per cent, followed by Bangladeshi men at 20.4 per cent. This compares to 7.2 per cent for Indian men, slightly higher than the white population. Overall, ethnic minority men have an unemployment rate of 13 per cent compared to 6.9 per cent for white men while for ethnic minority women it is 12.3 per cent, compared to 4.7 per cent for white women. Bangladeshi and Pakistani women have the highest rate of unemployment at 23.9 per cent. Even graduates fare comparatively worse, with black and Asian students facing discrimination as they look for work after university or college.[58] Not unnaturally, 60 per cent of ethnic minority students believe their employment prospects are not as good as others'. There is evidence that all ethnic minorities are disadvantaged in terms of occupational attainment and have difficulty in climbing up the managerial ladder. Africans, Caribbeans, Pakistanis and Bangladeshis fare particularly badly. British Indians tend to have better educational qualifications than their white colleagues and have no problem getting started in managerial and professional jobs. But their progress up the career ladder is slower than that of their white counterparts. Nor does social integration guarantee labour market success.[59] The fact is, as the

UN Committee on Economic, Social and Cultural Rights noted, Britain's race relations laws have failed significantly to combat de facto employment discrimination in the thirty years or so that they have been in force.

The Low Pay Commission's third report in 2001 showed that ethnic minority workers are over-represented in low-paying occupations and service industries.[60] Again there is a diversity of experience both in terms of different groups and between men and women. The introduction of the NMW in 1999 has therefore been particularly important for black workers. But it is simply one structural adjustment in the labour market when a panoply of structural changes across the whole range of disadvantage is required. It does not for example do anything to shift poor ethnic minority workers out of their low-paying environment. It does not give them the language skills and the education they need in the first place (although studies have shown there is often a disparity between educational attainment of black people and their position in the labour market). It does not compensate for bad housing in disadvantaged areas, social exclusion and poor transport (with black workers twice as dependent as white workers on using public transport to get to work).[61] It does not eradicate the discrimination that impacts on the way pay is determined, particularly performance-related pay, especially when two thirds of black workers are not covered by collective bargaining. Finally, it does not grapple with the underlying racial discrimination that British society and its laws have so far failed to overcome.

Asylum seekers, refugees and migrant workers
It is not possible to estimate the size of the shifting population living illegally in Britain. An official estimate, published in July 2003, could only say that it is probably hundreds of thousands. An EU estimate has put the figure at 560,000. The British government, like governments across Europe, is caught in the position of recognising that the economy urgently requires economic migrants to fill both professional and unskilled jobs and yet being wary of the political dangers of being perceived to be 'soft on immigration'. Thus the government takes an ambivalent posture, occasionally adopting positive attitudes – 'we are

a nation of immigrants, and all the better for it' – and actively recruiting nurses and public servants from abroad, while at the same time talking tough and taking punitive and restrictive measures to prevent economic migrants entering the UK or to stop refugees from working here. Unusually in the EU, the government has retained the right not to accept European legislation in this area, deciding entry on a case-by-case basis. Its ambivalence extends even to legal migrant workers, having refused to ratify the UN Migrants Workers Rights Convention and denying refugee women with professional qualifications as teachers, nurses and doctors the opportunity to work in Britain, as a report by the Greater London Authority in December 2002 found.[62] More than half the women surveyed actually had security of residence and full employment rights, but fewer than one in five of them were in work, thanks to restrictive Home Office regulations and the inability to convert overseas qualifications. There have admittedly been conversion schemes and even talk of amnesties for refugees working illegally, but tough policies predominate. But asylum seekers are prohibited from working and the right for them to work after six months from their application was withdrawn in July 2002; if they apply late for asylum, they are also denied benefits and emergency accommodation. In February 2004, the then Home Secretary, David Blunkett, responded to fears about immigrants from eastern Europe falsely receiving visas by placing tough restrictions on job-seekers coming to Britain after the accession of the ten new EU member states. Under his scheme, access to the full range of social security benefits was restricted until after a year's continuous employment; and workers were required to register their jobs and provide evidence they were being paid at least the NMW. Those who fail to find work are not able to claim benefit for two years. At the 2005 general election Labour proposed the introduction of a 'points' system to determine whether migrants can come and work in the country. In such an environment, those migrants and asylum seekers who do work illegally are particularly vulnerable to exploitation and desperately low pay and working conditions, being outside employment protection measures, health and safety regulations and the NMW. The dangers were highlighted by the deaths of twenty Chinese cockle pickers in Morecombe Bay in February 2004.

Prisoners

Prison labour in the UK fails to comply with the provisions of ILO Convention No. 29, the Convention Concerning Forced or Compuslory Labour. Prisoners in state-run and privately run prisons work for private enterprises, but not in a free employment relationship. The report of the ILO Committee of Experts for 2000 was strongly critical of the government's policy. At the ILO Conference Committee on the Application of Standards in June 2000, the TUC pointed out that prisoners were given the choice of being put to work or being put 'on report', which reduced their chances of early release, essentially denying them a free choice. The prisoners received between 8 and 20 per cent of the NMW in force outside prisons. The conference committee in its conclusions called for the government to ensure that any prison work was carried out in conformity with ILO Convention No. 29.

Older people

Growing old may well set off a less well-publicised 'demographic time-bomb' than the sheer number of old people. According to the ONS, nearly a third of people aged over 50 (some 2.8 million people) are currently not in a full-time job, and one third of the UK population will be aged over fifty by 2020. The cost of economic 'inactivity' amongst the over-fifties is already estimated to be at least £26 billion a year. There is therefore the prospect of a pre-pension 'unemployment trough' since at the same time the state pension age for women is being raised to sixty-five by 2020, and may be raised still further to sixty-eight by 2050, as proposed by Adair Turner in the second report of the independent Pensions Commission.[63] The aim of the government is certainly to move towards the US model, where it is the norm for people to work well into their seventies, or to combine retirement with part-time work. Thus while some people may choose to work beyond the traditional retirement age of sixty-five, more people may be forced to opt for a combination of retirement and work; and for jobless over-fifties, living on pre-pension benefits may no longer be possible, since a Cabinet Office report has already recommended (in 2000) that unemployed men over sixty should lose their benefits unless they are looking for jobs.

(There is currently of course no fixed state retirement age in the UK.)

Age Concern estimates that there are about 250,000 employees working over the age of sixty-five, but this figure is expected to grow as the population ages and new policies take shape. Currently UK workers aged over sixty-five are not protected from unfair dismissal or eligible for statutory redundancy payments, with discrimination on grounds of age not outlawed. The result is that attempts to challenge ageist dismissals by employers have, to date, been unsuccessful. Those who remain in work suffer frequent discrimination. Indeed it is the most common form of discrimination in the workplace, ahead of sex or race.[64] One in five workers told MORI that they had experienced discrimination at work, with 38 per cent citing ageism as the cause.[65] A voluntary code of practice was introduced in 2000 but has failed. The position should, however, improve in 2006 when the new EU directive outlawing discrimination on the grounds of age comes into force. The directive has already applied in the rest of the EU-15 since 2003.

Gay and lesbian people

Since December 2003 the Employment Equality (Sexual Orientation) Regulations have made it illegal to discriminate against someone on grounds of their sexuality. However, following lobbying from churches, the government included a clause in the regulations permitting religious organisations, including (publicly funded) faith schools, to refuse to employ gay workers on the basis that employment of such people would be at odds with the employers' convictions. The seriousness of the proposed measure was indicated by the fact that it was the first time in five years that the Joint Committee on Statutory Instruments, which scrutinises the legality of regulations before they are debated, had met to take oral evidence. The DTI has maintained that there would only be very limited circumstances when a faith school could be exempt from the discrimination laws. The school would have to show that the church has a significant role in the running of the school and that the employment of teachers is for the purposes of the church.

Appendix A

The International Covenant on Economic, Social and Cultural Rights

This is an edited and abridged version of the Covenant. The full text is available at the UN High Commission for Human Rights website, www.unhchr.ch.

The Preamble asserts that, under the principles of the Universal Declaration of Human Rights, the ideal of free human beings enjoying freedom from fear and want can only be achieved if everyone may enjoy their economic, social and cultural rights, as well as civil and political rights. Under the UN Charter states are obliged to promote universal respect for, and observance of, human rights and freedoms, and individuals owe duties to other individuals and to the community also to strive for the promotion and observance of the economic, social and cultural rights recognised in the covenant.

States ratifying the Covenant agree upon the following articles:

Part I

Article 1

All peoples have the right of self-determination. By virtue of that right they freely determine their political status and freely pursue their economic, social and cultural development.

Part II

Article 2
1. Each state that is party to the covenant undertakes to take steps, individually and through international assistance and co-operation, especially economic and technical, to the maximum of its available resources, with a view to achieving progressively the full realisation of the rights recognised in the covenant by all appropriate means, including particularly the adoption of legislative measures.
2. Each state undertakes to guarantee that the covenant rights will be exercised without discrimination of any kind as to race, colour, sex, language, religion, political or other opinion, national or social origin, property, birth or other status.

Article 3
Each state undertakes to ensure the equal right of men and women to the enjoyment of all economic, social and cultural rights set out in the covenant.

Article 4
Each state recognises that it may impose limits, determined by law, to the enjoyment of these rights only in so far as this may be compatible with the nature of these rights and solely for the purpose of promoting the general welfare in a democratic society.

Article 5
1. Nothing in the covenant may be interpreted as implying for any state, group or person any right to engage in any activity or to perform any act aimed at the destruction of these economic, social and cultural rights or freedoms, or to limit them to a greater extent than is provided for in the covenant.
2. No restriction upon or derogation from any of the fundamental human rights recognised or existing in any country in virtue of law, conventions, regulations or custom shall be admitted on the pretext that the covenant does not recognise such rights or that it recognises them to a lesser extent.

Part III

Article 6

1. Each state party to the covenant recognises the right to work, which includes the right of everyone to the opportunity to gain their living by work which they freely choose or accept, and will take appropriate steps to safeguard this right.

2. The measures that states take fully to realise this right shall include technical and vocational guidance and training programmes, policies and techniques to achieve steady economic, social and cultural development and full and productive employment under conditions safeguarding fundamental political and economic freedoms to the individual.

Article 7

Each state recognises the right of everyone to the enjoyment of just and favourable conditions of work which ensure, in particular:

a) Remuneration which provides all workers, as a minimum, with:
   i) Fair wages and equal remuneration for work of equal value without distinction of any kind, in particular women being guaranteed conditions of work not inferior to those enjoyed by men, with equal pay for equal work;
   ii) A decent living for themselves and their families in accordance with the provisions of the covenant;
b) Safe and healthy working conditions;
c) Equal opportunity for everyone to be promoted in their employment to an appropriate higher level, subject to no considerations other than those of seniority and competence;
d) Rest, leisure and reasonable limitation of working hours and periodic holidays with pay, as well as remuneration for public holidays.

Article 8

1. Each state undertakes to ensure:
a) The right of everyone to form trade unions and join the trade union of their choice, subject only to the rules of the

organisation concerned, for the promotion and protection of their economic and social interests. No restrictions may be placed on the exercise of this right, other than those prescribed by law and which are necessary in a democratic society in the interests of national security or public order or for the protection of the rights and freedoms of others;

b) The right of trade unions to establish national federations or confederations and the right of the latter to form or join international trade union organisations;

c) The right of trade unions to function freely subject to no limitations other than those prescribed by law and which are necessary in a democratic society;

d) The right to strike, provided that it is exercised in conformity with the laws of the particular country.

2. This article shall not prevent the imposition of lawful restrictions on the exercise of these rights by members of the armed forces, the police or the state administration.

3. Nothing in this article shall authorise states party to the International Labour Organization Convention of 1948 concerning freedom of association and protection of the right to organise to take legislative measures or apply the law in such a manner as would prejudice the guarantees provided for in that convention.

Article 9
Each state recognises the right of everyone to social security, including social insurance.

Article 10
Each state recognises that:
a) The widest possible protection and assistance should be accorded to the family, particularly while it is responsible for the care and education of dependent children. Marriage must be entered into with the free consent of the intending spouses;

b) Special protection should be accorded to mothers during a reasonable period before and after childbirth. During such period working mothers should be accorded paid leave or leave with adequate social security benefits;

c) Special measures of protection and assistance should be taken on behalf of all children and young persons without any discrimination. Children and young persons should be protected from economic and social exploitation. Their employment in work harmful to their morals or health or dangerous to life or likely to hamper their normal development should be punishable by law. States should also set age limits below which the paid employment of child labour should be prohibited and punishable by law.

Article 11

1. Each state recognises the right of everyone to an adequate standard of living for themselves and their family, including adequate food, clothing and housing, and to the continuous improvement of living conditions. States will take appropriate steps to ensure the realisation of this right.

2. Each state, recognising the fundamental right of everyone to be free from hunger, shall take, individually and through international co-operation, the measures and programmes needed:
   a) To improve methods of production, conservation and distribution of food;
   b) To ensure an equitable distribution of world food supplies in relation to need.

Article 12

1. Each state recognises the right of everyone to the enjoyment of the highest attainable standard of physical and mental health.

2. The steps taken by states to achieve the full realisation of this right shall include those necessary for:
   a) The provision for the reduction of the stillbirth rate and of infant mortality and for the healthy development of the child;
   b) The improvement of all aspects of environmental and industrial hygiene;
   c) The prevention, treatment and control of epidemic, endemic, occupational and other diseases;
   d) The creation of conditions which would assure to all medical service and medical attention in the event of sickness.

Article 13

1. Each state recognises the right of everyone to education that is directed to the full development of the human personality and the sense of its dignity and strengthens respect for human rights and freedoms. They further agree that education shall enable all persons to participate effectively in a free society, and promote understanding, tolerance and friendship among all nations and all racial, ethnic or religious groups.

2. Each state recognises that fully to realise this right:
   a) Primary education shall be compulsory and available free to all;
   b) Secondary education in its different forms, including technical and vocational secondary education, shall be made generally available and accessible to all by every appropriate means, and in particular by the progressive introduction of free education;
   c) Higher education shall be made equally accessible to all, on the basis of capacity, by every appropriate means, and in particular by the progressive introduction of free education;
   d) Fundamental education shall be encouraged or intensified as far as possible for those persons who have not received or completed the whole period of their primary education;
   e) The development of a system of schools at all levels shall be actively pursued, an adequate fellowship system shall be established, and the material conditions of teaching staff shall be continuously improved.

3. Each state undertakes to respect the liberty of parents to choose for their children schools, other than those established by the public authorities but which conform to minimum state educational standards, to ensure the religious and moral education of their children in conformity with their own convictions.

4. No part of this article shall be construed so as to interfere with the liberty of individuals and bodies to establish and direct educational institutions, subject to the principles set forth above and minimum state educational standards.

Article 14

Each state which, at the time of becoming party to the covenant, has not been able to secure in compulsory primary education, free of charge, undertakes to work out and adopt a detailed plan of action within two years for the progressive implementation of the principle of free compulsory education for all.

Article 15

1. Each state recognises the right of everyone:
    a) To take part in cultural life;
    b) To enjoy the benefits of scientific progress and its applications;
    c) To benefit from the protection of the moral and material interests resulting from any scientific, literary or artistic production of which they are the author.
2. The steps to be taken to achieve the full realisation of this right shall include those necessary for the conservation, the development and the diffusion of science and culture.
3. Each state undertakes to respect the freedom indispensable for scientific research and creative activity.

Part IV

Article 16

1. and 2. Each state party to the covenant undertakes to report to the Secretary-General of the United Nations on the measures which they have adopted and the progress made in achieving the observance of these rights.

Article 17

1. and 2. Each state shall furnish their reports in stages and reports may indicate factors and difficulties affecting the degree of fulfilment of obligations under the covenant.

Article 18

Pursuant to its responsibilities under the Charter of the United Nations in the field of human rights and fundamental freedoms, the Economic and Social Council may make arrangements with the specialised agencies in respect of their reporting to it on the progress made in achieving the observance of the provisions of the present covenant falling within the scope of their activities. These reports may include particulars of decisions and recommendations on such implementation adopted by their competent organs.

Articles 19 to 24

These articles deal with the powers and duties of the Economic and Social Council and the Commission on Human Rights to study, make general recommendations or pass on information deriving from states' reports and the rights of states party to the covenant to comment on such general recommendations. The Economic and Social Council may submit reports with recommendations to the UN General Assembly on the progress made in achieving general observance of the covenant rights and also bring to the attention of other UN organs matters which may assist them in deciding upon international measures likely to contribute to that progress.

Article 25

Nothing in the covenant shall be interpreted as impairing the inherent right of all peoples to enjoy and utilise fully and freely their natural wealth and resources.

Part V

Article 26

1. The present covenant is open for signature by any state member of the United Nations or member of any of its specialised agencies, by any state party to the Statute of the International Court of Justice, and by any other state which has been invited by the General Assembly of the United Nations to become a party to the present covenant.

2. The present covenant is subject to ratification. Instruments of ratification shall be deposited with the Secretary-General of the United Nations.

3. The present covenant shall be open to accession by any state referred to in Paragraph 1 of this article.

4. Accession shall be effected by the deposit of an instrument of accession with the Secretary-General of the United Nations.

5. The Secretary-General of the United Nations shall inform all states which have signed the present covenant or acceded to it of the deposit of each instrument of ratification or accession.

Articles 27 to 31
These articles set out formal measures regarding the coming into force of the covenant, provisions for its amendment and ancillary matters.

Appendix B

Economic or social right	*Circumstances of the case*
Disability rights and community care (the Barry case, (1997) 2 All ER 1)	Gloucester City Council withdrew laundry and cleaning services from an old immobile man on grounds that it did not have sufficient resources to meet his needs.
Residential housing for the elderly (the Blanchard case, (1997) 4 All ER 449)	Sefton Borough Council refused to pay for residential accommodation for an elderly resident in line with nationally agreed guidelines.

Judicial review and socio-economic rights (selected recent cases, 1997–2005)

Legal and resources questions	*The court's decision*
Could a council take its resources into account in determining whether to meet a disabled person's needs under Section 2 of the Chronically Sick and Disabled Persons Act 1970, which apparently creates legally enforceable rights for the disabled to receive such services as necessary to meet their individually assessed needs?	Though Section 2 is apparently mandatory, the House of Lords narrowly concluded that a council could take its resources into account, both in assessing someone's needs and deciding what was necessary to meet them. Otherwise councils would be liable to open-ended budgetary commitments. However, once a local authority had deemed it necessary to make certain arrangements to meet someone's needs under Section 2, it had an absolute duty to supply the services. They could not be withdrawn without a reassessment.
Could a council take its own resources into account in assessing an applicant's needs under the National Assistance Act 1948 and making arrangements to meet them under National Assistance regulations?	The Court of Appeal reluctantly accepted the Gloucester precedent (above), but held that once it had recognised the man's need for residential accommodation, it could not refuse to meet its lawful obligation to fund his future care.

Economic or social right	*Circumstances of the case*
Family housing (the Tammadge case, (1998) 1 CCLR 581)	Wigan Borough Council refused to provide a larger home for a single mother with three severely mentally disabled sons and a daughter, all of whom had serious behavourial problems.
Special educational needs (the Tandy case, (1998) 2 All ER 770)	East Sussex County Council reduced home tuition for a sick child who had been off school for seven years from five to three hours weekly under a new blanket policy.
Disability rights to home adaptations (the Mohammed case, (1998) All ER 788)	Birmingham City Council refused to provide housing adaptations that were deemed necessary for a disabled applicant on resource grounds.

Legal and resources questions	*The court's decision*
Could a council refuse on resources grounds to give larger accommodation to a family at the care planning stage after having already recognised the family's housing needs under the Children Act 1989?	No. Since Wigan had already recognised the family's housing needs, it could no longer take its own resources into account at a later stage. The court ordered the council to identify suitable housing within three months and provide it within another three months.
Could a local education authority take its own resources into account when assessing what a 'suitable education' would be under the arguably resource-sensitive Section 298 of the Education Act 1993?	The House of Lords unanimously interpreted the section as imposing an absolute mandatory obligation to deliver home tuition that met a child's individual 'age, ability and special needs' and refused to 'downgrade' mandatory duties to discretionary obligations. Resources were deemed to be irrelevant – perhaps because they were negligible in this instance as only two other children were affected. But lower courts have since fully followed the precedent in much more costly cases.
Did a housing authority have the discretion to take its own resources into account in considering grant aid under Section 23 of the Housing Grants and Construction Regeneration Act 1996, given	No. The divisional court held that a housing authority was under a mandatory duty to provide home adaptations under the wide-ranging Act in accordance with the assessed needs of a disabled person,

Economic or social right	*Circumstances of the case*
Homeless rights (the Kujtim case, (1999) 4 All ER 101)	A Kosovan asylum seeker, suffering from a depressive illness induced by stress, had been evicted twice from temporary bed and breakfast accommodation as a consequence of extremely anti-social behaviour.
Disability rights to residential accommodation (the Coughlan case, (2000) 51 BMLR 1)	Six severely disabled residents were moved from a hospital that was being closed to a new nursing home with the assurance that it would be 'their home for life'. But the health authority then closed the new facility.
Right to life and health treatment (the case of Child B, (1995) 2 All ER 129)	Child B, a young girl with acute leukaemia, was denied potentially life-saving treatment by her health authority under its priorities policy.

Legal and resources questions	*The court's decision*
the Act's wide-ranging purposes?	irrespective of the resources it had available for that purpose.
Could a housing authority evict a homeless person who had been assessed as being 'in urgent need of care and attention' under Section 21 of the National Assistance Act and therefore placed in emergency accommodation?	The Court of Appeal found that an authority had a continuing mandatory as opposed to a discretionary duty under Section 21 to provide shelter for the asylum seeker once it had recognised his urgent need for 'care and attention'.
Could the health authority close the home, mainly on economic grounds, and thus break its promise to the six people after consulting them and taking into account that the promise had been made?	The Court of Appeal decided that the closure of the home was a breach of the residents' 'legitimate expectations' and of their right to respect for their family and private life under Article 8 of the European Convention. A mandatory order was made to keep the nursing home open indefinitely.
Section 3 of the National Health Service Act 1977 creates a duty to provide for the diagnosis and treatment of 'illness' as far as deemed reasonably necessary. Could the health authority refuse costly treatment to a child on grounds of its priorities and scarce resources where the efficacy of the treatment was in doubt but the child's right to life was at stake?	In the first instance, the divisional court judge held that while the authority should determine how scarce resources should be distributed, there had to be a substantial public interest ground to justify infringing a child's right to life. The authority's priorities policy was too limited and not transparent enough to justify interfering with her right to life. But the

Economic or social right	*Circumstances of the case*
Right to health treatment (the case of A, D and G, (1999) LRMC 399)	The North West Lancashire health authority denied three transexuals gender reassignment surgery under a policy that gave such surgery low priority on grounds of its low health gains
Right to respect for family and private life (the Donoghue case, (2001) 2 FLR 284)	A pregnant single mother with three children aged under six was being evicted from a housing association home that had been temporarily granted to her pending a decision on whether she was 'intentionally homeless'. It was decided that she was.

Legal and resources questions	*The court's decision*
	Court of Appeal felt that the authority did not need to explain its decision so transparently and held that it alone could decide how its 'limited budget' should be spent.
Did the health authority's blanket policy of giving low priority to gender reassignment surgery justify the refusal of such surgery to the three transexual men under the National Health Services Act 1977?	The Court of Appeal held that the authority was under a duty in operating such a policy to assess the possible benefits of gender reassignment surgery individually in all three cases. It had failed to do so adequately and its refusal of treatment was quashed. The decision was remitted to the authority.
Was the decision of the housing association to evict the woman under Section 21 of the Housing Act 1988 a violation of her right to respect for her family and private life under Article 8 of the European Court (now made part of UK law by the Human Rights Act 1998)?	The Court of Appeal agreed with the trial judge that there had been no violation of Article 8 since the refusal to make an eviction order would violate the rights of others to housing and allow temporarily homeless people to jump the housing queue. The Court of Appeal added that it would be necessary to alter radically the purpose of the Housing Act to render it compatible with the European Convention and the court would be 'acting as a legislator' if it did so.

Economic or social right	*Circumstances of the case*
Right to respect for family and private life (the case of Mrs A (2002), 4 CCLR 487)	A mother with three children, two of whom were autistic and suffered from severe learning difficulties, lived in a damp and unsuitable council flat where the autistic children were at risk of being run over. Lambeth Borough Council social services recognised their urgent need for rehousing, but there was no real prospect of a move.
Right to respect for family and private life; protection against degrading and inhuman treatment (the Bernard case, (2003) 5 CCLR 557)	Mrs Bernard was a severely disabled and doubly incontinent diabetic living with her husband and six children in cramped and inaccessible emergency housing where she could not use her wheelchair. Her husband attended to all her needs. She had no privacy, was unable to access the WC and found it very hard to keep herself clean or even to move without assistance.

Legal and resources questions	*The court's decision*
Lambeth had assessed the family's needs under Section 17 of the Children Act 1989 and recognised that their present home severely impaired their health and well-being. But they were merely placed on the transfer list instead of being rehoused? Did the Section 17 assessment of need 'crystallise' into a mandatory duty that the council was bound to honour?	This was one of three homelessness appeals, all of which lost. The Court of Appeal held by a majority in Mrs A's case that the Children Act empowered social services to provide accommodation, but held unanimously that Section 17 did not, as in cases like Kujtim (see above), 'crystallise' into a mandatory duty on the council to meet her family's needs. A judge in the lower divisional court criticised Lambeth's 'less than satisfactory' treatment of Mrs A. The decision raised the issue of families being split and the case went with the others to the House of Lords (see below).
Enfield Borough Council originally gave the family notice to quit on the grounds that they were intentionally homeless but this was withdrawn. A council care plan recognised her multiple needs, especially her need for a suitable adapted home. But the family was left in intolerable conditions for nearly two years. It was agreed that the council owed her a duty under Section 21 of the National Assistance Act 1948, but	This was the first case in which the courts awarded damages for a breach of Convention rights under Article 8 through the council's delay in providing suitable accommodation. Mr Justice Sullivan gave Enfield three months in which to find a suitable property and another three months in which to adapt it. He held that the council's failure to act was due to corporate neglect and did not amount to deliberately

Economic or social right	*Circumstances of the case*
Right to respect for family and private life (the cases of Mrs A, G and W, (2003) UKHL)	Two families had been refused housing together; the third was refused a move to a suitable home. Lambeth and Barnet Borough Councils told G (a Dutch woman) and W (a mother deemed intentionally homeless because of her rent arrears), living in cramped conditions with an extended family, that they would only give accommodation to their children. Mrs A was housed, but needed a more appropriate home (see above).
Protection against inhuman and degrading treatment (the Limbuela case, (2005) UKHL 66).	Wayoka Limbuela, an Angolan refugee, was one of thousands of destitute asylum seekers refused benefits and not allowed to work. He was forced to sleep rough and beg. His case went

Legal and resources questions	*The court's decision*
Articles 3 and 8 of the EHRA were also invoked.	degrading treatment under Article 3 of the ECHR, deplorable though the conditions were. However, the council had failed to live up to its positive obligations under Article 8 as well as under the 1948 Act and awarded the family £10,000 damages.
Social services departments such as Lambeth's had adopted policies of refusing to provide accommodation for parents and children, offering only to provide housing for their children separately. Did Section 17 of the Children Act impose a duty on social services to rehouse the families, and should the social services departments accommodate both parents and children together?	The House of Lords recognised that local authorities had only limited funds to satisfy multifarious demands and ruled that Section 17 imposed a 'general' and not an 'absolute' duty on social services. But they also ruled against blanket social services policies refusing to provide accommodation only for the children of vulnerable families without their parents. In the case of Mrs A a Law Lord expressed the expectation that Lambeth would 'reconsider' its refusal to provide the family with permanent accommodation.
The government was seeking to deter refugees by refusing benefits to those who did not immediately register as asylum seekers while denying them the right to work. Did policies	The lower courts were at odds over such cases and the Court of Appeal first ruled that destitute asylum seekers must experience degrading conditions before their

Economic or social right	*Circumstances of the case*
	with others through the courts up to the House of Lords

References: All ER = All England Reports; BMLR = Butterworths Medical Law Reports; CCLR = Community Care Law Reports; CCR = Community Care Reports; FLR = Family Law Reports; LRMC = Lloyds Reports of Medical Cases; UKHL = House of Lords

Legal and resources questions	*The court's decision*
which made asylum seekers destitute amount to inhuman and degrading treatment under Article 3 of the ECHR? And how severe did their degrading living conditions have to be?	treatment by the government could be ruled unlawful. It was not enough to sleep rough with no income. But the Court of Appeal, and then the House of Lords, decided that to be without accommodation and income with no prospect of charitable assistance was sufficient to amount to inhuman and degrading treatment.

About the authors

Andrew Blick is research officer for Democratic Audit at the University of Essex. He was previously political researcher to Graham Allen MP. He is the author of *People Who Live in the Dark: The History of the Special Adviser in British Politics* (Politico's, 2004) and *How to Go to War: A Manual for Democratic Leaders* (Politico's, 2005), which was described in the *Guardian* as 'a mild-mannered Machiavellian tract for the 21st century'. He was a key researcher on *Not in Our Name: Democracy and Foreign Policy in the UK* (Politico's, 2006).

Iain Byrne is Commonwealth law officer at Interights, the international centre for the legal protection of human rights. He is a visiting fellow of the Human Rights Centre at the University of Essex. He has worked as a consultant and lecturer on human rights for the British Council and the United Nations in Brazil, Georgia, Palestine, Sri Lanka and Zimbabwe. He took part in the first international mission to Israel and the Occupied Territories during the 2000 intifada. He worked previously as a research officer with Democratic Audit and has written and co-authored numerous books, including *The Human Rights of Street and Working Children: A Practical Manual for Advocates* (London: Intermediate Technology, 1998), *Blackstone's Human Rights Digest* (with Keir Starmer QC; London: Blackstone Press, 2001) and *Democracy under Blair* (with David Beetham and others; Politico's, 2002). He is currently co-writing a cases-and-material textbook on the judicial protection of economic and social rights in south Asia.

Tufyal Choudhury is a lecturer in international human rights law at Durham University. His research focuses on equality law and in particular on racial and religious discrimination. He is a director of the Discrimination Law Association and adviser to the discrimination law project for JUSTICE, the human rights organisation. He was also director of the Open Society Institute's UK Muslims Research Project and editor of its 2005 report, *Muslims in the UK: Policies for Engaged Citizens*. He is currently engaged on a study of the UK's counter-terrorism legislation, practice and policy with Andrew Blick and Stuart Weir.

Jan Flaherty is based at Loughborough University. She is currently exploring 'discourses of poverty', specifically how people defined as living in poverty talk about poverty and social exclusion. She was co-author of *Poverty: The Facts* in 2004 with Paul Dornan and John Veit-Wilson for the Child Poverty Action Group.

John Fowler undertakes management work in local government and writes on current education policy and legislation.

Judith Mesquita is senior research officer and co-ordinator of the Right to Health Unit at the Human Rights Centre, University of Essex. For the past three years, she has worked with the United Nations Special Rapporteur on the right to the highest attainable standard of health. Her research interests and publications focus on issues of health and human rights, including the skills drain in the health profession, and on mental health. She previously worked as a consultant for various organisations, including Medact, UNICEF and the United Nations Office of the High Commissioner for Human Rights.

Ellie Palmer is a senior lecturer in the Law Department and member of the Human Rights Centre at the University of Essex. She is an expert in the law of public services and her articles on judicial review and the impact of the Human Rights Act have been published in the *Oxford Journal of Legal Studies*, the *Journal of Social Welfare and Family Law*, the *Modern Law Review* and the *European Human Rights Law Review*. She is the UK contributor to a wide-ranging comparative study on the justiciability of socio-economic rights in national legal systems, *Justiciability, Socio-Economic Rights: Experiences from Domestic Legal Systems* (Antwerp: Intersentia, 2006). Her latest book is on the impact of the Human Rights Act on access to public services in the UK, *Judicial Review, Socio-Economic Rights and the Human Rights Act* (Oxford: Hart, 2006).

Stuart Weir is director of Democratic Audit at the University of Essex (where he is also a senior research fellow and visiting professor). He is joint author and editor of several previous democratic audits of the UK, most recently Democracy under Blair (Politico's, 2002). He is also a consultant and facilitator on democracy and human rights and has worked for the UNDP, the DfID, the EU and the British Council in Namibia, Zimbabwe, Palestine, Malawi and Nigeria. Between 1998 and 2004 he worked with the inter-governmental International Institute for Democracy and Electoral Assistance as senior consultant for its State of Democracy project and co-authored The International IDEA Handbook on Democracy Assessment. He is a former editor of the New Statesman and in 1988 he founded Charter88, the domestic campaign for democratic renewal.

Notes

Introduction

1. See Dunleavy, P., Margetts, H., Smith, T. and Weir, S., *Voices of the People: Popular Attitudes to Democratic Renewal in Britain*, 2nd edn (London: Politico's, 2005).
2. Ibid. Respondents in the Rowntree polls were given a list of possible rights and asked whether they should be included in a Bill of Rights. The polls were conducted by ICM Research.
3. Beetham, D., Byrne, I., Ngan, P. and Weir, S., *Democracy under Blair: a Democratic Audit of the UK* (London: Politico's, 2002). See also Beetham, D., Bracking, S., Kearton, I. and Weir, S. (eds), *The International IDEA Handbook on Democracy Assessment*, (New York: Kluwer Law International, 2002).
4. See Beetham et al., *International IDEA Handbook on Democracy Assessment*, ch. 9.
5. Bradshaw, J., *Civic Involvement*, Poverty and Social Exclusion survey, 2000.
6. Burchardt, T., Le Grand, J. and Piachaud, D., 'Degrees of exclusion: Developing a dynamic, multi-dimensional measure', in Hills, J., Le Grand, J. and Piachaud, D (eds), *Understanding Social Exclusion* (Oxford: Oxford University Press, 2002).
7. Foreign and Commonwealth Office, *Annual Report on Human Rights*, Cm 5967, 2003.
8. See for example, 'Free and fair elections', in Beetham et al., *Democracy under Blair*, or *The UK General Election of 5 May 2005: Report and Analysis* (London: Electoral Reform Society, 2005).
9. Published in Joint Committee on Human Rights, *The International Covenant on Economic, Social and Cultural Rights*, Twenty-first Report, Session 2003–04, HL 183/HC 1188, p. 28.
10. *Concluding Observations of the Committee on Economic, Social and Cultural Rights: United Kingdom of Great Britain and Northern Ireland, United Kingdom of Great Britain and Northern Ireland – Dependent Territories* (Geneva: Office of the United Nations High Commissioner of Human Rights, 2002).
11. *Daily Telegraph*, 21 May 2003.
12. See Brand, D. and Heyns, C. (eds), *Socio-Economic Rights in South Africa* (Pretoria: Pretoria University Law Press, 2005) for an across-the-board account.
13. Kinney, E., 'The International Human Right to Health: What Does This Mean for Our Nation and World?', *Indiana Law Review* (2001), vol. 34, no. 4, pp. 1457–76.
14. See Beatty, D., 'The Lost Generation: When Rights Lose Their Meaning', in Beatty, D. (ed.), *Human Rights and Judicial Review: A Comparative Perspective* (Dordrecht: Martinus Nijhoff, 1994).

15. See Blaustein, A. and Franz, G. (eds), *Constitutions of the Countries of the World* (Dobbs Ferry, NY: Oceana, 1993).

Chapter 1

1. *R v. Secretary of State for the Home Department, ex parte Adam, Limbuela and Tesema.*
2. In this election, Labour was returned to power with 356 seats – that is 55 per cent of the seats in the House of Commons and a 66-seat majority – on the support of only 35.2 per cent of those voting. As a proportion of the eligible electorate, Labour had just 21.6 per cent support – that is, from 9.6 million out of the 44.4 million eligible electors.
3. Dunleavy, P., Margetts, H., Smith, T. and Weir, S., *Voices of the People: Popular Attitudes to Democratic Renewal in Britain*, 2nd edn (London: Politico's, 2005).
4. The Commission on the NHS Chaired by Will Hutton, *New Life for Health* (London: Vintage, 2000).
5. *Making a Bill of Rights for Northern Ireland: A Consultation* (Belfast: Northern Ireland Human Rights Commission, 2001).
6. *Progressing a Bill of Rights for Northern Ireland: An Update* (Belfast: Northern Ireland Human Rights Commission, 2004).
7. The description comes from the Institute for Public Policy Research's study, *Social Justice: Building a Fairer Britain*, edited by Pearce, N. and Paxton, W. (London: Politico's, 2005).
8. Toynbee, P. and Walker, D., *Better or Worse?: Has Labour Delivered?* (London: Bloomsbury, 2005).
9. Public Administration Select Committee, *On Target?: Government by Measurement*, Fifth Report, Session 2002–03, HC 62.
10. *Sunday Times*, 16 January 2006.
11. *Observer*, 16 January 2006.
12. Mandelson, P. and Liddle, R., *The Blair Revolution: Can New Labour Deliver?* (London: Faber and Faber, 1996).
13. Wilkinson, R., *The Impact of Inequality: How to Make Sick Societies Healthier* (London: Routledge, 2005).
14. *Guardian*, 2 May 2005.
15. Pearce, N. and Paxton, W. (eds), *Social Justice: Building a Fairer Britain* (London: Politico's, 2005).
16. *Guardian*, 2 May 2005.
17. Toynbee and Walker, *Better or Worse?*
18. See further Beetham, D., Byrne, I., Ngan, P. and Weir, S., *Democracy under Blair: a Democratic Audit of the UK*, 2nd edn (London: Politico's, 2003).
19. See also Miller, D., 'What Is Social Justice?', in Pearce and Paxton, *Social Justice*.
20. Cabinet Office, *Modernising Government*, Cm 4331, 1999.
21. Public Administration Select Committee, *Choice, Voice and Public Services*, Fourth Report, Session 2004–05, HC 49.
22. Ibid.
23. Toynbee and Walker, *Better or Worse?*
24. Committee on the Office of the Deputy Prime Minister, *Decent Homes*, Fifth Report, Session 2003–04, HC 46.
25. Toynbee and Walker, *Better or Worse?*
26. Wright, T. and Ngan, P., *A New Social Contract: From Targets to Rights in Public Services* (London: Fabian Society, 2004).

27. HM Treasury, *Public Services: Meeting the Productivity Challenge*, April 2003.
28. Beetham et al., *Democracy under Blair*. A brief supplementary pamphlet, *Failing Democracy* (Colchester: Democratic Audit, 2005), issued at the time of the 2005 general election, argues that democracy improved under the first Blair government, but regressed between 2001 and 2005.
29. Public Administration Select Committee, *On Target?*.
30. *Daily Telegraph*, 21 May 2003.

Chapter 2

1. Special rapporteurs are independent experts, appointed by the chair of the Commission on Human Rights, to examine human rights situations in particular countries or particular human rights issues. They conduct studies, advise on technical cooperation, respond to individual complaints and engage in promotional activities.
2. *The Domestic Application of the Covenant* (Geneva: Office of the United Nations High Commissioner of Human Rights, 1998).
3. *Daily Telegraph* editorial, 21 May 2003.
4. Joint Committee on Human Rights, *The International Covenant on Economic, Social and Cultural Rights*, Twenty-first Report, Session 2003–04, HL 183/HC 1188.
5. Ibid.
6. Ibid.
7. See Alston, P., 'The Committee on Economic, Social and Cultural Rights', in Alston, P. (ed.), *The United Nations and Human Rights: A Critical Appraisal* (Oxford: Clarendon Press, 1992); Craven, M., *The International Covenant on Economic, Social and Cultural Rights: A Perspective on Its Development* (Oxford: Oxford University Press, 1995).
8. Joint Committee on Human Rights, *The International Covenant on Economic, Social and Cultural Rights*.
9. These three layers of obligations are not set out in the covenant, but the committee has consistently referred to the obligation to respect, protect and fulfil socio-economic rights in recent general comments: e.g. see Committee on Economic, Social and Cultural Rights General Comment 12 on the right to adequate food, 12 May 1999, E/C.12/1999/5, para. 15; General Comment 13 on the right to education, 8 December 1999, E/C.12/1999/10, para. 46; General Comment 14 on the right to the highest attainable standard of health, 11 August 2000, E/C.12/2000/4; General Comment 15 on the right to water, 26 November 2002, E/C.12/20002/11.
10. CESCR General Comment 9 on the domestic application of the covenant, 3 December 1998, E/C.12/1998/24.
11. E/C.12/2002/SR.11, our translation from the original French.
12. See Article 25 of the ICCPR, Article 8 of the ICESCR, Article 5 of the CERD, Article 7 of the CEDAW and Article 12 of the CRC.
13. Hunt, P., Nowak, M. and Osmani, S., *Draft Guidelines: A Human Rights Approach to Poverty Reduction Strategies* (Geneva: Office of the United Nations High Commission for Human Rights, 2002).
14. CESCR General Comment 14, paras 37–41.

Chapter 3

1. See for example Pitt, G., *Employment Law*, 5th edn (London: Sweet and Maxwell, 2003).
2. Case 6/64 *Faminio Costa v. ENEL*, (1964) ECR 585; (1964) CMLR 425.
3. Case 152/84 *Marshall v. Southampton and South West Area Health Authority*, (1986) ECR 723; (1986) 1 CMLR 688.
4. Hills, J., *Income and Wealth: The Latest Evidence* (York: Joseph Rowntree Foundation, 1998).
5. Ewing, K., 'Social Rights and Human Rights: Britain and the Social Charter – the Conservative legacy', *European Human Rights Law Review*, no. 2, 2000.
6. Joint Committee on Human Rights, *The International Covenant on Economic, Social and Cultural Rights*, Twenty-first Report, Session 2003–04, HL 183/HC 1188, written evidence.
7. House of Lords European Union Select Committee, *The Charter of Fundamental Rights*, Eighth Report, Session 1999–2000, HL 67.
8. Ibid.
9. *Times*, 19 May 2004.
10. Goldsmith, Lord, 'A Charter of Rights, Freedoms and Principles', *Common Market Law Review* (2001), vol. 38, pp. 1201–16.
11. Under Section 108 of the Employment Rights Act 1996.
12. See Hervey, T. and Kenner, J., *Economic and Social Rights under the EU Charter of Fundamental Rights: A Legal Perspective* (Oxford: Hart, 2003).
13. Lester, Lord, 'Introduction', in *The EU Charter of Fundamental Rights: Text and Commentaries*, (London: Federal Trust, 2001).
14. See Hunt, J., 'Fair and Just Working Conditions' and Ryan, B., 'The Charter and Collective Labour Law', both in Hervey and Kenner, *Economic and Social Rights under the EU Charter of Fundamental Rights*.

Chapter 4

1. Joint Committee of Human Rights, *The International Covenant on Economic, Social and Cultural Rights*, Twenty-first Report, Session 2003–04, HL 183/HC 1188, written evidence.
2. Fredman, S, 'Social, Economic, and Cultural Rights', in Feldman, D. (ed.), *English Public Law* (Oxford: Oxford University Press, 2004).
3. Joint Committee of Human Rights, *The International Covenant on Economic, Social and Cultural Rights*.
4. Ibid.
5. Ibid.
6. Ibid.
7. See Palmer, E., 'Courts, the UK Constitution and the HRA' in Cooman, F. (ed.), *Comparative Socioeconomic Rights* (Insentia, 2006). This chapter draws heavily on her research. See also generally Palmer, E. *Socio-economic Rights, Judicial Review and the Human Rights Act* (Oxford: Hart, 2006).
8. See *Cyprus v. Turkey*, (1988) 27 EHRR 212; *D. v. UK*, (1997) 24 EHRR 423; *O'Rourke v. UK*, Application 39022/97, 2001 (unreported).
9. *Marzari v. Italy*, admissibility decision, 4 May 1999. The ECHR went on to hold that it was not for it to review the decisions taken by the local authorities as to the adequacy of the accommodation offered to the applicant and found that the state had fulfilled positive obligations under Article 8.

10. *Connors v. UK*, Application No. 66746/01, judgment, May 2004.
11. However, the courts generally regard the decisions of independent contractors engaged by local authorities to provide services as generally outside judicial review and public law proceedings for violations of convention rights. There are questions of whether social landlords providing housing are caught by the HRA and, in the case of *R. (on the application of Heather) v. Leonard Cheshire Foundation*, (2002) 2 All ER, the Court of Appeal held that the charitable organisation providing residential care services for the elderly was not performing a public function within the meaning of the HRA.
12. See Klug, F., Starmer, K. and Weir, S., *The Three Pillars of Liberty: Political Rights and Freedoms in the UK* (London: Routledge, 1996), ch. 6.
13. Prosser, T., *Test Cases for the Poor* (London: Child Poverty Action Group, 1983).
14. *R. v. Secretary of State for the Environment ex parte Nottingham CC*, (1986) AC 240, and *R. v. Secretary of State for the Environment ex parte Hammersmith and Fulham LBC*, (1991) AC 521.
15. See also *Begum v. Tower Hamlets*, (2003) UKHL 5, where the Law Lords ruled that Mrs Begum did have an enforceable right to accommodation under Section 102 of the Housing Act 1996 since she was homeless, eligible for assistance, in priority need and (most significant) had not become homeless intentionally.
16. In a case in 1998, *Botta v Italy* (26 EHHR 241), the European Court had ruled that 'private life' under Article 8 included 'a person's physical and psychological integrity'.
17. Under Section 8 of the Asylum and Immigration Act 1996. The grant of permission is governed by the Immigration (Restrictions on Employment) Order 1996 (SI 1996/3225).
18. *R. (on the application of Limbuela) v. Secretary of State for the Home Department*, (2005) 3 All ER 1–94.
19. *T v. Secretary of State for the Home Department*, (2003) EWCA 1941. By contrast, the judge in the High Court found that T's condition at Heathrow had reached Article 3 ill treatment, noting inter alia that he 'found it difficult to rest or sleep because of the noise and light and because he would be moved on by the police. Any ablutions were confined to public lavatories and he was unable to wash his hair or his clothes or to bathe or shower' ((2003) EWHC 1941).
20. Metcalfe, E., 'Destitution and ESC Rights', JUSTICE seminar on economic, social and cultural rights, 3 December 2003.
21. *N v. Secretary of State for the Home Department*, (2005) UKHL 31, and *ZT v. Secretary of State for the Home Department*, (2005) EWCA Civ 1421.
22. *Guardian*, 30 January 2006; *Guardian Unlimited*, 31 January 2006.
23. See See Klug et al., *Three Pillars of Liberty*, ch. 6. for a fuller description of the Wednesbury test.
24. See *R. on the application of Mahmood v. Secretary of State for the Home Department*, (2001) 1 WLR 840.
25. *R. v. DPP ex parte Kebilene*, (2002) 2AC 326 HL.
26. See for example Jowell, J. and Cooper, J., *Delivering Rights: How the Human Rights Act Is Working* (Oxford: Hart, 2003).
27. Hunt, M., 'Why Contemporary Public Law Needs a Concept of Due Deference', in Bamford, N. and Leyland, P. (eds), *Public Law in a Multi-layered Constitution* (Oxford: Hart, 2003).

28. In a dissenting speech in *International Transport Roth GmbH and Others v. Secretary of State for the Home Department*, (2002) EWCA Civ 158.
29. Joint Human Rights Committee, *Nationality, Immigration and Asylum Bill: Further Report*, Twenty-third Report, Session 2001–02, HC 125/HL 176.

Chapter 5

1. See further Weir, S. and Beetham, D., *Political Power and Democratic Control in Britain: The Democratic Audit of the United Kingdom*, (London: Routledge, 1998), ch. 15.
2. See further Klug, F., Starmer, K. and Weir, S., *The Three Pillars of Liberty: Political Rights and Freedoms in the UK* (London: Routledge, 1996).
3. On the electoral politics of 'Middle England', see Cruddas, J., 'Epilogue', in Cruddas, J., John, P., Lowles, N., Margetts, H., Rowland, D. and Weir, S., *The Far Right in London: A Challenge for Local Democracy?* (York: Joseph Rowntree Reform Trust, 2005). Generally on the UK electoral system, see Beetham, D., Byrne, I., Ngan, P. and Weir, S., *Democracy under Blair* (London: Politico's, 2002).
4. See also Weir and Beetham, *Political Power and Democratic Control in Britain*, ch. 4, for a statement of the indivisibility of civil and political and economic, social and cultural rights within a democratic perspective.
5. See Tushnet, M., 'Enforcing Socio-economic Rights: Lessons from South Africa', *ESR Review* (2005), vol. 6, no. 3.
6. One of the ironies of the government's case against socio-economic rights is that ministers are vehemently opposed to trade union and employment rights, which are capable of immediate resolution in the courts, but rest their case upon arguments against socio-economic rights involving resources.
7. Joint Committee of Human Rights, *The International Covenant on Economic, Social and Cultural Rights*, Twenty-first Report, Session 2003–04, HL 183/HC 1188.
8. Ibid.
9. Ibid.
10. Under Article 25 of the International Covenant on Civil and Political Rights, Article 8 of the ICESCR; Article 5 of the International Convention on the Elimination of All Forms of Racial Discrimination, Article 7 of the Convention on the Elimination of All Forms of Discrimination against Women and Article 12 of the Convention on the Rights of the Child.
11. Committee on Economic, Social and Cultural Rights General Comment No. 9 on the domestic application of the covenant, E/C.12/1998/24. In Britain, tribunals and quasi-judicial bodies are often very much beholden to the executive and their processes are not always open; there is a need for a major review of their role and functions, which we cannot undertake here.
12. *Grootboom v. Oostenberg Municipality*, (2000) 3 BCLR 277; *Government of the Republic of South Africa v. Grootboom*, (2000) 11 BCLR 1169.
13. *Minister of Health and Others v. Treatment Action Campaign and others*, (2002) 10 BLCR 1033 (CC); (2002) SA 721 (CC) (TAC).
14. See further Brand, D. and Heyns, C. (eds), *Socio-economic Rights in South Africa* (Pretoria: Pretoria University Law Press, 2005).
15. *Soobramoney v. Minister of Health, KwaZulu-Natal*, (1997) 12 BCLR 1696 (CC).
16. See Ngwena, C. and Cook, R., 'Rights Concerning Health', in Brand and Heyns, *Socio-economic Rights in South Africa*.

17. See further Klug, F., Starmer, K. and Weir, S., *The Three Pillars of Liberty: Political Rights and Freedoms in the UK* (London: Routledge, 1996), ch. 2 & 6; and Palmer, E., 'Courts, the UK Constitution and the HRA', in Cooman, F. (ed.), *Comparative Socioeconomic Rights* (Insentia, 2006).

18. *R v. Secretary of State for the Home Department, ex parte Daly*, (2001) 3 All ER 417.

19. *R (Mahmood) v. Secretary of State for the Home Department*, (2000) 1 WLR 840.

20. CESCR General Comment 3.

21. Joint Committee of Human Rights, *International Covenant on Economic, Social and Cultural Rights*, Appendix 9.

22. Wilkinson, R., *The Impact of Inequality: How to Make Sick Societies Healthier* (London: Routledge, 2005).

23. Department for Constitutional Affairs, *International Human Rights Instruments: The UK's Position*, July 2004.

24. Joint Committee on Human Rights, *International Covenant on Economic, Social and Cultural Rights*; see Appendices 2, 5 and 6.

25. *Wilson and others v. United Kingdom*, (2002) 35 EHRR 523.

26. *National Minimum Wage: Low Pay Commission Report*, Cm 6759, 2006.

27. See the websites of Sane, the mental health charity (www.sane.org.uk), or the Mental Health Foundation (www.mentalhealth.org.uk). For a patient's eye view, see also Wield, C., *Life after Darkness: A Doctor's Journey through Severe Depression* (Oxford: Radcliffe, 2006).

28. See Dunleavy, P., Margetts, H., Smith, T. and Weir, S., *Voices of the People: Popular Attitutes to Democratic Renewal in Britain*, 2nd edn (London: Politico's, 2005).

29. See Cruddas, 'Epilogue', note 3.

Chapter 6

1. Jowell, J., 'Is Equality a Constitutional Principle?', (1994) 47 CLP 1, p. 4.

2. Ibid.

3. Ibid., p. 7.

4. (1999) 1 AC 98, p. 109. Although this case concerned the constitution of Mauritius these views are clearly expressed as having universal relevance.

5. McColgan, A., 'Discrimination Law and the Human Rights Act 1998', in Campbell, T., Ewing, K. and Tomkins, A. (eds), *Sceptical Essays on Human Rights* (Oxford: Oxford University Press, 2001).

6. Ibid.

7. This was opened for signature on 4 November 2000.

8. Hansard, HL Deb, 9 November 2000, vol. 618, col. WA 174; see also 11 October 2000, vol. 617, col. WA 37; 23 October 2000, vol. 618, col. WA 14; and 25 October 2000, vol. 618, col. WA 45.

9. Hansard, HL Deb, 11 October 2000, vol. 617, col. WA 37.

10. Hansard, HL Deb, 23 October 2000, vol. 618, col. WA 14.

11. Hansard, HL Deb, 25 October 2000, vol. 618, col. WA 45.

12. Lester, A., 'Equality and the United Kingdom Law: Past, Present and Future', *Public Law* (2001), vol. 46, p. 80; and Fredman, S., 'Why the Government Should Sign and Ratify Protocol 12', (2002) 105 EOR 21.

13. Human Rights Act, Section 3(2)(b).

14. (2002) 4 All ER 1162.

15. See Hepple, B., Coussey, M. and Choudhury, T., *Equality: A New Framework* (Oxford: Hart, 2000).

16. Sex Discrimination Act 1975 (SDA), Section 1; Sex Discrimination (Northern Ireland) Order (SD(NI)O), Article 3.

17. SDA, Section 2A (1), as amended by the Sex Discrimination (Gender Reassignment) Regulation (SI 1999/1102); SD(NI)O, Article 4A, as amended by the Sex Discrimination (Gender Reassignment) Regulations (Northern Ireland) (SI 1999/311).

18. SDA, Section 3; SD(NI)O, Article 5; this is not the same as 'marital status' as it only covers discrimination against a married person, but not against single or unmarried persons.

19. Race Relations Act 1976 (RRA), Section 3; Race Relations (Northern Ireland) Order (SI 1997/869 (NI 6)) (RR(NI)O), Article 5(1).

20. Disability Discrimination Act 1995.

21. Fair Employment and Treatment Order 1998 (SI 1998/3162 (NI 21)) (FETO).

22. Article 5(3)(a), RR(NI)O.

23. See Trade Union and Labour Relations (Consolidation) Act 1992.

24. Part-time Workers (Prevention of Less Favourable Treatment) Regulations (SI 2000/1551).

25. Religion and Belief Discrimination Regulations 2003 (SI 2003/1660).

26. Employment Equality (Sexual Orientation) Regulations 2003 (SI 2003/1661); Employment Equality (Sexual Orientation) Regulations (Northern Ireland) 2003 (SR 2003/497).

27. Equality Act 2006, passim.

28. *R v. Entry Clearance Officer, Bombay, ex parte Amin*, (1983) 2 AC 818.

29. *The Stephen Lawrence Inquiry: Report of an Inquiry by Sir William MacPherson of Cluny*, Cm 4262-I, 1999.

30. Hansard, HC Deb, 24 February 1999, vol. 326, col. 391.

31. RRA, Section 19B, as amended by Race Relations (Amendment) Act 2000, Section 1.

32. Northern Ireland Act 1998, Section 76.

33. Joint Committee on Human Rights, *Equality Bill*.

34. Leverton, S., *Monitoring the Disability Discrimination Act 1995 (Phase 2), Final Report* (Department of Work and Pensions, 2002).

35. Hansard, HL Deb, 19 January 2004, vol. 656, col. WA 122.

36. Advice and Assistance (Assistance by Way of Representation) (Scotland) Amendment Regulations 2001.

37. The case (Case C–271/91 (1993) ECR I–4367) was the follow-up of a previous case in which Miss Marshall obtained a ruling from the court that it was unlawful for her employer, a health authority, to require her to retire at 60 while male employees could work until the age of 65.

38. Law Commission, *Aggravated, Exemplary and Restitutionary Damages* (London: Law Commission, 1997).

39. SDA, Sections 57–9; RRA, Sections 48–50.

40. *R v. CRE ex parte Prestige Group PLC*, (1984) ICR 472.

41. *Hillingdon LBC v. CRE*, (1982) AC 779.

42. FETO, Article 11.

43. Joint Committee on Human Rights, *Equality Bill*.

44. Ibid.

45. O'Cinneide, C., *Taking Equality of Opportunities Seriously: The Extension of Positive Duties to Promote Equality* (London: Equality and Diversity Forum, 2004).

46. RRA, Section 71.
47. Schneider Ross and the Commission for Racial Equality, *Towards Racial Equality: An Evaluation of the Public Duty to Promote Race Equality and Good Race Relations in England and Wales (2002)* (London: Commission for Racial Equality, 2003).
48. Equality Act 2006, Section 84.
49. Government of Wales Act 1998.
50. Greater London Authority Act 1999.
51. Scotland Act 1998.
52. O'Cinneide, *Taking Equality of Opportunities Seriously.*
53. Standards in Scotland's Schools Act 2000, Section 5(2)(b); Housing (Scotland) Act 2001, Section 106; Regulation of Care (Scotland) Act 2001, Section 1(2)(b).
54. O'Cinneide, *Taking Equality of Opportunities Seriously.*

Chapter 7

1. Department for Work and Pensions, *Opportunity For All: Sixth Annual Report*, Cm 6239, 2004.
2. United Nations Committee on Economic, Social and Cultural Rights, *Poverty and the International Covenant on Economic, Social and Cultural Rights*, E/C.12/2001/10.
3. Declaration made at the Conference on Access to Social Rights, held in Malta in November 2002.
4. *Progressing a Bill of Rights for Northern Ireland: An Update* (Belfast: Northern Ireland Human Rights Commission, 2004).
5. See Lister, R., *Poverty* (Cambridge: Polity Press, 2004), ch. 7 for a full discussion.
6. Kenner, J., 'Economic and Social Rights in the EU Legal Order: The Mirage of Indivisibility', in Hervey, T. and Kenner, J., *Economic and Social Rights under the EU Charter of Fundamental Rights: A Legal Perspective* (Oxford: Hart, 2003).
7. Under the Employment Act 2002 maternity rights were extended and payments increased, two weeks' paid paternity leave became a statutory requirement and the right to request flexible working times (for parents of children under six or of disabled children under eighteen) was introduced. However, while the employer has to take applications seriously, there is no obligation to fulfil the employee's request.
8. Ruxton, S. and Karim, R., *Beyond Civil Rights: Developing Economic, Social and Cultural Rights in the United Kingdom* (Oxford: Oxfam, 2001).
9. Foreign and Commonwealth Office, *White Paper on the Treaty Establishing a Constitution for Europe*, Cm 6309, 2004.
10. Kenner, 'Economic and Social Rights in the EU Legal Order'.
11. For a detailed definition of 'public authority' and discussion of potential weaknesses of the HRA, see Joint Committee on Human Rights, *The Meaning of Public Authority under the Human Rights Act*, Seventh Report, Session 2003–04, HL 39/HC 382.
12. Ruxton and Karim, *Beyond Civil Rights*.
13. *Progressing a Bill of Rights for Northern Ireland*.
14. Ibid. This criticism came from the main Unionist parties among others.
15. UN Committee on Economic, Social and Cultural Rights.
16. Tribunals (in social security, employment, health and housing) do offer some

means of claiming rights but they are not always independent.

17.	Gordon, D., Adelman, L., Ashworth, K., Bradshaw, J., Levitas, R., Middleton, S., Pantazis, C., Patsios, D., Payne, S., Townsend, P. and Williams, J., *Poverty and Social Exclusion in Britain* (York: Joseph Rowntree Foundation, 2000).

18.	Hillyard, P., Kelly, G., McLaughlin, E., Patsios, D. and Tomlinson, M., *Bare Necessities: Poverty and Social Exclusion in Northern Ireland – Key Findings* (Belfast: Democratic Dialogue, 2003).

19.	Office for National Statistics, *Family Spending (2004–2005): A Report on the 2004–2005 Expenditure and Food Survey* (Basingstoke: Palgrave Macmillan, 2006).

20.	*Low Cost but Acceptable Budget for Families with Children April 2005* (York: University of York Family Budget Unit, 2005). LCA budget D is for a local authority tenant couple family with two children and includes work, housing and travel costs (a car) and a small entertainment allowance but no budget for alcohol. It represents a costing for an 'adequate' but basic standard of living in April 2005.

21.	*2005 Annual Survey of Hours and Earnings* (corrected version) (London: National Statistics, 2005).

22.	Palmer, G., North, J., Carr, J. and Kenway, P., *Monitoring Poverty and Social Exclusion 2003* (York: Joseph Rowntree Foundation, 2003).

23.	A further fifth remained on a low income (i.e. below 60 per cent of median income after deducting housing costs) despite the tax credits and the remaining three-fifths would not have been on a low income even if they had not received tax credits. See the New Policy Institute's Policy and Social Exclusion website, www.poverty.org.uk.

24.	Brewer, M., Goodman, A., Myck, M., Shaw, J. and Shephard, A., *Poverty and Inequality in Britain: 2004* (London: Institute for Fiscal Studies, 2004).

25.	Hirsch, D., 'Trends in poverty and inequality', *Prospect*, May 2004; Hills, J. and Stewart, K. (eds), *A More Equal Society?: New Labour, Poverty, Inequality and Exclusion* (Bristol: Policy Press, 2005).

26	An income below 60 per cent of the national median income after adjustment for household size and composition (HBAI, 2005).

27.	See the New Policy Institute's Policy and Social Exclusion website, www.poverty.org.uk.

28.	Watson, A., *Food Poverty: Policy Options for the New Millennium* (London: Sustain, 2001).

29.	Gill, O. and Sharma, N., *Food Poverty in the School Holidays* (Ilford: Barnardo's, 2004).

30.	Burchett, H. and Seeley, A., *Good Enough to Eat?: The Diet of Pregnant Teenagers* (London: Maternity Alliance / Food Commission, 2003).

31.	*'If They Don't Eat a Healthy Diet It's Their Own Fault!'*: Myths about Food and Low Income (London: National Food Alliance, 1997); Christie, I., Harrison, M., Hitchman, C. and Lang, T., *Inconvenience Food: The Struggle to Eat Well on a Low Income* (London: Demos, 2002).

32.	Hawkes, C. and Webster, J., *Debates on Surplus Food Redistribution: Too Much and Too Little?* (London: Sustain, 2000). Food poverty is defined by Hawkes and Webster as 'the inability to acquire or consume an adequate quality or sufficient quantity of food in socially acceptable ways, or the uncertainty that one will be able to do so'.

33.	Ibid.

34. *Fuel Poverty Advisory Group (for England) Second Annual Report, 2003/04* (Department of Trade and Industry, 2004).
35. Department for Work and Pensions, *Opportunity for All.*
36. *Excess Winter Mortality: By Age Group and Region* (London: National Statistics, 2005).
37. *Hypothermia and Excess Winter Deaths* (London: Age Concern England, 2002); National Audit Office, *Warm Front: Helping to Combat Fuel Poverty*, Session 2002–03, HC 769.
38. A vulnerable household is one containing older, disabled or chronically ill people, or children.
39. Lupton, R., 'School Quality, Free School Meals and Area Deprivation: Reading between the Lines,' paper presented at the LSE Research Laboratory All-Centre event, July 2002. Households in receipt of income support or jobseeker's allowance, and some low-income households receiving child tax credit, are entitled to free school meals.
40. See the New Policy Institute's Policy and Social Exclusion website, www.poverty.org.uk.
41. *Child Poverty and Education* (London: End Child Poverty, 2003).
42. Tanner, E., Bennett, F., Churchill, H., Ferres, G., Tanner, S. and Wright, S., *The Costs of Education: A Local Study* (London: Child Poverty Action Group, 2003); Harker, L., Kober, C. and Stearn, J., *Poverty in a Land of Plenty: Five Years On* (London: End Child Poverty, 2004).
43. *Tackling Health Inequalities: Summary of the Cross-cutting Review* (Department of Health, 2002).
44. Glasgow, an area of significant deprivation, has the lowest life expectancy (68.7 years for men and 76.2 for women) and North Dorset (79.3 for men, 83.4 for women), in the south of England, the highest. *Life Expectancy at Birth: Local Health Authorities in the UK, 1991–1993 to 1999–2001* (London: National Statistics, 2003).
45. Klein, G., Whyley, C. and O'Reilly, N., *Paying More, Getting Less: Overview* (London: National Consumer Council, 2004).
46. This is because home owners constitute the largest housing sector. Burrows, R. *Poverty and Home Ownership in Contemporary Britain* (Bristol: Policy Press, 2003).
47. *No Room to Play: Children and Homelessness* (London: Shelter, 2002).
48. This number is for England only. *Statutory Homelessness: 3rd Quarter 2005, England* (Office of the Deputy Prime Minister, 2005).
49. The other component of the Social Fund is a regulated scheme made up of maternity, funeral, cold weather and winter fuel payments.
50. Department for Work and Pensions, *Annual Report by the Secretary of State for Work and Pensions on the Social Fund 2004/2005*, Cm 6595, 2005.
51. Kempson, E., Collard, S. and Taylor, S., *Experiences and Consequences of Being Refused a Community Care Grant* (Department for Work and Pensions, 2004).
52. Finch, N. and Kemp, P., *The Use of the Social Fund by Families with Children* (Department for Work and Pensions, 2004).
53. Department for Work and Pensions, *Annual Report by the Secretary of State for Work and Pensions on the Social Fund 2003/2004*, The Stationery Office, 2005.
54. *Social Action Plan: Annual Review 2005* (London: Ofgem, 2005). Of these disconnections, 15,973 were from the electricity supply and 1,361 from gas. This figure is lower than the average, which is above 20,000, as the halt in disconnections mentioned in the main text began in the final quarter of 2003.

55. Trade and Industry Committee, *Debt and Disconnection: Gas and Electricity Supply Companies*, Fifth Report, Session 2004–05, vol. 2, HC 297-II.
56. See the Energywatch website, www.energywatch.org.uk.
57. Klein et al., *Paying More, Getting Less*.
58. See the Energywatch website, www.energywatch.org.uk.
59. *Social Action Plan Indicators* (London: Ofgem, 2004).
60. Klein et al., *Paying More, Getting Less*.
61. Low-income customers often need to borrow and repay small amounts over a short period, a circumstance not catered for by mainstream credit services.
62. *Forgive Us Our Debts* (Manchester: Church Action on Poverty, 2002).
63. *Tackling Over-indebtedness: Action Plan 2004* (Department of Trade and Industry / Department for Work and Pensions, 2004).
64. *Households below Average Income 1994/95–2003/04* (Department for Work and Pensions, 2005).
65. Paxton, W. and Dixon, M., *The State of the Nation: An Audit of Injustice in the UK* (London: Institute of Public Policy Research, 2004).
66. *Poverty Street: The Dynamics of Neighbourhood Decline and Renewal* (London: Centre for Analysis of Social Exclusion, 2003); Department for Work and Pensions, *Opportunity for All*.
67. Social Exclusion Unit, *A New Commitment to Neighbourhood Renewal: National Strategy Action Plan* (Cabinet Office, 2001).
68. *Poverty Street*.
69. Fahmy, E., 'Civic Capacity, Social Exclusion and Political Participation in Britain: Evidence from the 1999 Poverty & Social Exclusion Survey', paper presented at the Political Studies Association Annual Conference, University of Leicester, April 2003.
70. Young, S., *Poverty in Nottingham 2001* (Nottingham: Observatory, 2001).
71. Tax credits are means-tested, in-work benefits, which function as part of the tax system and are administered by HM Revenue and Customs (formerly the Inland Revenue).
72. *European Social Statistics: Social Protection: Expenditure and Receipts: Data 1992–2001* (Luxembourg: Office for Official Publications of the European Communities, 2004).
73. The EES was introduced in 1997 and renewed employment guidelines in 2003.
74. New Deal programmes exist for young people, lone parents, the over-25s and over-50s, disabled people and partners (of those on jobseeker's allowance, income support, incapacity benefit, carer's allowance or severe disablement allowance).
75. Figures for May 2005. Department for Work and Pensions.
76. Figures for May 2005. Department for Work and Pensions.
77. Adelman, L., Middleton, S. and Ashworth, K., *Britain's Poorest Children: Severe and Persistent Poverty and Social Exclusion* (London: Save the Children, 2003).
78. Low Pay Commission, *The National Minimum Wage: Building on Success Fourth Annual Report of the Low Pay Commission* (Norwich: Stationery Office, 2003).
79. *Households below Average Income 1994/95–2003/04*.
80. Millar, J. and Gardiner. K., *Low Pay, Household Resources and Poverty* (York: Joseph Rowntree Foundation, 2004).
81. The income poverty measure is on an after-housing-costs basis, although before-housing-costs figures will be used in the new measurement of child poverty.

82. Child poverty was 12 per cent in 1979.

83. *Households below Average Income 1994/95–2003/04.*

84. Paxton and Dixon, *State of the Nation.*

85. *Child Poverty Review* (HM Treasury, 2004).

86. *Households below Average Income 1994/95–2003/04.*

87. Paxton and Dixon, *State of the Nation*. There is little difference in the child poverty rates of the five worst-performing countries but a drop of 6 percentage points between the UK's rate and the next best performing country.

88. Ermisch, J. Francesconi, M. and Pevalin, D., *Outcomes for Children of Poverty* (Department for Work and Pensions, 2001).

89. Social Exclusion Unit, *A Better Education for Children in Care* (Office of the Deputy Prime Minister, 2003).

90. Bradshaw, J., Finch, N., Kemp, P., Mayhew, E. and Williams, J., *Gender and Poverty in Britain* (London: Equal Opportunities Commission, 2003); National Statistics, *Low-income Dynamics* (Department for Work and Pensions, 2004).

91. Women and Equality Unit, *Individual Incomes of Men and Women 1996–2001/02* (Department of Trade and Industry, 2003).

92. Office for National Statistics, 'Patterns of Low Pay', *Labour Market Trends* (2003), vol. 111, no. 4.

93. *Households below Average Income 1994/95–2003/04.*

94. National Statistics, *Low-income Dynamics.*

95. Palmer, G., Carr, J. and Kenway, P., *Monitoring Poverty and Social Exclusion* (York: Joseph Rowntree Foundation, 2005).

96. Department for Work and Pensions, *Opportunity for All.*

97. *Disability in Scotland 2002: Key Facts and Figures* (Stratford-upon-Avon: Disability Rights Commission, 2004.

98. *Households below Average Income 1994/95–2003/04.*

99. Hills and Stewart, *A More Equal Society?.*

100. Under Section 55 of the Nationality, Immigration and Asylum Act 2002.

101. Brewer et al., *Poverty and Inequality in Britain*. Income inequality as measured on the Gini co-efficient. The Gini co-efficient is a general measure of inequality: the higher the number the greater the income inequality.

102. Brewer et al., *Poverty and Inequality in Britain.*

103. Donald Hirsch argues that passive redistribution has occurred by means of an unadjusted tax rate threshold for high earners, despite a rise in the number of high-rate taxpayers (Hirsch, 'Trends in poverty and inequality').

104. *Key Findings from the 2003/04* Households below Average Income *Series* (London: Child Poverty Action Group, 2005).

105. *Personal Wealth: Distribution among the Adult Population of Marketable Wealth (Series C)* (HM Revenue and Customs, 2004).

106. Dennis, I. and Guio, A., 'Monetary Poverty in New Member States and Candidate Countries', *Statistics in Focus* (2004), no. 12.

107. Dennis, I. and Guio, A., 'Poverty and Social Exclusion in the EU', *Statistics in Focus* (2004), no. 16.

108. Howarth, C., Kenway, P. and Palmer, G., *Responsibility for All: A National Strategy for Social Inclusion* (London: New Policy Institute / Fabian Society, 2001).

109. The suggestion of minimum standards was an issue in the consultation over child poverty measures. See *Measuring Child Poverty: Preliminary Conclusions* (Department for Work and Pensions, 2003).

Chapter 8

1. Eurocare-3 study, 2003.
2. This chapter was last updated in terms of new material in July 2005.
3. See for example McHale, J., 'Enforcing Health Care Rights in the English Courts', in Burchill, R., Harris, D. and Owers, A. (eds), *Economic, Social and Cultural Rights: Their Implementation in United Kingdom Law* (Nottingham: University of Nottingham Human Rights Law Centre, 1999); Montgomery, J., 'Recognising a Right to Health', in Beddard, R. and Hill, D. (eds), *Economic, Social and Cultural Rights: Progress and Achievements* (London: Macmillan, 1992).
4. See CESCR General Comment 14 on the right to health, 11 August 2000, E/CN.4/2000/4.
5. *Interim Report of the Special Rapporteur on the Right to Health, Paul Hunt, to the General Assembly*, October 2003, A/58/427, para. 5.
6. CESCR General Comment 14, paras 57–8.
7. A/58/427, paras 14–28.
8. Ibid., para. 10.
9. *Interim Report of the Special Rapporteur on the Right to Health, Paul Hunt, to the General Assembly*, October 2004, A/49/522.
10. E/C.12/2000/4, para. 60.
11. See Hervey, T., 'The Right to Health in European Union Law', in Hervey, T. and Kenner, J. (eds), *Economic and Social Rights under the EU Charter of Fundamental Rights* (Oxford: Hart, 2003).
12. McHale, 'Enforcing Health Care Rights in the English Courts'.
13. For example *Mariela Cecilia Viceconte v. Ministry of Health and Social Welfare*, National Court of Appeals for the Federal Contentious-Administrative Jurisdiction of Argentina, Fourth Chamber, 2 June 1998.
14. See (1995) 2 All ER 129.
15. *R v. Cambridge Health Authority ex parte B*, (1995) 2 AC 129.
16. *N v. Secretary of State for the Home Department*, opinions of the Law Lords of 5 May 2005.
17. (2003) EWCA Civ 663.
18. (2002) EWCA Civ 388.
19. ECtHR Application 22009/93 and ECtHR Application 20837/92 respectively.
20. E/C.12/2000/4, paras 12 and 23.
21. ECtHR Application 16798/90.
22. E/C.12/2000/4, para. 4.
23. (2003) EWHC 2228 Admin.
24. Ibid. See also *Human Rights Act Information Service Newsletter* (2003), no. 3.
25. (2000) 1 WLR 977.
26. The Commission on the NHS (chaired by Will Hutton), *New Life for Health* (London: Vintage, 2000).
27. Ibid.
28. *Human Rights: Improving Public Service Delivery* (London: Audit Commission, 2003).
29. Ibid.
30. See Leatherman, S. and Sutherland, K., *The Quest for Quality in the NHS: A Mid-term Evaluation of the Ten-year Quality Agenda* (London: Nuffield Trust, 2003).
31. Wanless, D., *Securing Our Future Health: Taking a Long-term View* (HM Treasury, 2002).

32. See Guardian Unlimited, 26 April 2002.
33. *Tackling Health Inequalities: Summary of the Cross-cutting Review* (Department of Health, 2002).
34. CERD Concluding Observations on the UK, 18 August 2003, CERD/C/63/CO/11.
35. Acheson, D., *Independent Inquiry into Inequalities in Health* (Norwich: Stationery Office, 1998).
36. See Office for National Statistics, 'General Household Survey', unpublished analysis, 1997, reported in Acheson, *Independent Inquiry into Inequalities in Health*.
37. Study by Cancer Research UK and the Office for National Statistics, see Cancer Research UK press release, 'New statistics show poverty gap in cancer survivors has widened', 9 March 2004.
38. Hansard, HC Deb, 11 June 1997, vol. 295, cols 1139–40. See also Acheson, *Independent Inquiry into Inequalities in Health*.
39. See *Tackling Health Inequalities*, p. 11.
40. CESCR General Comment 14, para. 4.
41. Lister, S., 'British children top league for unhealthy living', *Times*, 4 June 2004.
42. Batty, D., 'Fruit and veg campaign fails to make an impact', *Guardian*, 20 January 2003.
43. Wanless, *Securing Our Future Health*.
44. Ibid.
45. Ibid.
46. Ibid.
47. BBC, 30 March 2005.
48. CRC Concluding Observations on the UK, 9 October 2002, CRC/C/15/Add.188.
49. Ibid.
50. National Survey Division of Office for National Statistics and Medical Research Council, *National Diet and Nutritional Survey: Young People Aged 4–18*, (Norwich: The Stationery Office, 2000).
51. *Guardian*, 9 December 2003.
52. Ibid.
53. See *Comments on the Second Report to the UN Committee on the Rights of the Child by the United Kingdom 1999* (London: Save the Children, 2002).
54. Ibid.
55. CESCR General Comment 14, para. 14.
56. United Kingdom Second Periodic Report to the CRC, CRC/C/83/Add.3, para. 8.18.1, 1999.
57. See Dawe, F. and Meltzer, M., *Contraception and Sexual Health 1999: A Report on Research for the Department of Health Using the ONS Omnibus Survey* (London: National Statistics, 2001); also *The National Health Strategy for Sexual Health and HIV* (Department of Health, 2001).
58. A/54/38/Rev.1, part II, paras 309–10.
59. Teenage Pregnancy Unit, *Conception Statistics for Local Authorities 1998-2002* (Newport: National Statistics, 2004).
60. CRC Concluding Observations on the UK.
61. Ibid., para. 42.
62. Terrence Higgins Trust.
63. See *The UK, HIV and Human Rights: Recommendations for the Next Five Years*

(London: All-Party Parliamentary Group on AIDS, 2001).

64. See International Planned Parenthood Federation, *UK Country Profile*, available at www.ippf.org.

65. See *Sexually Transmitted Infections: Policy Brief* (London: Family Planning Association, 2004).

66. *A Strategic Framework for Promoting Sexual Health in Wales* (National Assembly for Wales, 2000).

67. CRC, Article 19.

68. *Highlights on Health in the United Kingdom* (Copenhagen: WHO Regional Office for Europe, 1997).

69. Sen, P., Humphreys, C. and Kelly, L., *CEDAW Thematic Shadow Report 2003: Violence Against Women in the UK* (London: Womankind Worldwide, 2003).

70. CEDAW Concluding Observations on the UK's 3rd and 4th Periodic Reports, contained in report of CEDAW on its 20th and 21st sessions, A/54/38/Rev.1, part II, para. 311, 1999.

71. CRC/C/15/Add.188, paras 39–40.

72. Ibid., paras 35–8.

73. Wanless, *Securing Our Future Health*.

74. See Ham, C., *Health Policy in Britain: The Politics and Organisation of the National Health Service*, 4th edn (Basingstoke: Macmillan Press, 1999).

75. *Guardian*, 14 November 2003.

76. 'NHS needs 5,000 extra dentists', BBC News Online, 5 May 2004.

77. Department of Health, *The NHS Plan: A Plan for Investment, a Plan for Reform*, Cm 4818-I, 2000, p. 31.

78. See Leatherman and Sutherland, *Quest for Quality in the NHS*.

79. Duckworth, L., *Independent*, 21 May 2001.

80. European Committee on Social Rights, Conclusions XV-2 – the United Kingdom.

81. 'A sick NHS: the diagnosis', *Observer*, 7 April 2002.

82. See Carvel, J., *Guardian*, 28 July 2000.

83. BBC News online, 26 November 2002.

84. *Whose Charity? Africa's Aid to the NHS* (London: Save the Children / Medact, 2005).

85. See Carvel, J., *Guardian*, 12 May 2004.

86. ICESCR, Article 2(1); CESCR General Comment 14, paras 39–42. See also *An Action Plan to Prevent Brain Drain: Equitable Health Systems in Africa* (Boston: Physicians for Human Rights, 2004).

87. CESCR General Comment 14.

88. Survey, Age Concern England, 15 January 2002.

89. Roberts, E., Robinson, J. and Seymour, L., *Old Habits Die Hard: Tackling Age Discrimination in Health and Social Care* (London: King's Fund, 2002).

90. *Guardian*, 27 March 2001.

91. *National Services Framework for Older People* (Department of Health, 2001), para. 6.

92. See *Social Exclusion and HIV: A Report* (London: Terrence Higgins Trust, 2001).

93. See Apoola, A., tenHof, J. and Allan, P., 'Access to Infertility Investigations and Treatment in Couples infected with HIV: Questionnaire Survey', *British Medical Journal* (2001), vol. 323, p. 1285.

94. See *Report to the UN Committee on Economic, Social and Cultural Rights: Response to the UK Government's Fourth Report Under ICESCR: Article 12 the Right to*

Health (Dundee: Physicians for Human Rights UK, 2002).

95. *Proposals to Exclude Overseas Visitors from Eligibility to Free NHS Primary Medical Services: A Consultation* (Department of Health, 2004).

96. See *Report to the UN Committee on Economic, Social and Cultural Rights*.

97. *The UK, HIV and Human Rights*, paras 41–43.

98. CESCR General Comment 14, para. 12(b).

99. Ibid., para 12(c).

100. Ibid., para. 12(d).

101. Leatherman and Sutherland, *The Quest for Quality in the NHS*.

102. *A First Class Service: Quality in the New NHS* (Department of Health, 1998).

103. Roberts, M., 'How big a threat is MRSA really?', BBC News Online, 23 June 2005.

104. *Guardian*, 27 March 2001.

105. *Independent*, 14 January 2001.

106. McGauran, A., 'Foundation Hospitals: Freeing the Best or Dividing the NHS?', *British Medical Journal* (2002), vol. 324, p. 1298.

107. See Lister, J., *Health Policy Reform: Driving the Wrong Way?* (Enfield: Middlesex University Press, 2005).

108. See McFadyean, M. and Rowland, D., *PFI vs Democracy?: The Case of Birmingham's Hospitals* (London: Menard Press, 2002).

Chapter 9

1. Article 2(2) of the Swedish constitution inserts socio-economic rights, including housing, as 'fundamental aims'. It reads: 'The personal, economic and cultural welfare of the individual shall be fundamental aims of public activity. In particular, it shall be incumbent upon the public administration to secure the right to work, housing and education, and to promote social care and social security and a good living environment.'

2. Ofwat's jurisdiction covers only England and Wales; the Scottish equivalent is the Water Industry Commission for Scotland.

3. Joint Committee on Human Rights, *Homelessness Bill*, Second Report, Session 2001–02, HL30/HC314.

4. 'Council house queue grows to 1.5m families', *Observer*, 13 November 2005.

5. Jowell, R., Curtice, J., Park, A., Thomson, K., Jarvis, L., Bromley, C. and Stratford, N. (eds), *British Social Attitudes: Focusing on Diversity* (London: Sage, 2000).

6. Barker, K., *Review of Housing Supply: Delivering Stability: Securing Our Future Housing Needs, Final Report – Recommendations* (the Barker review) (HM Treasury, 2004).

7. As noted by the Barker review.

8. Study by the Cambridge Centre of Housing, Planning and Research, December 2000.

9. Source: National Housing Federation.

10. *Housing in England*, 4 vols (Office of the Deputy Prime Minister, 2005–6).

11. Shelter press release, 17 June 2003.

12. Kemp, P. and Rigg, J., *The Single Room Rent : Its Impact on Young People* (York: University of York Centre for Housing Policy, 1998).

13. Shelter press release, 15 September 2003.

14. See page 198 below.

15. Wilkinson, P., Landon, M., Armstrong, B., Stevenson, S., Pattenden, S.,

Fletcher, T. and McKee, M., *Cold Comfort: The Social and Environmental Determinants of Excess Winter Deaths in England, 1986–96* (Bristol: Policy Press, 2002).

16. Revell, K. and Leather, P., *The State of UK Housing: A Fact-file on Housing Conditions and Housing Renewal Policies in the UK* (Bristol: Policy Press, 2000).

17. Ibid.

18. Gordon, D., Levitas, R., Pantazis, C., Patsios, D., Payne, S., Townsend, P., Adelman, L., Ashworth, K., Middleton, S., Bradshaw, J. and Williams, J., *Poverty and Social Exclusion in Britain* (York: Joseph Rowntree Foundation, 2000).

19. Eurostat – European Community Household Panel 1996.

20. See the Campaign for More and Better Homes website, www.moreandbetter.org.uk.

21. Eurostat – European Community Household Panel 1996.

22. Revell and Leather, *State of UK Housing*.

23. Jowell et al., *British Social Attitudes*.

24. Revell and Leather, *State of UK Housing*.

25. Jowell et al., *British Social Attitudes*.

26. Revell and Leather, *State of UK Housing*.

27. *Guardian*, 29 November 2000.

28. See Power, A. and Mumford, K., *The Slow Death of Great Cities? Urban Abandonment or Urban Renaissance* (York: Joseph Rowntree Foundation, 1999).

29. *Scottish House Condition Survey 1996* (Edinburgh: Scottish Homes, 1997).

30. This is probably an underestimate since the survey was conducted during the warmest months.

31. As outlined on the Department of Environment, Transport and the Regions website, February 2001.

32. DTI Public Service Agreement Targets for 2005–08, PSA Target 4, Energy.

33. *Sustainable Communities: Building for the Future* (Office of the Deputy Prime Minister, 2003).

34. Housing, Planning, Local Government and the Regions Committee, *Homelessness*, Third Report, Session 2004–05, HC 61-I.

35. E/C.12/1/Add.19, para. 17.

36. Department of the Environment, Transport and the Regions, homelessness statistics, 2000.

37. Ibid.

38. Shelter research, 1998.

39. *Hidden Homelessness: Britain's Invisible City* (London: Crisis, 2004).

40. *Roof*, January–February 2005.

41. Source: Crisis, December 2002.

42. *Homelessness: Responding to the New Agenda* (London: Audit Commission, 2003).

43. E/C.12/1/Add.79, para. 6.

44. See page 199.

45. Study by Shelter Scotland and the Chartered Institute of Housing in Scotland.

46. See page 200.

47. *Emergency Hostels: Direct Access Accommodation in London* (London: Resource Information Service, 1996).

48. See Davies, J., Lyle, S. and Deacon, A., *Discounted Voices: Homelessness among Young Black and Ethnic People in England* (Leeds: Leeds University School of Sociology and Social Policy, 1996).

49. *English Housing Condition Survey 2001: Building the Picture* (Office of the Deputy Prime Minister, 2003).
50. *Racial Discrimination* (Department of the Environment, Transport and the Regions, 1998).
51. Source: Audit Commission figures, July 2000.
52. Garvie, D., *Far from Home: The Housing of Asylum Seekers in Private Rented Accommodation* (London: Shelter, 2001).
53. CERD Concluding Observations on the UK, 18 August 2003, CERD/C/63/CO/11, paras 22 and 23.
54. Open letter by travellers in *Travellers Times*, August 2000.
55. Crawley, H., *Moving Forward* (London: Institute of Public Policy Research, 2003).
56. Neier, P., *Local Authority Gypsy/Traveller Sites in England* (Office of the Deputy Prime Minister, 2003).
57. Crawley, *Moving Forward*.
58. The last major study in this area found that almost half of households in temporary accommodation were headed by women. Niner, P., *Homelessness in Nine Local Authorities: Case Studies of Policy and Practice* (London: HMSO, 1989).
59. See Rao, N., *Black Women in Public Housing: A Report on the Housing Problems of Black Women in the London Boroughs of Wandsworth and Southwark* (London: Black Women in Housing Group, 1990).
60. Kemp and Rigg, *Single Room Rent*.
61. 'Children and Families', Shelter website.
62. *The Victoria Climbié Inquiry, Report of an Inquiry by Lord Laming*, Cm 5730, 2003.
63. *Homelessness: Responding to the New Agenda* (London: Audit Commission, 2003).
64. *Child Poverty Review* (HM Treasury, 2004).
65. Revell and Leather, *State of UK Housing*.
66. See further Tinker, A., *Older People in Modern Society*, 4th edn (Harlow: Longman, 1997), ch. 7.
67. Housing, Planning, Local Government and the Regions Committee, *Homelessness*, op. cit. Government response, Cm 6490.
68. *English Housing Condition Survey 2001*.
69. Bevan, M., *Housing and disabled children: the art of the possible* (Joseph Rowntree Foundation, 2002.
70. Gordon et al., *Poverty and Social Exclusion in Britain*.

Chapter 10

1. Report submitted by Katarina Tomaševski, special rapporteur on the right to education, Mission to the United Kingdom of Great Britain and Northern Ireland (England) 18–22 October 1999 to the United Nations Economic and Social Council Commission on Human Rights, 9 December 1999, E/CN.4/2000/6/Add.2.
2. The negative formulation is important. It is summed by the European Court of Human Rights in the *Belgian Linguistics* case, (1968) EHRR 252, as follows: 'The negative formulation of the right includes that the contracting parties do not recognise such a right to education as would require them to establish at their own expense, or to subsidise, education of any particular type or at any particular level. There never was, nor is now, therefore any question of requiring each state to establish a system (of general and official education) but merely of guaranteeing to persons subject to the jurisdiction of the contracting

parties the right, in principle, to avail themselves of the means of instruction existing at a given time.' In other words, the European Convention does not require individual states to provide education but only a right of access to educational institutions existing at a given time.

3. For a full discussion see Whitbourn, S., *Education and the Human Rights Act* (Slough: EMIE, 2003).

4. Ibid.

5. United Nations Economic and Social Council, *Implementation of the International Covenant on Economic, Social and Cultural Rights*, General Comment No. 13, 8 December 1999, E/C.12/1999/10.

6. The instruments are the World Declaration on Education for All, Article 1; the Convention on the Rights of the Child, Article 29(1); the Vienna Declaration and Programme of Action, Part I, para. 33 and Part II, para. 80; and the Plan of Action for the United Nations Decade for Human Rights Education, para. 2.

7. *The Annual Report of Her Majesty's Chief Inspector of Schools 2004/05* (London: Ofsted, 2005).

8. Para. 85.

9. Lennon, F., in 'Organisation and Management in the Secondary School', in Bryce, T. and Humes, W. (eds), *Scottish Education, 2nd Edition: Post Devolution* (Edinburgh: Edinburgh University Press, 2003), notes that 'children in Scotland must, as of right, have a school education that is "directed to the development of [their] personality, talents and mental and physical abilities . . . to their fullest potential". This right to an education is not conditional upon the child's socio-economic status, racial origin, cultural background or religious belief.'

10. Section 7, Education Act 1996.

11. *Exclusion from Schools and Pupil Referral Units*, National Assembly for Wales Circular 1/2004.

12. *Education at a Glance: OECD Indicators 2005* (Paris: Organisation for Economic Co-operation and Development, 2005).

13. 13 September 2005.

14. *Statistics of Education: Schools in England* (Department for Education and Skills, 2004), Table 1b.

15. *Education at a Glance*.

16. *The Cost of a Free Education* (London: Citizens Advice, 2005).

17. *Pupil Absence in Schools in England 2004/05 (Provisional)* (Department for Education and Skills, 2005).

18. *Provision for Children under Five Years of Age in England: January 2005 (Provisional)* (Department for Education and Skills, 2005).

19. *Childcare Bill Consultation* (Department for Education and Skills, 2005).

20. *Education at a Glance*.

21. Department for Education and Skills, *14-19 Education and Skills*, Cm 6476, 2005.

22. *Education at a Glance*.

23. *A Fresh Start: Improving Literacy and Numeracy* (Department for Education and Employment, 1999).

24. *Education at a Glance*.

25. Department for Education and Skills, *Higher Standards, Better Schools for All*, Cm 6677, 2005.

26. *GCSE and Equivalent Results for Young People in England 2004/05 (Provisional)* (Department for Education and Skills, 2005).

27. 'Private schools standards attacked', BBC News online, 29 April 2003.
28. Joint Committee on Human Rights, *The International Covenant on Economic, Social and Cultural Rights*, Twenty-first Report, Session 2003–04, HL 183/HC 1188.
29. The DfES Research and Statistics website (www.dfes.gov.uk/rsgateway) contains a wealth of administrative statistics: for example, *Statistical First Release 08/2005* records that for the assessment of eleven-year-olds in mathematics, 89 per cent of pupils of Chinese ethnicity achieve the expected level 4. Compared to the national figure of 73 per cent for all ethnic groups, the figure for black Caribbean pupils is 61 per cent, for black African pupils 64 per cent, for other black pupils 64 per cent and pupils of mixed white and black origin 69 per cent. The site also contains information on DfES-sponsored research done by or in collaboration with higher education, for example, Bhattacharyya, G., Ison, L. and Blair, M., *Minority Ethnic Attainment and Participation in Education and Training: The Evidence* (2003) contains a comprehensive analysis of participation by ethnic minorities. Independent academic analyses can be found on the Democratic Audit website (www.democraticaudit.com), especially Choudhury, T., *Discrimination in Economic and Social Rights* (2003), and from non-governmental organisations, such as the annual survey by the Children's Rights Alliance for England, *State of Children's Rights in England*, at www.crae.org.uk. UN reports include that of Katarina Tomaševski, the former UN special rapporteur on the right to education.
30. 'Quality and Equality in Schooling – Miliband', DfES press notice, 30 January 2003.
31. *The Social Composition of Top Comprehensive Schools* (London: Sutton Trust, 2006).

Chapter 11

1. *European Labour Force Survey* (Luxembourg: Eurostat, 1999).
2. Sylvia Carr, 'Teleworking a popular choice for the self-employed', *Silicon.com*, 6 October 2005.
3. See 'Stretching the red tape', *Guardian*, 23 April 2004.
4. Figures for 2000, *European Labour Force Survey* (Luxembourg: Eurostat, 2003).
5. 'How New Labour buried the dustbin people', *Guardian*, 7 June 2004.
6. Beatty, C., Fothergill, S., Gore, T. and Green, A., *The Real Level of Unemployment 2002* (Sheffield: Sheffield Hallam University Centre for Regional Economic and Social Research, 2004).
7. See Gordon, D., Adelman, L., Ashworth, K., Bradshaw, J., Levitas, R., Middleton, S., Pantazis, C., Patsios, D., Payne, S., Townsend, P. and Williams, J., *Poverty and Social Exclusion in Britain* (York: Joseph Rowntree Foundation, 2000), Table 18, p.55.
8. See Berthoud, R., *Multiple Disadvantage in Employment* (York: Joseph Rowntree Foundation, 2003).
9. Speech to Amalgamated Engineering and Electrical Union, 6 January 2001.
10. Survey of 72,000 employers for the National Employer Skill Survey 2003.
11. 'New Deal', Briefing No. 94, Trades Union Congress, 11 November 2005.
12. 'Young pay the price as job hopes plummet', *Guardian*, 6 August 2005.
13. Department for Work and Pensions, *Welfare Green Paper: A New Deal for Welfare: Empowering People to Work*, Cm 6730, 2006.
14. See for example 'Minimum wage comes of age', *Guardian*, 20 March 2004.

15. See TUC and Low Pay Network research, October 2003.
16. See analysis of 700 cases reported by the National Association of Citizens Advice Bureaux, *Guardian*, 27 February 2001.
17. See *A League Table of Child Poverty in Rich Nations* (Florence: UNICEF Innocenti Research Centre, 2000); Morris, J., Donkin, A., Wonderling, D., Wilkinson, P. and Dowler, E., 'A Minimum Income for Healthy Living', *Journal of Epidemiology and Community Health* (2000.), vol. 54, no. 12, pp. 885–8.
18. *Work–Life Balance 2000* (Department for Education and Skills, 2000).
19. Source: Chartered Institute of Personnel and Development, March 2001.
20. Compton-Edwards, M., *Living to Work?* (London: Institute of Personnel and Development, 1999).
21. Research by University of Kent Economics Department; see *Guardian*, 21 June 2000.
22. Professor Green, University of Kent Economics Department, ibid.
23. John Monks, the then general secretary of the TUC, following publication of a report into the working conditions in call centres, *Calls for Change* (London: TUC, 2001).
24. One place for every 6.9 children under eight in 2001 compared to one for every nine in 1998.
25. *Statistics of Workplace Fatalities and Injuries in Great Britain: International Comparisons 2000* (London: Health and Safety Executive, 2000).
26. See the Centre for Corporate Accountability website, www.corporate accountability.org.
27. 'Vive la différence', *People Management*, 17 May 2001.
28. Trade and Industry Select Committee, *Vehicle Manufacturing in the UK*, Third Report, Session 2000–01, HC 128.
29. Though exact figures are unavailable, it is estimated that some one million people, including 700,000 temps, may be employed through 17,000 agencies.
30 *Made at Home: British Homeworkers in Global Supply Chains* (Oxford: Oxfam, 2004).
31. See memorandum from the Institute of Employment Rights in Joint Committee on Human Rights, *The International Covenant on Economic, Social and Cultural Rights*, Twenty-first Report, Session 2003–04, HL 183/HC 1188.
32. Joint Committee on Human Rights, *International Covenant on Economic, Social and Cultural Rights*.
33. Memorandum from the National Union of Rail, Maritime and Transport Workers, Joint Committee on Human Rights, *International Covenant on Economic, Social and Cultural Rights*.
34. International Labour Organization, Twenty-ninth Report (para. 68), March 2002.
35. Memorandum from the Communication Workers Union, Joint Committee on Human Rights, *International Covenant on Economic, Social and Cultural Rights*.
36. Ibid.
37. Memorandum from the National Union of Rail, Maritime and Transport Workers, Joint Committee on Human Rights, *International Covenant on Economic, Social and Cultural Rights*.
38. Joint Committee on Human Rights, *International Covenant on Economic, Social and Cultural Rights*.
39. See *Wilson v. United Kingdom*, (2002) IRLR 568.

40. Joint Committee on Human Rights, *International Covenant on Economic, Social and Cultural Rights*.

41. A survey for the Joseph Rowntree Foundation found that in 1999 disabled people made up half of all those who were not employed but said they would like to work and one-third of those who were available to start in a fortnight.

42. While 57 per cent of the population participate in the labour market, this proportion declines to 35 per cent for those with a long-standing illness/disability. Gordon et al., *Poverty and Social Exclusion in Britain*.

43. Burchardt, T., *Enduring Economic Exclusion: Disabled People, Income and Work* (York: Joseph Rowntree Foundation, 2000).

44. Education and Employment Select Committee, *Opportunities for Disabled People*, Ninth Report, Session 1998–99, HC 111-I.

45. Survey conducted by MIND.

46. Focus on Mental Health forum.

47. Report by Higher Education Funding Council on graduate employment for 2000, 4 April 2001.

48. Source: Gordon, D., Levitas, R., Pantazis, C., Patsios, D., Payne, S., Townsend, P., Adelman, L., Ashworth, K., Middleton, S., Bradshaw, J. and Williams, J., *Poverty and Social Exclusion in Britain* (York: Joseph Rowntree Foundation, 2000).

49. Research published by Department of Education and Employment, December 2000.

50. Source: ONS report 16 October 2003.

51. Low Pay Commission, *Making a Difference*, Third Report, 2001.

52. *Next Steps* (London: Unison, 2000).

53. Income Data Services' pay report no. 838, Aug 2001.

54. From 38 per cent in 1975 to 37 per cent in 2000 (Calculations by Low Pay Unit using New Earnings Survey 2000 data).

55. Calculations by National Council for One Parent Families, October 2001.

56. Source: *Child Labour in Britain: Report to the International Working Group on Child Labour* (1995).

57. Survey for the Industrial Society in January 2001.

58. *Graduates in the Eyes of Employers 2002* (London: Park / London: Guardian / Warwick: Association of Graduate Recruiters).

59. *Ethnic Minorities and the Labour Market: Interim Analytical Report* (Cabinet Office, 2005).

60. Department of Trade and Industry, *The National Minimum Wage: Making a Difference: The Next Steps*, Cm 5175, 2001.

61. See Owen, D. and Green, A., 'Estimating Commuting Patterns for Minority Ethnic Groups in England and Wales', *Journal of Ethnic and Migration Studies* (2000), vol. 26, no.4.

62. *Missed Opportunities: A Skills Audit of Refugee Women in London from the Teaching, Nursing and Medical Professions* (London: Greater London Authority, 2002).

63. See *A New Pensions Settlement for the Twenty-first Century* (London: Pensions Commission, 2005).

64. Survey by MORI Social Research Institute for the Association of Retired and Persons over 50, December 2002.

65. It is estimated by Age Concern that ageist hiring and firing costs the UK economy £31 billion a year.

Index